Small Business Legal Forms

Simplified

The Ultimate Guide to Small Business Legal Forms

Small Business Legal Forms *Simplified*

DANIEL SITARZ, ATTORNEY-AT-LAW

Nova Publishing Company
Small Business and Consumer Legal Books
Carbondale Illinois

ISBN 13: 978-1-892949-62-2
Book w/CD-Rom Price: $29.95

Library of Congress Cataloging-in-Publication Data
    Small Business Legal Forms Simplified / Daniel Sitarz. -- 5th ed. -- Carbondale, Ill. : Nova Publishing, c2011.
    Formerly titled: *The Complete Book of Small Business Legal Forms*
    p. ; cm. + CD-ROM
    (Small Business Made Simple series)
    ISBN: 978-1-892949-62-2
    1. Small business--Law and legislation--United States--Forms. 2. Forms (Law)--United States--Popular works.
    I. Title. III. Series.
        KF 1659.A65S43 2011   346.73'0652'0269--dc20 [347.3066520269]

Nova Publishing Company is dedicated to providing up-to-date and accurate legal information to the public. All Nova publications☐ ☐ ☐ ☐
periodically revised to contain the latest available legal information.

5th Edition; 1st Printing: June 2011
4th Edition; 1st Printing: January, 2005
3rd Edition; 2nd Printing: October, 2001
3rd Edition; 1st Printing: December, 2000
2nd Edition; 2nd Printing: April, 1998

2nd Edition; 1st Printing: September, 1996
1st Edition; 4th Printing: August, 1994
1st Edition; 3rd Printing: May, 1992
1st Edition; 2nd Printing: October, 1991
1st Edition; 1st Printing August, 1991

This publication is designed to provide accurate and authoritative information in regard to the subject matter covered. It is sold with the understanding that the publisher and author are not engaged in rendering legal, accounting, or other professional services. If legal advice or other expert assistance is required, the services of a competent professional person should be sought.
—From a Declaration of Principles jointly adopted by a Committee of
the American Bar Association and a Committee of Publishers

DISCLAIMER (Please also see DISCLAIMER and WARNING on Page 20)

Because of possible unanticipated changes in governing statutes and case law relating to the application of any information contained in this book, the author, publisher, and any and all persons or entities involved in any way in the preparation, publication, sale, or distribution of this book disclaim all responsibility for the legal effects or consequences of any document prepared or action taken in reliance upon information contained in this book. No representations, either express or implied, are made or given regarding the legal consequences of the use of any information contained in this book. Purchasers and persons intending to use this book for the preparation of any legal documents are advised to check specifically on the current applicable laws in any jurisdiction in which they intend the documents to be effective.

Nova Publishing Green Business Policies

Nova Publishing Company takes seriously the impact of book publishing on the Earth and its resources. Nova Publishing Company is committed to protecting the environment and to the responsible use of natural resources. As a book publisher, with paper as a core part of our business, we are very concerned about the future of the world's remaining endangered forests and the environmental impacts of paper production. We are committed to implementing policies that will support the preservation of endangered and ancient forests globally and to advancing 'best practices' within the book and paper industries. Our company's policy is to print all of our books on 100% recycled paper, with 100% post-consumer waste content, de-inked in a chlorine-free process. In addition, all Nova Publishing Company books are printed using soy-based inks. As a result of these environmental policies, Nova Publishing Company has saved hundreds of thousands of gallons of water, hundreds of thousands of kilowatts of electricity, thousand of pounds of pollution and carbon dioxide, and thousands of trees that would otherwise have been used in the traditional manner of publishing its books. Nova Publishing Company is very proud to be one of the first members of the Green Press Initiative, a nonprofit program dedicated to supporting publishers in their efforts to reduce their use of fiber obtained from endangered forests. (see www.greenpressinitiative.org). Nova Publishing Company is also proud to be an initial signatory on the Book Industry Treatise on Responsible Paper Use. In addition, Nova Publishing Company uses all compact fluorescent lighting; recycles all office paper products, aluminum and plastic beverage containers, and printer cartridges; uses 100% post-consumer fiber, process-chlorine-free, acid-free paper for 95% of in-house paper use; and, when possible, uses electronic equipment that is EPA Energy Star-certified. Nova's freight shipments are coordinated to minimize energy use whenever possible. Finally, all carbon emissions from Nova Publishing Company office energy use are offset by the purchase of wind-energy credits that are used to subsidize the building of wind turbines (see www.nativeenergy.com). We strongly encourage other publishers and all partners in publishing supply chains to adopt similar policies.

Nova Publishing Company
Small Business and Consumer Legal Books and Software
1103 West College St.
Carbondale, IL 62901
Editorial: (800) 748-1175
www.novapublishing.com

Distributed by:
National Book Network
4501 Forbes Blvd., Suite 200
Lanham, MD 20706
Orders: (800) 462-6420

Table of Contents

8

LIST of FORMS ON CD

(All forms on CD are both PDF and text forms unless noted)

APPENDICES of State Laws
    Business Registration Laws (on CD only as PDF form)
    Real Estate Laws (on CD only as PDF form)

Chapter 1: Business Operations
    Agreement for Sale of Business
    Agreement for Sale of Business Assets
    Notice of Intention to Use Fictitious Business Name
    Affidavit of Use of Fictitious Business Name
    Partnership Agreement

Chapter 2: Contracts
    General Contract
    Extension of Contract
    Modification of Contract
    Termination of Contract
    Assignment of Contract
    Consent to Assignment of Contract

Chapter 3: Signatures and Notary Acknowledgments (all forms text only)
    Corporate Acknowledgment
    Corporate Signature Line
    Partnership Acknowledgment
    Partnership Signature Line
    Limited Liability Company Acknowledgment
    Limited Liability Company Signature Line
    Sole Proprietorship Acknowledgment
    Sole Proprietorship Signature Line
    Power of Attorney Acknowledgment
    Power of Attorney Signature Line
    Individual Acknowledgment
    Individual Signature Line
    Husband and Wife Acknowledgment
    Husband and Wife Signature Line

Chapter 4: Powers of Attorney
    General Power of Attorney
    Unlimited Power of Attorney
    Limited Power of Attorney
    Revocation of Power of Attorney

California Notary Acknowledgment (on CD only): California notary acknowledgement form that is required to be used on documents that are intended to be valid in the state of California. On CD in separate folder as both text and PDF form.

Introduction to Small Business Legal Forms

The contracts and other various legal documents that are used in this book are written in plain English. Standard legal jargon, as used in most lawyer-prepared documents, is, for most people, totally incomprehensible. The vast majority of such legalese is absolutely unnecessary. Clarity, simplicity, and readability should be the goal in legal documents. In most contexts, "buyer" and "seller," "landlord" and "tenant," or some other straightforward term of definition of the parties involved is possible. Unfortunately, certain obscure legal terms are the only words that accurately and precisely describe some things in certain legal contexts. In those few cases, the unfamiliar legal term will be defined when first used. Generally, however, simple terms are used. Although this book will provide an overview of the uses of legal documents in many standard situations, it is not intended to be a complete reference on the subject and you may still need to seek legal help in some situations.

All of the legal documents contained in this book have been prepared in essentially the same manner that attorneys use to create legal forms. This book provides individuals with a set of legal forms that have been prepared with the problems and normal transactions of everyday business in mind. These forms are intended to be used in those situations that are clearly described by the specific terms of the particular form. Of course, while most transactions will fall within the bounds of these normal situations, some legal circumstances will present non-standard situations. The forms in this book are designed to be readily adaptable to most usual situations. They may be carefully altered to conform to the particular transaction that you may be confronted with. You should seek the advice of a competent lawyer if you intend to rely on any of the forms in this book. You may create your legal document and have a lawyer check it for any local legal circumstances or requirements. See also the Disclaimer and Warning on Page 20.

The proper and cautious use of the forms provided in this book will allow the typical person to save considerable money on legal costs. Perhaps more importantly, these forms will provide a method for the person to avoid costly misunderstandings about what exactly was intended in a particular situation or transaction. By using the forms provided to clearly set out the terms and conditions of everyday business dealings, disputes over what was really meant can be avoided.

How to Use This Book

In each chapter of this book, you will find an introductory section that will give you an overview of the types of situations in which the forms in that chapter will generally be used. Following that overview, there will be a brief explanation of the specific uses for each form. Included in the information provided for each form will be a discussion of the legal terms and conditions provided in the form. For each form, there is a numbered listing of the information that must be compiled to complete the form. After this information, a sample numbered form is provided that corresponds to the numbered listing of information needed to complete the form correctly.

For purposes of simplification, most of the forms in this book are set out as a form that would be used by two individuals. If businesses are parties to the contract, please identify the name and type of business entity (for example: Jackson Car Stereo, a New York sole proprietorship, etc.) in the first section of the contract. Many of the forms in this book have blanks for inserting the state or county. If you are a resident of Louisiana, substitute "parish" for "county." If you are a resident of Pennsylvania, Massachusetts, Virginia, or Kentucky, substitute "Commonwealth" for "state." If you are a resident of Washington D.C., please substitute "District of Columbia" for "state." In most cases, masculine and feminine terms have been eliminated and the generic "it" or "them" is used instead. In the few situations where this leads to awkward sentence construction, "his or her" or "he or she" may be used instead.

It is recommended that you review the table of contents of this book in order to gain a broad overview of the range and type of legal documents that are available. Then, before you prepare any of the forms for use, you should carefully read the introductory information and instructions in the chapter containing the particular form that you wish to use. Try to be as detailed and specific as possible as you fill in these forms. The more precise the description, the less likelihood that later disputes may develop over what was actually intended by the language chosen. The careful preparation and use of the legal forms in this book should provide the typical individual with most of the legal documents necessary for day-to-day life. If in doubt as to whether a particular form will work in a specific application, please consult a competent lawyer.

State Law Appendices Provided on CD

On the CD that accompanies this book are provided appendices that contain detailed information about differences in state laws regarding many of the forms in this book are provided. Please refer to them for information regarding your particular state's laws. The following state laws are outlined in these appendices:

- Real Estate Laws
- Business Registration Laws

Installation Instructions for Installing Forms-on-CD

Installation Instructions for PCs

1. Insert the enclosed CD in your computer.
2. The installation program will start automatically. Follow the onscreen dialogue and make your appropriate choices.
3. If the CD installation does not start automatically, click on START, then RUN, then BROWSE, and select your CD drive, and then select the file "Install.exe." Finally, click OK to run the installation program.
4. During the installation program, you will be prompted as to whether or not you wish to install the Adobe Acrobat Reader® program. This software program is necessary to view and fill in the PDF (potable document format) forms that are included on the Forms-on-CD. If you do not already have the Adobe Acrobat Reader® program installed on your hard drive, you will need to select the full installation that will install the program on your computer.

Installation Instructions for MACs®

1. Insert the enclosed CD in your computer.
2. Copy the folder "Forms for Macs" to your hard drive. All of the PDF and text-only forms are included in this folder.
3. If you do not already have the Adobe Acrobat Reader® program installed on your hard drive, you will need to download the version of this software that is appropriate for your particular MAC operating system from www.adobe.com. Note: The latest versions of the MAC operating system (OS-X) has PDF capabilities built into it.

Instructions for Using Forms-on-CD

All of the forms that are included in this book have been provided on the Forms-on-CD for your use if you have access to a computer. If you have completed the Forms-on-CD installation program, all of the forms will have been copied to your computer's hard drive. By default, these files are installed in the C:\SmallBusinessLegalForms\ Forms folder which is created by the installation program. (Note for MAC users: see instructions above). Opening the Forms folder will provide you with access to folders for each of the topics corresponding to chapters in the book. Within each chapter, the forms are provided in two separate formats:

Text forms may be opened, prepared, and printed from within your own word processing program (such as Microsoft Word®, or WordPerfect®). The text forms all have the file extension: .txt. These forms are located in the TEXT FORMS folders supplied for each chapter's forms. You will use the forms in this format if you will be making changes to any of the text on the forms.

PDF forms may be filled in on your computer screen and printed out on any printer. This particular format provides the most widely-used format for accessing computer files. Files in this format may be opened as images on your computer and printed out on any printer. The files in PDF format all have the file extension: .pdf. Although this format provides the easiest method for completing the forms, the forms in this format can not be altered (other than to fill in the information required on the blanks provided). To access the PDF forms, please see below. If you wish to alter the language in any of the forms, you will need to access the forms in their text-only versions.

To Access PDF Forms

1. You must have already installed the Adobe Acrobat Reader® program to your computer's hard drive. This program is installed automatically by the installation program. (MAC users will need to install this program via www.adobe.com).

2. On your computer's desktop, you will find a shortcut icon labeled "Acrobat Reader®" Using your mouse, left double- click on this icon. This will open the Acrobat Reader® program. When the Acrobat Reader® program is opened for the first time, you will need to accept the Licensing Agreement from Adobe in order to use this program. Click "Accept" when given the option to accept or decline the Agreement.

3. Once the Acrobat Reader® program is open on your computer, click on FILE (in the upper left-hand corner of the upper taskbar). Then click on OPEN in the drop down menu. Depending on which version of Windows or other operating system you are using, a box will open which will allow you to access files on your computer's hard drive. The files for small business forms are located on your computer's "C" drive, under the folder "Small Business Legal Forms." In this folder, you will find a subfolder "Forms." (Note: if you installed the forms folder on a different drive, access the forms on that particular drive).

4. If you desire to work with one of the forms, you should then left double-click your mouse on the sub-folder: "Forms." A list of form topics (corresponding to the chapters in the book) will appear and you should then left double-click your mouse on the topic of your choice. This will open two folders: one for text forms and one for PDF forms. Left double click your mouse on the PDF forms folder and a list of the PDF forms for that topic should appear. Left double- click your mouse on the form of your choice. This will open the appropriate form within the Acrobat Reader® program.

To Fill in and Use PDF Forms

1. Once you have opened the appropriate form in the Acrobat Reader® program, filling in the form is a simple process. A 'hand tool' icon will be your cursor in the Acrobat Reader® program. Move the 'hand tool' cursor to the first blank space that will need to be completed on the form. A vertical line or "I-beam" should appear at the beginning of the first space on a form that you will need to fill in. You may then begin to type the necessary information in the space provided. When you have filled in the first blank space, hit the TAB key on your keyboard. This will move the 'hand' cursor to the next space which must be filled in. Please note that some of the spaces in the forms must be completed by hand, specifically the signature, witness and notary blanks.

2. Move through the form, completing each required space, and hitting TAB to move to the next space to be filled in. For details on the information required for each blank on the forms, please read the instructions in this book. When you have completed all of the fill-ins, you may print out the form on your computer's printer. (Please note: hitting TAB after the last fill-in will return you to the first page of the form.)

3. If you wish to save a completed form, you should "save as" a renamed form. This will allow you to retain a blank form on your hard drive for later use.

To Access and Complete Text Forms

For your convenience, all of the forms in this book (except certain state-specific forms) are also provided as text-only forms which may be altered and saved. To open and use any of the text forms:

1. First, open your preferred word processing program. Then click on FILE (in the upper left-hand corner of the upper taskbar). Then click on OPEN in the drop down menu. Depending on which version of Windows or other operating system you are using, a box will open which will allow you to access files on your computer's hard drive. The files for small business forms are located on your computer's "C" drive, under the folder "Small Business Legal Forms." In this folder, you will find a sub-folder: "Forms."

2. If you desire to work with one of the forms, you should then left double-click your mouse on the sub-folder: "Forms." A list of form topics (corresponding to the chapters in the book) will appear and you should then left double-click your mouse on the topic of your choice. This will open two folders: one for text forms and one for PDF forms. Left double-click your mouse on the text forms folder and a list of the text forms for that topic should appear. Left double-click your mouse on the form of your choice. This will open the appropriate form within your word processing program.

3. You may now fill in the necessary information while the text-only file is open in your word processing program. You may need to adjust margins and/or line endings of the form to fit your particular word processing program. Note that there is an asterisk (*) in every location in these forms where information will need to be included. Replace each asterisk with the necessary information. When the form is complete, you may print out the completed form and you may save the completed form. If you wish to save the completed form, you should rename the form so that your hard drive will retain an unaltered version of the original form.

Technical Support

Please also note that Nova Publishing Company cannot provide legal advice regarding the effect or use of the forms in this book or on the CD. For questions about installing the Forms-on-CD and software, you may access the Nova Publishing Website for support at www.novapublishing.com.

DISCLAIMER AND WARNING: Any Nova legal product, whether book, CD, kit, or individual legal form should only be a starting point for you and should not be used nor relied upon without consulting with an attorney first. Nova legal products are not intended as a substitute for legal advice. Nova legal products contains the basic terms and language that should be included in similar legal documents. However, laws vary from time to time and from state to state. Purchasers and persons intending to use this Nova legal product for the preparation of any legal document are advised to check specifically on the current applicable laws in any jurisdiction in which they intend the documents to be effective and to determine the existence of any state-specific requirements. Although Nova Publishing Company and its authors try to keep Nova legal products accurate and up-to-date, the accuracy of any of these products can not be guaranteed. Because of differing interpretations of law in different jurisdictions and possible unanticipated changes in governing statutes and case law relating to the application of any information contained in any Nova legal product, the author, publisher, and any and all persons or entities involved in any way in the preparation, publication, sale, or distribution of this book disclaim all responsibility for the legal effects or consequences of any document prepared or action taken in reliance upon information contained in any Nova product. These legal products are provided 'as-is" and are used at your own risk. No representations or warranties either express or implied, are made or given regarding suitability, merchantability, fitness for a particular purpose, or completeness for a particular purpose, nor regarding the legal consequences of a particular use of any information contained in any Nova legal product. Neither Nova Publishing Company, nor its authors, shall be responsible or liable for any direct or indirect, incidental, special, exemplary, or consequential damages (including, but not limited to, procurement of substitute goods or services; loss of use, data, or profits; or business interruption) however used, and on any theory of liability whatsoever, whether in contract, strict liability, or tort (including negligence or otherwise) arising in any way out of the use of any Nova legal product or materials. Nova legal products are not printed, published, sold, circulated, or distributed with the intention that it be used to procure or aid in the procurement of any legal effect or ruling in any jurisdiction in which such procurement or aid may be restricted by statute.

California Residents: Please note that a California Notary Acknowledgement form is required to be used on documents that are intended to be valid in California. The California Notary Acknowledgment form is included on the CD.

Florida and Georgia Residents: Please note that there are state-specific forms for the Claim of Lien that must be used in your particular states. These forms are contained on the CD only.

All Users: Please check in the provided Appendices for any state-specific laws/forms.

Chapter 1

Business Operations Agreements

One of the first decisions that a potential business owner must confront is how the business should be structured and operated. This crucial decision must be made even before the business has actually begun operations. The legal documents which will generally accompany the formation of a business can follow many different patterns, depending on the particular situation and the type of business to be undertaken. There are two initial decisions which must be made in order to begin a business operation: the type of business entity to be used and from where the business assets will come.

First, the type of business entity to be used must be selected. There are many basic forms of business operating entities. The five most common forms are:

- Sole proprietorship
- Partnership
- Corporation
- S-corporation
- Limited liability company

The choice of entity for a particular business depends on many factors. Which of these forms of business organization is chosen can have a great impact on the success of the business. The structure chosen will have an effect on how easy it is to obtain financing, how taxes are paid, how accounting records are kept, whether personal assets are at risk in the venture, the amount of control the "owner" has over the business, and many other aspects of the business.

Keep in mind that the initial choice of business organization need not be the final choice. It is often wise to begin with the most simple form, the sole proprietorship, until the business progresses to a point where another form is clearly indicated. This allows the business to begin in the least complicated manner and allows the owner to retain total control in the important formative period of the business. As the business grows and the potential for liability and tax burdens increase, circumstances may dictate a re-examination of the business structure.

Sole Proprietorship

A sole proprietorship is both the simplest and the most prevalent form of business organization. An important reason for this is that it is the least regulated of all types of business structures. Technically, the *sole proprietorship* is the traditional unincorporated one-person business. For legal and tax purposes, the business is the owner. It has no existence outside the owner. The liabilities of the business are personal to the owner and the business ends when the owner dies. On the other hand, all of the profits are also personal to the owner and the sole owner has full control of the business. For more information on sole proprietorships, please see Nova Publishing Company's *Sole Proprietorship: Small Business Start-Up Kit*.

Partnership

A *partnership* is a relationship existing between two or more persons who join together to carry on a trade or business. Each partner contributes money, property, labor, or skill to the partnership and, in return, expects to share in the profits or losses of the business. A partnership is usually based on a partnership agreement of some type, although the agreement need not be a formal document. It may simply be an oral understanding between the partners, although this is not recommended.

A simple joint undertaking to share expenses is not considered a partnership, nor is a mere co-ownership of property that is maintained and leased or rented. To be considered a partnership for legal and tax purposes, the following factors are usually considered:

- The partner's conduct in carrying out the provisions of the partnership agreement
- The relationship of the parties
- The abilities and contributions of each party to the partnership

- The control each partner has over the partnership income and the purposes for which the income is used

Note: a basic Partnership Agreement is included later in this chapter.

Corporation

A *corporation* is a creation of law. It is governed by the laws of the state of incorporation and the state or states in which it does business. In recent years it has become the business structure of choice for many small businesses. Corporations are, generally, a more complex form of business operation than either a sole proprietorship or partnership. They are also subject to far more state regulations regarding both their formation and operation. Because of this, legal documents for the formation of a corporation are beyond the scope of this book and are not included. Legal forms for the formation and operation of a corporation are contained in Nova Publishing's *Corporation: Small Business Start-up Kit*. The following discussion is provided in order to allow the potential business owner an understanding of this type of business operation.

The corporation is an artificial entity. It is created by filing Articles of Incorporation with the proper state authorities. This gives the corporation its legal existence and the right to carry on business. Adoption of *corporate bylaws*, or internal rules of operation, is often the first business of the corporation. In its simplest form, the corporate organizational structure consists of the following levels:

- **Shareholders:** who own shares of the business but do not contribute to the direct management of the corporation, other than by electing the directors of the corporation

- **Directors:** who may be shareholders, but as directors do not own any of the business. They are responsible, jointly as members of the board of directors of the corporation, for making the major business decisions of the corporation, including appointing the officers of the corporation

- **Officers:** who may be shareholders and/or directors, but, as officers, do not own any of the business. The officers (generally the president, vice president, secretary, and treasurer) are responsible for the day-to-day operation of the business

S-Corporation

The *S-corporation* is a certain type of corporation that is available for specific tax purposes. It is a creature of the Internal Revenue Service. Its purpose is to allow small corporations to choose to be taxed like a partnership, but to also enjoy many of the benefits of a corporation. Formation of an S-corporation is beyond the scope of this book. Legal forms for the formation and operation of an S-corporation are contained in Nova Publishing's *S-Corporation: The Small Business Start-Up Kit.* The following discussion is provided in order to allow the potential business owner an understanding of this type of business operation.

In general, to qualify as an S-corporation under current IRS rules, a corporation must have no more than 100 shareholders, all of whom must be individuals; it must only have one class of stock; and each of the shareholders must consent to the choice of S-corporation status.

The S-corporation retains all of the advantages and disadvantages of the traditional corporation except in the area of taxation. For tax purposes, S-corporation shareholders are treated similarly to partners in a partnership. The income, losses, and deductions generated by an S-corporation are "passed through" the corporate entity to the individual shareholders. Thus, there is no "double" taxation of an S-type corporation. In addition, unlike a standard corporation, shareholders of S-corporations can deduct personally any corporate losses.

Limited Liability Company

A relatively new business form is the *limited liability company.* This business form has been adopted in some manner in all states. It is, essentially, a non-incorporated business form which has been given limited legal liability by legislative mandate. Thus, this hybrid type of business has the pass-through taxation advantages of a partnership and the limited legal liability of a corporation. This type of company consists of one or more members/owners who manage the company. There may also be non-member managers employed to handle the business. As a hybrid-type business structure, this form has many of the same advantages and disadvantages as both corporations (particularly S-corporations) and partnerships. One unique advantage that the limited liability company has over standard corporations is the increased flexibility to allocate profits and losses to its members. As this is a new form of business, you are advised to consult a competent business lawyer for assistance in operating as a limited liability company or check out Nova Publishing Company's *Limited Liability Company: Small Business Start-up Kit.*

Instructions for Business Operations Forms

In addition to selecting the type of structure that the business will take, the other important factor in the initial start-up of a business is where the basic assets of the business will come from. From the point of view of someone who is starting a business, the equipment and supplies needed to begin a business are often purchased from an on-going concern. A purchase of business assets for the purpose of beginning an enterprise will generally take two forms: the purchase of an entire business or the purchase of specific assets and equipment only. There are two legal agreements included in this chapter for these situations. Their use is outlined below.

The following documents are included in this chapter for use in purchasing, selling, or forming a business:

Agreement for Sale of Business: This form should be used when one party is purchasing an entire business from another party. The form, as shown in this book, is set up for use in the sale of a sole proprietorship to an individual. This structure can be easily adapted to fit other particular situations if necessary. For example, if the business being sold is a partnership and the buyer is a corporation, a few simple substitutions will be necessary to change the document to the appropriate form. Simply substitute the name and address of the partnership for the seller's name wherever indicated and substitute the name and address of the corporate buyer where necessary. If changes are made in the type of entity doing the buying or selling on this form, the appropriate notarization and signature line from Chapter 3 must be used also. *Note:* The notarization on this form is only necessary if the sale of the business includes the sale of real estate. A notarization will be needed in order to record this document with the appropriate county office. A sample numbered version of this form is found on page 33.

The following information will have to be used to fill in this form:

① Date of agreement
② Name of seller
③ Address of seller with name of city and state
④ Name of buyer
⑤ Address of buyer with name of city and state
⑥ Type of business
⑦ Name of business
⑧ Address of business with name of city and state
⑨ Address of business premises with name of city and state
⑩ Amount of full purchase

⑪ Amount for premises
⑫ Amount for equipment/furniture
⑬ Amount for goodwill
⑭ Amount for stock-in-trade/inventory
⑮ Amount for notes/accounts receivable
⑯ Amount for any outstanding contracts
⑰ Breakdown of purchase price : amount of earnest money
⑱ Amount of cash down payment
⑲ Amount of promissory note
⑳ Amount of total price
㉑ Amount of promissory note
㉒ Interest rate of promissory note
㉓ Number of years to pay on note
㉔ Amount of payment per month of note
㉕ Amount of earnest money
㉖ Date of closing
㉗ Time of closing
㉘ Address of closing with name of city and state
㉙ List all other documents provided to buyer
㉚ State where sale takes place
㉛ Date of balance sheet
㉜ Radius from business that seller cannot compete
㉝ Number of years that seller cannot compete
㉞ Amount of insurance
㉟ Any additional terms
㊱ State where business is sold
㊲ Date of signatures
㊳ Signature of seller
㊴ Printed name of seller
㊵ Name of Business (Doing Business As)
㊶ Type of business
㊷ State where business will operate
㊸ Signature of buyer
㊹ Printed name of buyer
㊺ Notary will complete this section

The sale of a complete and ongoing business is one of the most complex business transactions that a small businessperson will encounter. It may incorporate many other the legal documents.

Agreement for Sale of Business Assets: This form should be used when one party is purchasing only certain business assets from another party. As in the previous form, this form, as it is shown in this book, is set up for use in the sale of sole proprietorship assets to an individual. This structure may be easily adapted to fit other particular situations if necessary. For example, if the business assets are being sold by a partnership and the buyer is a corporation, a few simple substitutions will be necessary to change the document to the appropriate form. Simply substitute the name and address of the partnership for the seller's name wherever indicated, substitute the name and address of the corporate buyer where necessary, and provide the proper signature lines as shown in Chapter 4. *Note*: Notarization is not provided for this form. Notarization of this form is only necessary if the sale of the business assets includes the sale of real estate. In that case, a notarization will be needed in order to record this document with the appropriate county real estate records office. A sample numbered version of this form is found on page 38.

The following information will have to be used to fill in this form:

① Date of agreement
② Name of seller
③ Address of seller with name of city and state
④ Name of buyer
⑤ Address of buyer with name of city and state
⑥ Type of business
⑦ Name of business
⑧ Adress of business with name of city and state
⑨ Amount of full purchase
⑩ Breakdown of purchase price : amount of earnest money
⑪ Amount of cash down payment
⑫ Amount of promissory note
⑬ Amount of total price
⑭ Amount of promissory note
⑮ Interest rate of promissory note
⑯ Number of years to pay on note
⑰ Amount of payment per month of note
⑱ Amount of earnest money
⑲ Date of closing
⑳ Time of closing
㉑ Address of closing with name of city and state
㉒ List all other documents provided to buyer
㉓ Other adjustments to purchase price
㉔ Amount of insurance
㉕ Any additional terms

㉖ State where business assets are sold
㉗ Date of signatures
㉘ Signature of seller
㉙ Printed name of seller
㉚ Name of Business (Doing Business As)
㉛ Type of business
㉜ State where business will operate
㉝ Signature of buyer
㉞ Printed name of buyer

Note that you may also need additional documents in conjunction with the basic Agreement for Sale of Business Assets form.

Notice of Intention to Use Fictitious Name: This form is a notice to be published in a local newspaper a certain number of times which publicly declares the intention of using a fictitious name in a business. It is generally used for setting up a sole proprietorship or partnership. This form is completed by filling in the address of the business, the fictitious name of the business, and the name and percent of interest of all owners of the business.

The general method of registration follows two steps. First, a legal notice (Notice of Intention to Use Fictitious Name) containing the information in the filed document must, generally, be run in a local newspaper for a specified number of times. Second, the Affidavit, or registration form, is actually filed with the appropriate county records office. The legal affidavit provided for this registration should be valid in virtually all jurisdictions. However, certain locales may have slightly differing forms which must be used. Check with your local newspaper and with your county records office to see if the form provided is acceptable in your area. A sample numbered version of this form is found on page 41.

The following information will have to be used to fill in this form:

① Address of business
② Fictitious name
③ Name of all owners with interest in business
④ Percent of business
⑤ Date of signatures
⑥ Signatures of all owners
⑦ Printed names of all owners

Affidavit of Use of Fictitious Business Name: The registration of the use of a fictitious name is, in most jurisdictions, one of the only documents that needs to be completed prior to operating a business as a sole proprietorship. The purpose of this document is to place on a public record a statement verifying the actual name of the owner of a business that operates under a fictitious name. For example: if Ms. Jill Smith operates Golden Scissors Hair Styling Salon as a sole proprietorship, she would need to register her use of the fictitious name "Golden Scissors Hair Styling." This registration will allow any third party to check the public records and determine who is actually responsible for the business liabilities and debts. The rationale for this registration is to provide a public record of the name of the owner for the purpose of lawsuits. A sample numbered version of this form is found on page 42.

The following information will have to be used to fill in this form:

① State of Affidavit
② County of Affidavit
③ Address of business
④ Fictitious name
⑤ Name of all owners with interest in business
⑥ Percent of business
⑦ Date of signatures
⑧ Signatures of all owners
⑨ Printed names of all owners
⑩ Notary will complete the following section

Partnership Agreement: This legal agreement is for use in beginning a partnership. This particular agreement provides for four partners to join into a partnership. Any number of partners, however, can be used with this agreement by simple addition or deletion of names and signature lines. A sample numbered version of this form is found on page 43.

The information necessary to complete this form is as follows:

① Date of the Partnership Agreement

② State in which the Partnership will be operating under. In general, the partnership should be begun in the state in which it will conduct business.

③ Partnership Name: The selection of a name is often crucial to the success of a partnership. The name must not conflict with any existing company names, nor can it be deceptively similar to other names. It is often wise to clearly explain the business of the partnership through the choice of name. Many states require or allow the registration of the use of a fictitious partnership name. Check the Appendix on the enclosed CD for the listing for your state on partnership name registration.

④ Partnership Office: This must be the address of the actual physical location of the main business. It may not be a post office box. If the partnership is home-based, this address should be the home address.

⑤ Purpose of the Partnership: Here you may note the specific business purpose of the partnership. In your Partnership Agreement you will also note that your partnership has a general purpose of engaging in any and all lawful business in your state.

⑥ Term of the Partnership: Proposed date to begin partnership business. This should be the date on which you expect the partnership to begin its legal existence. Decide if the partnership is to be for a certain term, to end on a certain date, or to continue until the partners' death.

⑦ Contributions and Start-Up Capital: Start with the total initial investment. This figure is the total amount of money or property that will be transferred, or services that will be rendered to the partnership by each partner upon the beginning of partnership business. List also the dates on which the contributions must be made.

⑧ Additional Contributions: If there are to be planned additional partner contributions of money, services, or property, list them here.

⑨ Failure to make Contributions: Select appropriate action

⑩ Interest on Contributions: Select appropriate action

⑪ Loans to Partnership: List any addition contributions that will be loaned to the Partnership

⑫ Share of the Partnership: Under this heading, list the proportionate share of the profits and losses of the partnership for each partner. The shares can be equal, or related to the proportionate contributions of each partner.

⑬ Distribution of Profits and Losses: Here decide how the partnership will distribute its profits and cover its losses. If the partnership will retain a portion of the profits for reinvestment, note that here.

⑭ Management of the Partnership: If the business will be managed equally or in differing proportions by the partners, note that here.

⑮ Managing Partners: If one or more partners will be appointed as managing partners, also make note of that decision.

⑯ Date and Time of Annual Partnership Meeting: This will be the date proposed for holding the first meeting of the partnership.

⑰ Financial Matters: Here list the authority of each proposed partner to sign checks, borrow money in the partnership's name, or sign documents in the name of the partnership.

⑱ Bank Account: In advance of partnership, you should determine the bank that will handle the partnership account. Obtain from the bank the necessary bank paperwork, that will be signed by partners at the first partners meeting.

⑲ Loans to Partners: In this item, decide if you wish the partnership to have the ability to make loans directly to the partners.   .

⑳ Draws of Partners: In this listing, make note of the ability of partners to obtain draws against their individual shares of the annual profits of the partnership. These draws can be monthly, quarterly, annual, or on some other basis.

㉑ Salaries of Partners: Here you should decide if the partners will earn a salary for their work on behalf of the partnership.

㉒ Partner Expense Accounts: Here note if partners are allowed expense accounts for the normal expenses of the business. If so, note the maximum monthly amount of the expense account.

㉓ Transfer of Partnership Interests: Under this listing, a decision should be made as to whether and how partners are allowed to transfer their ownership interest in the partnership. This may range from "not at all" to "freely" or may be by unanimous or majority consent of the other partners.

㉔ Expulsion of Partners: Here you should consider the terms and conditions for removing a partner.

㉕ Insurance: Under this heading, consider the types of insurance that you will need, ranging from general casualty to various business liability policies. Also consider the need for the partners or the partnership to provide the partners with life and/or disability insurance.

㉖ Mediation or Arbitration: Select appropriate action that partners will use during times of mediation.

㉗ Admission of New Partners: Will new partners be allowed into the partnership? Here note the terms and conditions for their entry.

㉘ Responsibility New Partners: Select appropriate situation for any new partner.

㉙ Withdrawl from the Partnership: Select appropriate action for partner with-drawls.

㉚ Outside Activities of Partnership: Select appropriate situation for partnership activity and possible competition.

㉛ Termination of Partnership: How will the partnership end? Here list any considerations relating to the dissolution of the partnership that you may wish to be considered.

㉜ Amendments to Partnership Agreement: Here should be the determination of how to amend the Partnership Agreement. The forms in this book are designed to allow the Partnership Agreement to be amended either by unanimous or majority vote of the partners.

㉝ Additional Provisions: List any additional provisions.

㉞ Modification of Agreement: select appropriate modifications agreement (all partners or just majority)

㉟ State in which the Partnership will be operating under. In general, the partnership should be begun in the state in which it will conduct business.

㊱ Date that patnership agreement was signed

㊲ Signature and Printed Name of Partner #1

㊳ Signature and Printed Name of Partner #2

㊴ Signature and Printed Name of Partner #3

AGREEMENT FOR SALE OF BUSINESS

This agreement is made on ①_____ , 20 _____ , between ②_____ , seller, of ③_____ , City of _____ , State of _____ , and ④_____ , buyer, of ⑤_____ , City of _____ , State of _____ .

The seller now owns and conducts a ⑥_____ business, under the name of ⑦_____ , located at ⑧_____ , City of _____ , State of _____ .

For valuable consideration, the seller agrees to sell and the buyer agrees to buy this business for the following price and on the following terms:

1. The seller will sell to the buyer, free from all liabilities, claims, and indebtedness, the seller's business, including the premises located at ⑨_____ , City of _____ , State of _____ , and all other assets of the business as listed on Exhibit A, which is attached and is a part of this agreement.

2. The buyer agrees to pay the seller the sum of $ ⑩_____ , which the seller agrees to accept as full payment. The purchase price will be allocated to the assets of the business as follows:

a. The premises $ ⑪_____
b. Equipment/furniture $ ⑫_____
c. Goodwill $ ⑬_____
d. Stock-in-trade/inventory $ ⑭_____
e. Notes/accounts receivable $ ⑮_____
f. Outstanding contracts $ ⑯_____

3. The purchase price will be paid as follows:

Earnest money $ ⑰_____
Cash down payment $ ⑱_____
Promissory note payable $ ⑲_____
TOTAL Price $ ⑳_____

The $ ㉑_____ Promissory Note will bear interest at ㉒_____ % (_____ percent) per year, payable monthly for

㉓_____ years at $ ㉔_____ per month with the first payment due one (1) month after the date of closing. The Promissory Note will be secured by a U.C.C. Financing Statement and a Security Agreement in the usual commercial form. The Promissory Note will be prepayable without limitation or penalty.

4. The seller acknowledges receiving the earnest money deposit of $ ㉕_____ from the buyer. If this sale is not completed for any valid reason, this money will be returned to the buyer without penalty or interest.

5. This agreement will close on ㉖_____ , 20 _____ , at ㉗____ o'clock ___ . m., at ㉘_____ , City of _____ , State of _____ .

At that time, and upon payment by the buyer of the portion of the purchase price then due, the seller will deliver to buyer the following documents:

a. A Bill of Sale for all personal property (equipment, inventory, parts, supplies, and any other personal property)
b. A Warranty Deed for any real estate
c. All accounting books and records
d. All customer and supplier lists
e. A valid assignment of any lease
f. All other documents of transfer as listed below: ㉙

At closing, adjustments to the purchase price will be made for the following items:

a. Changes in inventory since this agreement was made
b. Insurance premiums
c. Payroll and payroll taxes
d. Rental payments
e. Utilities
f. Property taxes
g. The following other items:

6. The seller represents and warrants that it is duly qualified under the laws of the State of ㉚_____ to carry on the business being sold, and has complied with and is not in violation of any laws or regulations affecting the seller's business, including any laws governing bulk sales or transfers.

7. Attached as part of this agreement as Exhibit B is a Balance Sheet of the seller as of ㉛_____ , 20 _____ , which has been prepared according to generally accepted accounting principles. The seller warrants that this Balance Sheet fairly represents the financial position of the seller as of that date and sets out any contractual obligations of the seller. If this sale includes the sale of inventory of the business, the seller has provided the buyer with a completed Bulk Transfer Affidavit containing a complete list of all creditors of the seller, together with the amount claimed to be due to each creditor.

8. Seller represents that it has good and marketable title to all of the assets shown on Exhibit A, and that those assets are free and clear of any restrictions on transfer and all claims, taxes, indebtedness, or liabilities except those specified on the Exhibit B Balance Sheet. The seller also warrants that all equipment will be delivered in working order on the date of closing.

9. Seller agrees not to participate in any way, either directly or indirectly, in a business similar to that being sold to the buyer, within a radius of ㉜____ __ miles from this business, for a period of ㉝_____ years from the date of closing.

10. Between the date of this agreement and the date of closing of the sale, the seller agrees to carry on the business in the usual manner and agrees not to enter into any unusual contract or other agreement affecting the operation of the business without the consent of the buyer.

11. The buyer represents that it is financially capable of completing the purchase of this business and fully understands its obligations under this agreement.

12. Buyer agrees to carry hazard and liability insurance on the assets of the business in the amount of $ ㉞_____ and to provide the seller with proof of this coverage until the Promissory Note is paid in full. However, the risk of any loss or damage to any assets being sold remain with the seller until the date of closing.

13. Any additional terms: ㉟

14. No modification of this agreement will be effective unless it is in writing and is signed by both the buyer and seller. This agreement binds and benefits both the buyer and seller and any successors. Time is of the essence of this agreement. This document, including any attachments, is the entire agreement

between the buyer and seller. This agreement is governed by the laws of the State of ㊱_____ .

Dated: ㊲_____ , 20 _____

㊳_____
Signature of Seller

㊴_____
Printed Name of Seller

DBA
㊵_____
Name of Business

A(n) ㊶_____ (type of business)

State of Operation ㊷_____

㊸_____
Signature of Buyer

㊹_____
Printed Name of Buyer

㊺
State of _____
County of _____
On _____ , 20 _____ , _____
personally came before me and, being duly sworn, did state that he or she is the person who owns the business described in the above document and that he or she signed the above document in my presence on behalf of the business and on his or her own behalf.

_____
Signature of Notary Public

Notary Public, In and for the County of _____
State of _____
My commission expires: _____ , 20 _____
Notary Seal

㊺

State of _____

County of _____

On _____ , 20 _____ , _____

personally came before me and, being duly sworn, did state that he or she is the person described in the above document as the buyer and that he or she signed the above document in my presence.

_____

Signature of Notary Public

Notary Public, In and for the County of _____

State of _____

My commission expires: _____ , 20 _____ Notary Seal

AGREEMENT FOR SALE OF BUSINESS ASSETS

This agreement is made on ① _____ , 20 _____ , between
② _____ , seller, of ③ _____ , City of
_____ , State of _____ , and ④ _____ ,
buyer, of ⑤ _____ , City of _____ , State of
_____ .

The seller now owns and conducts a ⑥ _____ business, under the
name of ⑦ _____ , located at ⑧ _____
, City of _____ , State of _____ .

For valuable consideration, the seller agrees to sell and the buyer agrees to
buy certain assets of this business for the following price and on the following
terms:

1. The seller will sell to the buyer certain assets of the business as listed on
Exhibit A, which is attached and is a part of this agreement. The assets will be
transferred free from all liabilities, claims, and indebtedness, unless listed on
Exhibit A.

2. The buyer agrees to pay the seller the sum of $ ⑨ _____ ,
which the seller agrees to accept as full payment.

3. The purchase price will be paid as follows:

Earnest money	$ ⑩ _____
Cash down payment	$ ⑪ _____
Promissory note payable	$ ⑫ _____
TOTAL Price	$ ⑬ _____

The $ ⑭ _____ Promissory Note will bear interest at ⑮ _____ %
(_____ percent) per year, payable monthly for ⑯ _____ years at
$ ⑰ _____ per month with the first payment due one (1)
month after the date of closing. The Promissory Note will be secured by a
UCC Financing Statement and a Security Agreement in the usual commercial
form. The Promissory Note will be prepayable without limitation or penalty.

4. The seller acknowledges receiving the earnest money deposit of
$ ⑱ _____ from the buyer. If this sale is not completed for any valid reason,

this money will be returned to the buyer without penalty or interest.

5. This agreement will close on ⑲_____ , 20 _____ , at ⑳_____ o'clock ____ . m., at ㉑_____, City of _____ , State of _____ .

At that time, and upon payment by buyer of the portion of the purchase price then due, the seller will deliver to buyer the following documents:

a. A Bill of Sale for all personal property (equipment, inventory, parts, supplies, and any other personal property)
b. All other documents of transfer as listed below: ㉒

At closing, adjustments to the purchase price will be made for changes in inventory since this agreement was made, and for the following other items: ㉓

6. The seller represents and warrants that it is in full compliance with and is not in violation of any laws or regulations affecting the seller's business, including any laws governing bulk sales or transfers.

7. Seller represents that it has good and marketable title to all of the assets shown on Exhibit A, and that those assets are free and clear of any restrictions on transfer, claims, taxes, indebtedness, or liabilities except those specified on the Exhibit A. If this sale includes the sale of inventory of the business, the seller has provided the buyer with a completed Bulk Transfer Affidavit containing a complete list of all creditors of the seller, together with the amount claimed to be due to each creditor. Seller also warrants that all equipment will be delivered in working order on the date of closing.

8. Between the date of this agreement and the date of closing of the sale, the seller agrees to carry on the business in the usual manner and agrees not to enter into any unusual contract or other agreement affecting the business assets being sold without the consent of the buyer.

9. The buyer represents that it is financially capable of completing the purchase of these business assets and fully understands its obligations under this agreement.

10. Buyer agrees to carry hazard and liability insurance on the assets of the

business in the amount of $ ㉔_____ and to provide the seller with proof of this coverage until the Promissory Note is paid in full. However, the risk of any loss or damage to any assets being sold remain with the seller until the date of closing.

11. Any additional terms: ㉕

12. No modification of this agreement will be effective unless it is in writing and is signed by both the buyer and seller. This agreement binds and benefits both the buyer and seller and any successors. Time is of the essence of this agreement. This document, including any attachments, is the entire agreement between the buyer and seller. This agreement is governed by the laws of the State of ㉖_____ .

Dated: ㉗_____ , 20 _____

㉘_____
Signature of Seller

㉙_____
Printed Name of Seller

DBA
㉚_____
Name of Business

A(n) ㉛_____ (type of business)

State of Operation ㉜_____

㉝_____
Signature of Buyer

㉞_____
Printed Name of Buyer

NOTICE OF INTENTION TO USE FICTITIOUS BUSINESS NAME

NOTICE is hereby given that the undersigned intends to engage in business at the following address: ①

under the fictitious business name of: ②

The full and true name of every person with an interest in this business and the ownership interest of each person is as follows:

③ *Name*   ④ *Percent of*
Interest

_____   _____
_____   _____
_____   _____
_____   _____
_____   _____
_____   _____

Dated: ⑤_____ , 20 _____

⑥ *Signature of Owner(s)*   ⑦ *Printed Name of Owner(s)*

_____   _____
_____   _____
_____   _____
_____   _____
_____   _____

AFFIDAVIT OF USE OF FICTITIOUS BUSINESS NAME

State of ①_____

County of ②_____

It is hereby stated, under oath, that pursuant to law:

1. The undersigned intends to engage in business at the following address:③

under the fictitious name of: ④

2. The full and true name of every person with an interest in this business and the ownership interest of each person is as follows:

⑤Name   ⑥Percent of Interest

_____   _____

_____   _____

3. A Proof of Publication of a Notice of Intention to Use a Fictitious Name is filed with this affidavit.

Dated: ⑦_____ , 20 _____

⑧Signature of Owner(s)   ⑨Printed Name of Owner(s)

_____   _____

_____   _____

⑩
State of _____
County of _____
On _____ , 20 _____ , _____
personally came before me and, being duly sworn, did state that he, she, or they is or are the person(s) who own(s) the business described in the above document and that he, she, or they signed the above document in my presence.

_____
Signature of Notary PublicNotary Public,
In and for the County of _____
State of _____

My commission expires: _____ , 20 _____
Notary Seal

PARTNERSHIP AGREEMENT

This Partnership Agreement is made on ①_____ , 20 _____ , by and between the partners whose signatures are on this agreement.

Agreement. ②

The parties to this Agreement agree to carry on a partnership operating under the laws of the State of _____ under the following terms and conditions:

Partnership Name. ③

The partnership shall be known as: _____
This name shall be property of the partnership.

Partnership Office. ④

The partnership's principal place of business shall be: _____

Purpose of the Partnership. ⑤

The purpose of this partnership is to: _____

In addition, the partners agree that the partnership may also engage in any lawful business under the laws of the State of _____ as the partners may agree to, from time to time.

Term of the Partnership. ⑥

☐ The partnership will begin on _____ , 20 ____, and end on _____ , 20 _____ .

☐ The partnership will begin on _____ , 20 ____, and end when terminated by agreement of all of the partners.

☐ The partnership will begin on _____ , 20 ____, and end on the death or withdrawal of any partner.

Contributions and Start-up Capital. ⑦

The start-up capital will be a total of $ _____ . Each partner of the partnership agrees to contribute the following property, services, or cash to this total amount:

Name   Cash/Services/Property   Value
_____
_____
_____
_____

If the partner's contribution is cash, the contribution shall be delivered to the partnership on or before _____ , 20 _____ .

If the partner's contribution is property, the contribution shall be delivered to the partnership on or before _____ , 20 _____ .

If the partner's contribution is in the form of services, the services which are to be performed are as follows: _____ .

and shall be performed according to the following schedule: _____

Additional Contributions. ⑧

☐ If additional capital is required by the partnership and is determined by a majority vote of the partners, then each partner shall be required to contribute to such additional capital in proportion to each partner's interest in the partnership as set forth in this Agreement.

☐ If additional capital is required by the partnership and is determined by a unanimous vote of the partners, then each partner shall be required to contribute to such additional capital in proportion to each partner's interest in the partnership as set forth in this Agreement.

☐ Each partner shall be required to contribute a _____ percent share of his or her profits to the partnership on an annual basis.

☐ Each partner shall contribute the following property, cash, or services to the partnership on an annual basis:

Name	Cash/services/property	Value

☐ If the partner's contribution is cash, the contribution shall be delivered to the partnership on or before _____ , 20 _____ .

☐ Additional Contributions. If the partner's contribution is property, the contribution shall be delivered to the partnership on or before ___ , 20 ___ .

☐ If the partner's contribution is in the form of services, the services which are to be performed are as follows: _____ , and shall be performed according to the following schedule: _____

☐ Each partner shall be required to work in the partnership business as follows: _____

Failure to Make Contributions. ⑨

☐ If any partner shall fail to make their initial or additional contributions as indicated by this Agreement, any Amendment to this Agreement, or any additional Agreement between the partners, whether such contributions were to be cash, services, or property, then this partnership shall be immediately terminated and each partner who has made a contribution shall be entitled to an immediate return of any property or cash contributed or for reimbursement from the partnership for any services provided.

☐ If any partner shall fail to make their initial or additional contributions as indicated by this Agreement, any Amendment to this Agreement, or any additional Agreement between the partners, then this partnership shall continue as a partnership of only those partners who have satisfied their contribution requirements. Any partner who has failed to satisfy their contribution requirements will not be a partner of this partnership. Each partner who has made a contribution shall then be entitled to a share of partnership profits and losses in proportion to the amount of their contribution to the total contributions. If any additional partnership contributions are necessary, such additional contributions shall be determined by the remaining partners as specified under the terms of this Agreement regarding Additional Contributions.

Interest on Contributions. ⑩

❑ No interest shall be paid to any partner for any capital contributions.

❑ Interest at the rate of _____ percent per annum shall be paid on each partner's capital contributions that were paid in cash. The interest shall be an expense of the partnership and paid to the partner who is entitled to it on an annual basis.

Loans to Partnership. ⑪

In addition to capital contributions, the following cash or property will be loaned to the partnership under the terms specified:

Name of Partner   Cash/Property Loaned   Terms of Loan
_____
_____
_____
_____

Share of the Partnership. ⑫

❑ Each partner's proportional share of the profits and losses of the partnership shall be as follows:

Name   Percent of Ownership of Partnership
_____
_____
_____
_____
_____

❑ Each partner's share of the profits and losses of the partnership shall be equal.

❑ Each partner's proportional share of the profits of the partnership shall be as follows: _____

And each partner's proportional share of the losses of the partnership shall be as follows: _____

Distribution of Profits and Losses. ⑬

☐   Any profits or losses of the partnership shall be determined and distributed to the partners on a monthly basis according to their proportionate share of the profits and losses of the partnership.

☐   Any profits or losses of the partnership shall be determined and distributed to the partners on a quarterly basis according to their proportionate share of the profits and losses of the partnership.

☐   Any profits or losses of the partnership shall be determined and distributed to the partners on an annual basis according to their proportionate share of the profits and losses of the partnership.

☐   Any profits or losses of the partnership shall be determined and distributed to the partners on a monthly basis according to their proportionate share of the profits and losses of the partnership. However, the first $ _____ of the profits each month shall be retained by the partnership for reinvestment in the partnership.

☐ Any profits or losses of the partnership shall be determined and distributed to the partners on a quarterly basis according to their proportionate share of the profits and losses of the partnership. However, the first $ _____ of the profits each quarter shall be retained by the partnership for reinvestment in the partnership.

☐   Any profits or losses of the partnership shall be determined and distributed to the partners on an annual basis according to their proportionate share of the profits and losses of the partnership. However, the first $ _____ of the profits each year shall be retained by the partnership for reinvestment in the partnership.

☐   Any profits or losses of the partnership shall be determined and distributed to the partners on a monthly basis according to their proportionate share of the profits and losses of the partnership. However, _____ percent of the profits each month shall be retained by the partnership for reinvestment in the partnership.

☐   Any profits or losses of the partnership shall be determined and distributed to the partners on a quarterly basis according to their proportionate share of the profits and losses of the partnership. However,

_____ percent of the profits each quarter shall be retained by the partnership for reinvestment in the partnership.

☐ Any profits or losses of the partnership shall be determined and distributed to the partners on an annual basis according to their proportionate share of the profits and losses of the partnership. However, _____ percent of the profits each year shall be retained by the partnership for reinvestment in the partnership.

Management of the Partnership. ⑭

☐ Each partner shall have an equal right to manage and control the partnership. All partnership decisions will be made by majority vote, except the following major decisions, which must be decided by unanimous vote:

The partners can select, by unanimous vote, one or more of the partners to act as managing partners of the partnership.

☐ Each partner shall have an equal right to manage and control the partnership. All partnership decisions will be made by majority vote. The partners can select, by majority vote, one or more of the partners to act as managing partners of the partnership.

☐ Each partner shall have an equal right to manage and control the partnership. Partnership decisions will be made by unanimous vote. The partners can select by unanimous vote, one or more of the partners to act as managing partners of the partnership.

☐ Each partner shall have a right to manage and control the partnership in the following proportions: _____

All partnership decisions will be made by majority vote, except the following major decisions, which must be decided by unanimous vote:

The partners can select, by unanimous vote, one or more of the partners to act as managing partners of the partnership.

☐ Each partner shall have a right to manage and control the partnership in the following proportions: _____

All partnership decisions will be made by majority vote.

The partners can select, by majority vote, one or more of the partners to act as managing partners of the partnership.

☐ Each partner shall have a right to manage and control the partnership in the following proportions: _____

Partnership decisions will be made by unanimous vote.

The partners can select, by unanimous vote, one or more of the partners to act as managing partners of the partnership.

Managing Partner(s). ⑮

☐ One or more managing partners may be selected under the terms of this Agreement. The salary of the managing partner(s) shall be $ _____ . The managing partner(s) shall have the authority to conduct the day-to-day business of the partnership, without consultation with the other partners. This shall include hiring and firing employees, signing partnership checks, withdrawing funds from partnership accounts, borrowing money up to the amount of $ _____, and maintaining the books and records of the partnership. The managing partner(s) shall not have the authority to make major decisions for the partnership without the majority approval of the other partners. Major decisions are defined as follows: _____

☐ One or more managing partners may be selected under the terms of this Agreement. The salary of the managing partner(s) shall be $ _____ . The managing partner(s) shall have the authority to conduct the day-to-day business of the partnership, without consultation with the other partners. This shall include hiring and firing employees, signing partnership checks, withdrawing funds from partnership accounts, borrowing money up to the amount of $ _____ , and maintaining the books and records of the partnership. The managing partner(s) shall not have the authority to make major decisions for the partnership without the unanimous approval of the other partners. Major decisions are defined as follows: _____ .

Date and Time of Annual Partnership Meeting. ⑯

The annual partnership meeting will be held on the _____ of every year at _____. m. This meeting is for the purpose of assessing the current status of the partnership and transacting any necessary business. If this day is a legal holiday, the meeting will be held on the next day.

Place of Partnership Meetings.

The place for the meeting will be the principal office of the partnership.

Partners Quorum.

A quorum for a partners meeting will be a majority of the partners. Once a quorum is present, business may be conducted at the meeting, even if partners leave prior to adjournment.

Partners Proxies.

At all meetings of partners, a partner may vote by signed proxy or by power of attorney. To be valid, a proxy must be filed with the partnership prior to the stated time of the meeting. No proxy may be valid for more than 11 months, unless the proxy specifically states otherwise. Proxies may always be revoked prior to the meeting for which it is intended. Attendance at the meeting for which a proxy has been authorized always revokes the proxy.

Partners Voting.

The vote of the holders of a majority of partnership interests entitled to vote will be sufficient to decide any matter, unless a greater number is required by the Partnership Agreement or by state law. Adjournment shall be by majority vote of those entitled to vote.

Partners Consent Agreements.

Any action that may be taken at a Partnership meeting may be taken instead without a meeting if an agreement is consented to, in writing, by all of the partners who would be entitled to vote.

Powers of the Partners.

The partners will have all powers available under state law, including the power to appoint and remove managers and employees; the power to change the offices; the power to borrow money on behalf of the partnership, including the power to execute any evidence of indebtedness on behalf of the partnership; and the power to enter into contracts on behalf of the partnership.

Fiduciary Duty of the Partners.

Each director owes a fiduciary duty of good faith and reasonable care with regard to all actions taken on behalf of the partnership. Each partner must perform her/his duties in good faith in a manner which she/he reasonably believes to be in the best interest of the partnership, using ordinary care and prudence.

Accounting Matters.

The partnership will maintain accounting records which will be open to any partner for inspection at any reasonable time. These records will include separate income and capital accounts for each partner. The accounting will be on the accrual basis and on a calendar year basis. The capital account of each partner will consist of no less than the value of the property, cash, or services that the partner shall have contributed with their initial or additional contributions to the partnership.

Financial Matters. ⑰

☐ The partners will determine the accounting methods and fiscal year of the partnership. All checks, drafts, or other methods of payment shall be signed by all of the partners. All notes, mortgages, or other evidence of indebtedness shall be signed by all of the partners. No money will be borrowed or lent by the partnership unless authorized by a unanimous vote of the partners. No contracts will be entered into on behalf of the partnership unless authorized by a unanimous vote of the partners. No documents may be executed on behalf of the partnership unless authorized by a unanimous vote of the partners.

☐ The partners will determine the accounting methods and fiscal year of the partnership. All checks, drafts, or other methods of payment shall be signed by all of the Partners or by a partner selected as manager to carry on the day-to-day business of the partnership. All notes, mortgages, or other evidence of indebtedness shall be signed by all of the partners. No money will be borrowed or lent by the partnership unless authorized by a majority vote of the partners. No contracts will be entered into on behalf of the partnership unless authorized by a majority vote of the partners. No documents may be executed on behalf of the partnership unless authorized by a majority vote of the partners.

Bank Account. ⑱

The partnership will maintain a business checking bank account at: _____

Loans to Partners. ⑲

☐ The partnership may not lend any money to any partner unless the loan has been approved by a unanimous vote of all partners of the partnership.

☐ The partnership may not lend any money to any partner unless the loan has been approved by a majority vote of all partners of the partnership.

Draws to Partners. ⑳

☐ All partners are entitled to monthly draws from the expected profits of the partnership. The draws will be debited against the income account of the partner. The amount of the draws shall be determined by a majority vote of the partners.

☐ All partners are entitled to monthly draws from the expected profits of the partnership. The draws will be debited against the income account of the partner. The amount of the draws shall be determined by unanimous vote of the partners.

☐ All partners are entitled to quarterly draws from the expected profits of the partnership. The draws will be debited against the income account of the partner. The amount of the draws shall be determined by a majority vote of the partners.

☐ All partners are entitled to quarterly draws from the expected profits of the partnership. The draws will be debited against the income account of the partner. The amount of the draws shall be determined by unanimous vote of the partners.

☐ No partners are entitled to draws against the expected profits of the partnership.

Salaries to Partners. ㉑

☐ All partners are eligible to be paid reasonable salaries for work or services they perform in the partnership business.

❑ No partners are eligible to be paid salaries for any work or services they perform in the partnership business. Such work or services shall be considered contributions to the partnership.

Partnership Expense Accounts. ㉒

❑ No partner shall have an expense account. Reimbursement for business expenses may be made by majority vote of the partners.

❑ No partner shall have an expense account. Reimbursement for business expenses may be made by unanimous vote of the partners.

❑ Each partner shall receive an expense account of up to $ _____ per month for the payment of reasonable and necessary business expenses in the regular course of partnership business. Each partner shall provide the partnership with a written record of such expenses in order to obtain reimbursement.

Transfers of Partnership Interests. ㉓

❑ A partner may transfer all or part of his or her interest in the partnership to any other party without the consent of the other partners.

❑ A partner may transfer all or part of his or her interest in the partnership to any other party without the consent of the other partners. However, the partnership has the right of first refusal to purchase the partner's interest on the same terms and conditions as the partner's offer from the third party. This option to buy must be exercised by the partnership within 30 days from notice of the offer to buy by a third party.

❑ A partner may transfer all or part of his or her interest in the partnership to any other party only with the unanimous consent of the other partners.

❑ A partner may transfer all or part of his or her interest in the partnership to any other party only with the majority consent of the other partners.

❑ A partner may not transfer any or all of his or her interest in the partnership.

Expulsion of Partners. 24

A partner may be expelled from the partnership at any time by the unanimous consent of the other partners. Upon expulsion, the expelled partner shall cease to be a partner and shall have no interest, rights, authority, power, or ownership in the partnership or any partnership property. The expelled partner shall be entitled to receive value for his or her interest in the partnership as determined by the terms of this Agreement. The partnership shall continue in business without interruption without the expelled partner. Automatic Expulsion of Partners. A partner is automatically expelled from the partnership at any time upon the occurrence of any of the following:

a. A partner files a petition for or becomes subject to an order for relief under the Federal Bankruptcy Code.
b. A partner files for or becomes subject to any order for insolvency under any state law.
c. A partner makes an assignment for the benefit of creditors.
d. A partner consents to or becomes subject to the appointment of a receiver over a substantial portion of his or her assets.
e. A partner consents to or becomes subject to an attachment or execution of a substantial portion of his or her assets.

On the date of any of the above events, the expelled partner shall cease to be a partner and shall have no interest, rights, authority, power, or ownership in the partnership or any partnership property. The expelled partner shall be entitled to receive value for his or her interest in the partnership as determined by the terms of this Agreement. The partnership shall continue in business without interruption without the expelled partner.

Limit on Remedies of Expelled Partners.

The expulsion of a partner shall be final and shall not be subject to mediation, arbitration, or review by any court of any jurisdiction.

Insurance. 25

☐ Each partner shall buy and maintain life insurance on the life of each other partner in the amount of $ _____ .

☐ Each partner shall buy and maintain disability insurance on the life of each other partner in the amount of $ _____ .

☐ The partnership shall buy and maintain life insurance on the life of each partner in the amount of $ _____ and such insurance shall be considered assets of the partnership.

☐ The partnership shall buy and maintain disability insurance on the life of each partner in the amount of $ _____ and such insurance shall be considered assets of the partnership.

☐ On the withdrawal, termination, or expulsion of any partner for any reason other than their death or disability, any insurance policies on the partner's life or health on which the partnership paid premiums shall become the personal property of the departing partner and the cash value (if any) of such policy shall be considered as a draw against the departing partner's income account.

Mediation or Arbitration. ㉖

☐ Except as otherwise provided by this Agreement, the partners agree that any dispute arising related to this Agreement will be settled by voluntary mediation, if possible. The mediator shall be chosen by a majority vote of the partners. All costs of mediation will be shared equally by all partners involved in the dispute.

☐ Except as otherwise provided by this Agreement, the partners agree that any dispute arising related to this Agreement will be settled by voluntary mediation, if possible. The mediator shall be chosen by a unanimous vote of the partners. All costs of mediation will be shared equally by all partners involved in the dispute.

☐ Except as otherwise provided by this Agreement, the partners agree that any dispute arising related to this Agreement will be settled by binding arbitration, if possible. The arbitrator shall be chosen by a majority vote of the partners. All costs of arbitration will be borne by all partners involved in the dispute as directed by the arbitrator.

☐ Except as otherwise provided by this Agreement, the partners agree that any dispute arising related to this Agreement will be settled by binding arbitration, if possible. The arbitrator shall be chosen by a unanimous vote of the partners. All costs of arbitration will be borne by all partners involved in the dispute as directed by the arbitrator.

Admission of New Partners. ㉗

☐ A new partner may be admitted to the partnership only by unanimous consent of the partners. Admission of a new partner shall not cause the termination of the original partnership entity, but it shall continue with the additional partner.

☐ A new partner may be admitted to the partnership by majority consent of the partners. Admission of a new partner shall not cause the termination of the original partnership entity, but it shall continue with the additional partner.

Responsibility of New Partners. ㉘

Any new partner to the partnership shall be responsible for and assume full personal liability equal to all other partners for all partnership debts, liabilities, and obligations whenever incurred.

☐ Any new partner to the partnership shall be responsible for and assume full personal liability for all partnership debts, liabilities, and obligations whenever incurred only up to the amount of the value of the initial and any additional contributions of the new partner.

☐ Any new partner to the partnership shall be responsible for and assume full personal liability only for those partnership debts, liabilities, and obligations incurred after the date of their acceptance as a new partner.

Withdrawal from the Partnership. ㉙

☐ If any partner withdraws from the partnership for any reason (including the death or disability of the partner), the partnership shall continue and be operated by the remaining partners. The withdrawing partner or his or her personal representative will be obligated to sell his or her interest to the remaining partners, and the remaining partners will be obligated to buy that interest. The value of the withdrawing partner's interest will be his or her proportionate share of the total value of the partnership. If necessary, the total value of the partnership will be made by an independent appraisal made within 90 days of the partner's withdrawal. The costs of the appraisal will be shared equally by all partners, including the withdrawing partner.

☐ If any partner withdraws from the partnership for any reason (including the death or disability of the partner), the partnership shall cease to exist. All partnership assets and liabilities will be divided by the partners as provided by the terms of this Agreement relating to the termination of the partnership.

Outside Activities of Partnership. ㉚

☐ No partner, during or after the partnership, shall engage in any business that is in competition with the partnership in any manner. The prohibition against competition shall continue for a period of _____ years after the partner leaves the partnership and for any business within _____ miles of the partnership's principal place of business. This non-competition agreement shall end with the termination of the partnership.

☐ During or after the partnership, each partner may engage in any other business activities, even if such activities compete with the partnership.

Termination of the Partnership. ㉛

☐ The partnership may be terminated at any time by unanimous consent of the partners. Upon termination, the partners agree to apply the assets and money of the partnership in the following order:

a. To pay all the debts and obligations of the partnership
b. To distribute the partners' income accounts to the partners in their proportional share
c. To distribute the partners' capital accounts to the partners in their proportional share
d. To distribute any remaining assets to the partners in their proportional share

☐ The partnership may be terminated at any time by majority vote of the partners. Upon termination, the partners agree to apply the assets and money of the partnership in the following order:

a. To pay all the debts and obligations of the partnership
b. To distribute the partners' income accounts to the partners in their proportional share
c. To distribute the partners' capital accounts to the partners in their proportional share

d. To distribute any remaining assets to the partners in their proportional share.

Amendments to the Partnership Agreement. ㉜

☐ This Partnership Agreement may be amended in any manner by unanimous vote of the partners.

☐ This Partnership Agreement may be amended in any manner by majority vote of the partners.

Additional Provisions. ㉝

The following additional provisions are part of this Agreement: _____

Modification of Agreement. ㉞

☐ No modification of this Agreement shall be effective unless it is in writing and signed by all partners.

☐ No modification of this Agreement shall be effective unless it is in writing and signed by a majority of the partners.

This Agreement binds and benefits all partners and any successors, inheritors, assigns, or representatives of the partners. Time is of the essence of this Agreement. This document is the entire Agreement between the partners. Any attached papers that are referred to in this Agreement are part of this Agreement. Any alleged oral agreements shall have no force or effect. This Agreement is governed by the laws of the State of ㉟_____ . If any portion of this Agreement is held to be invalid, void, or unenforceable by any court of law of competent jurisdiction, the rest of the Agreement shall remain in full force and effect.

Dated ㊱_____

(37)_____
Partner Signature

_____
Printed Name of Partner

(38)_____
Partner Signature

_____
Printed Name of Partner

(39)_____
Partner Signature

_____
Printed Name of Partner

Chapter 2

Contracts

The foundation of most agreements is a contract. A *contract* is merely an agreement by which two or more parties each promise to do something. This simple definition of a contract can encompass incredibly complex agreements. The objective of a good contract is to clearly set out the terms of the agreement. Once the parties have reached an oral understanding of what their agreement should be, the terms of the deal should be put in writing. Contrary to what many attorneys may tell you, the written contract should be clearly written and easily understood by both parties to the agreement. It should be written in precise and unambiguous terms. The most common causes for litigation over contracts are arguments over the meaning of the language used. Remember that both sides of the agreement should be able to understand and agree to the language being used.

A contract has to have certain prerequisites to be enforceable in court. These requirements are relatively simple and most will be present in any standard agreement. However, you should understand what the various legal requirements are before you prepare your own contracts. To be enforceable, a contract must have *consideration*. In the context of contract law, this simply means that both parties to the contract must have promised to do something or forego taking some type of action. If one of the parties has not promised to do anything or forego any action, he or she will not be able to legally force the other party to comply with the terms of the contract. There has to be some form of mutual promise for a contract to be valid. For example: Andy agrees to pay Bill if Bill paints a car. Andy's promise is to pay Bill if the job is completed. Bill's promise is to paint the car. If Bill paints the car and is not paid, Andy's promise to pay Bill can be enforced in court. Similarly, if Bill fails to paint the car, Andy can have the contract enforced in court. Andy and Bill's mutual promises are the consideration necessary to have a valid and enforceable contract.

Another requirement is that the parties to the contract be clearly identified and the terms of the contract also be clearly spelled out. The terms and description need not be complicated, but they must be spelled out in enough detail to enable the parties to the contract (and any subsequent court) to clearly determine what exactly the parties were referring to when they made the contract. In the prior example, the names and addresses of the parties must be included for the contract to be enforceable. In addition, a description of the car must be incorporated in the contract. Finally, a description of the type of paint job and the amount of money to be paid should also be contained in the contract.

The following documents are included for use in situations requiring a basic contract. There are documents for assigning, modifying, extending, and terminating a basic contract. Finally, elsewhere in this book are numerous other contract forms for specific circumstances, which should be used if the legal situation fits the particulars of these forms. Chapter 9 contains a Contract for Sale of Personal Property; Chapter 10 contains a Contract for Deed (for the sale of real estate); Chapter 11 contains an Employment Contract; and Chapter 18 contains both a Contract for the Sale of Goods and a Contract for the Sale of Goods on Consignment. *Note*: If you are at all unsure of the correct use of any forms in this chapter, please consult a competent attorney.

Instructions for Contract Forms

General Contract: This basic document can be adapted for use in many situations. The terms of the contract that the parties agree to should be carefully spelled out and inserted where indicated. The other information that is required are the names and addresses of the parties to the contract and the date the contract is to take effect. This basic contract form is set up to accommodate an agreement between two individuals. If a business is party to the contract, please identify the name and type of business entity (for example: Jackson Car Stereo, a New York sole proprietorship, etc.) in the first section of the contract. A sample numbered version of this form is found on page 66.

In order to complete this form, fill in the following information:

① Date of contract
② Name of first party to the contract [If a business is party to the contract, please identify the name and type of business entity (for example: Jackson Car Stereo, a New York sole proprietorship, etc.)]
③ Address of first party
④ City of first party

⑤ State of first party
⑥ Name of second party
⑦ Address of second party
⑧ City of second party
⑨ State of second party
⑩ Exact terms of the contract to which Party One agrees
⑪ Exact terms of the contract to which Party Two agrees
⑫ Any additional terms
⑬ State whose laws will govern this contract (Generally, where the contract actions will take place)
⑭ Date of contract
⑮ Signature of Party One
⑯ Printed name of Party One
⑰ Signature of Party Two
⑱ Printed name of Party Two

Extension of Contract: This document should be used to extend the effective time period during which a contract is in force. The use of this form allows the time limit to be extended without having to entirely redraft the contract. Under this document, all of the other terms of the contract will remain the same, with only the expiration date changing. You will need to fill in both the original expiration date and the new expiration date. Other information necessary will be the names and addresses of the parties to the contract and a description of the contract. A copy of the original contract should be attached to this form. A sample numbered version of this form is found on page 67.

In order to complete this form, fill in the following information:

① Date of extension of contract
② Name of first party to the contract [If a business is party to the contract, please identify the name and type of business entity]
③ Address of first party
④ Name of second party
⑤ Address of second party
⑥ Date that the original contract will end
⑦ Date that the extension will end
⑧ Signature of Party One
⑨ Printed Name of Party One
⑩ Signature of Party Two
⑪ Printed Name of Party Two

Modification of Contract: Use this form to modify any other terms of a contract (other than the expiration date). The modification can be used to change any portion of the contract. Simply note what changes are being made in the appropriate place on this form. If a portion of the contract is being deleted, make note of the deletion. If certain language is being substituted, state the substitution clearly. If additional language is being added, make this clear. For example, you may wish to use language as follows:

- "Paragraph _____ is deleted from this contract."
- "The following new paragraph is added to this contract:"

A copy of the original contract should be attached to this form. A sample numbered version of this form is found on page 68.

In order to complete this form, fill in the following information:

1. Date of modification contract
2. Name of first party to the contract [If a business is party to the contract, please identify the name and type of business entity]
3. Address of first party
4. Name of second party
5. Address of second party
6. Describe the original contract
7. Describe what modifications are being made to the original contract
8. Signature of Party One
9. Printed Name of Party One
10. Signature of Party Two
11. Printed Name of Party Two

Termination of Contract: This document is intended to be used when both parties to a contract mutually desire to end the contract prior to its original expiration date. Under this form, both parties agree to release each other from any claims against each other based on anything in the contract. This document effectively ends any contractual arrangement between two parties. Information necessary to complete this form are the names and addresses of the parties to the contract, a description of the contract, and the effective date of the termination of the contract. A sample numbered version of this form is found on page 69.

In order to complete this form, fill in the following information:

1. Date of the termination contract
2. Name of first party to the contract [If a business is party to the contract, please identify the name and type of business entity]

③ Address of first party
④ Name of second party
⑤ Address of second party
⑥ Describe the original contract
⑦ Signature of Party One
⑧ Printed Name of Party One
⑨ Signature of Party Two
⑩ Printed Name of Party Two

Assignment of Contract: This form is for use if one party to a contract is assigning its full interest in the contract to another party. This effectively substitutes one party for another under a contract. This particular assignment form has both of the parties agreeing to indemnify and hold each other harmless for any failures to perform under the contract while they were the party liable under it. This *indemnify and hold harmless* clause simply means that if a claim arises for failure to perform, each party agrees to be responsible for the period of their own performance obligations.

 A description of the contract which is assigned should include the parties to the contract, the purpose of the contract, and the date of the contract. Other information that is necessary to complete the assignment is the name and address of the *assignor* (the party who is assigning the contract), the name and address of the *assignee* (the party to whom the contract is being assigned), and the date of the assignment. A copy of the original contract should be attached to this form. A copy of a Consent to Assignment of Contract should also be attached, if necessary. A sample numbered version of this form is found on page 70.

In order to complete this form, fill in the following information:

① Date of the assignment of contract
② Name of first party to the contract [If a business is party to the contract, please identify the name and type of business entity]
③ Address of first party
④ Name of second party
⑤ Address of second party
⑥ Describe the original contract
⑦ Signature of Assignor
⑧ Printed Name of Assignor
⑨ Signature of Assignee
⑩ Printed Name of Assignee

Consent to Assignment of Contract: This form is used if the original contract states that the consent of one of the parties is necessary for the assignment of the contract to be valid. A description of the contract and the name and signature of the person giving the consent are all that is necessary for completing this form. A copy of the original contract should be attached to this form. A sample numbered version of this form is found on page 71.

In order to complete this form, fill in the following information:

① Date of the consent to assignment of contract
② Name of person assigning contract interest
③ Describe the original contract
④ Signature
⑤ Printed Name

GENERAL CONTRACT

This Contract is made on ①_____ , between ②_____ ,
Party One, of ③_____ , City of ④_____ , State of
⑤_____ , and ⑥_____ , Party Two, of ⑦_____ ,
City of ⑧_____ , State of ⑨_____ .

For valuable consideration, the parties agree to the following:

Party One agrees to: ⑩

Party Two agrees to: ⑪

Any additional terms: ⑫

No modification of this Contract will be effective unless it is in writing and is signed by both parties. This Contract binds and benefits both parties and any successors or assigns. Time is of the essence of this Contract. This document, including any attachments, is the entire agreement between the parties. This Contract is governed by the laws of the State of ⑬_____ .

Dated: ⑭_____

⑮_____
Signature of Party One

⑯_____
Printed Name of Party One

⑰_____
Signature of Party Two

⑱_____
Printed Name of Party Two

EXTENSION OF CONTRACT

This Extension of Contract is made on ①_____ , between ②_____ _____ , whose address is ③_____ , and ④_____ , whose address is ⑤_____ .

For valuable consideration, the parties agree as follows:

1. The following described contract will end on ⑥_____ :

This contract is attached to this Extension and is a part of this Extension.

2. The parties agree to extend this contract for an additional period, which will begin immediately on the expiration of the original time period and will end on ⑦_____ .

3. The Extension of this contract will be on the same terms and conditions as the original contract. This Extension binds and benefits both parties and any successors. This document, including the attached original contract, is the entire agreement between the parties.

The parties have signed this Extension on the date specified at the beginning of this Extension of Contract.

⑧_____
Signature
⑨_____
Printed Name

⑩_____
Signature
⑪_____
Printed Name

MODIFICATION OF CONTRACT

This Modification of Contract is made on ①_____ , between ②_____
_____ , whose address is ③_____ , and ④_____ , whose
address is ⑤_____ .

For valuable consideration, the parties agree as follows:

1. The following described contract is attached to this Modification and is made
a part of this Modification: ⑥

2. The parties agree to modify this contract as follows: ⑦

3. All other terms and conditions of the original contract remain in effect without
modification. This Modification binds and benefits both parties and any successors. This document, including the attached contract, is the entire agreement
between the parties.

The parties have signed this Modification on the date specified at the beginning
of this Modification of Contract.

⑧_____
Signature
⑨_____
Printed Name

⑩_____
Signature
⑪_____
Printed Name

TERMINATION OF CONTRACT

This Termination of Contract is made on ①_____ , between ②_____
_____ , whose address is ③_____ , and ④_____ , whose
address is ⑤_____ .

For valuable consideration, the parties agree as follows:

1. The parties are currently bound under the terms of the following described
contract, which is attached and is part of this Termination: ⑥

2. They agree to mutually terminate and cancel this contract effective on this
date. This Termination Agreement will act as a mutual release of all obligations
under this contract for both parties, as if the contract has not been entered into
in the first place.

3. This Termination binds and benefits both parties and any successors. This
document, including the attached contract being terminated, is the entire agreement between the parties.

The parties have signed this Termination on the date specified at the beginning
of this Termination of Contract.

⑦_____
Signature
⑧_____
Printed Name

⑨_____
Signature
⑩_____
Printed Name

ASSIGNMENT OF CONTRACT

This Assignment of Contract is made on ①_____ , between ②_____
_____ , whose address is ③_____ , and ④_____ , whose
address is ⑤_____ .

For valuable consideration, the parties agree to the following terms and conditions:

1. The Assignor assigns all interest, burdens, and benefits in the following described contract to the Assignee: ⑥

    This contract is attached to this Assignment and is a part of this Assignment.

2. The Assignor warrants that this contract is in effect, has not been modified, and is fully assignable. If the consent of a third party is necessary for this Assignment to be effective, such consent is attached to this Assignment and is a part of this Assignment. Assignor agrees to indemnify and hold the Assignee harmless from any claim which may result from the Assignor's failure to perform under this contract prior to the date of this Assignment.

3. The Assignee agrees to perform all obligations of the Assignor and receive all of the benefits of the Assignor under this contract. Assignee agrees to indemnify and hold the Assignor harmless from any claim which may result from the Assignee's failure to perform under this contract after the date of this Assignment.

4. This Assignment binds and benefits both parties and any successors. This document, including any attachments, is the entire agreement between the parties.

The parties have signed this Assignment on the date specified at the beginning of this Assignment of Contract.

⑦_____
Signature of Assignor
⑧_____
Printed Name of Assignor

⑨_____
Signature of Assignee
⑩_____
Printed Name of Assignee

CONSENT TO ASSIGNMENT OF CONTRACT

Date: ①_____

To: ②_____

I am a party to the following described contract: ③

This contract is the subject of the attached Assignment of Contract.

I consent to the Assignment of this Contract as described in the attached Assignment, which provides that the Assignee is substituted for the Assignor.

④_____
Signature
⑤_____
Printed Name

Chapter 3

Signatures and Notary Acknowledgments

Signatures and notary acknowledgments for legal forms serve similar but slightly different purposes. Both are used to document the formal signing of a legal instrument, but the notarized acknowledgment also serves as a method of providing a neutral witness to the signature, and so, authenticates the signature. In addition, a notarized acknowledgment can serve an additional purpose of providing a statement under oath. For example, a notarized acknowledgment can be used to assert that a person states, under oath, that he has read the document that she or he is signing and believes that what it contains is the truth. The use of a notary acknowledgment is not required for all legal forms. The notary acknowledgments contained in this chapter are to be used only for the purpose of providing a notarization required for recording a document. Generally, notarization is only necessary if the document is intended to be recorded with an official government office in some manner. For example, all documents which intend to convey real estate should be recorded in the county recorder's office or register of deeds office in the county (or parish) where the property is located. In virtually all jurisdictions, such documents must be notarized before they will be recorded. Similarly, some states require automobile titles and similar documents to be notarized. **Note:** Always check with your local county clerk and/or with an attorney to determine the specific recording and/or notarization requirements in your locale. You should also check the Real Estate Law Appendix that is included on the CD that accompanied this book.

Another unofficial purpose of notarization of legal documents is to make the document seem more important to the parties. By formally having their signatures witnessed by a notary public, they are attesting to the fact that they ascribe a powerful purpose to the document. Although this type of notarization carries with it no legal value, it does serve a valid purpose in solemnizing the signing of an important business document. For all of the notary acknowledgment forms contained in this chapter, the following information is necessary:

- The name of the state in which the document is signed
- The name of the county in which the document is signed
- The date on which the document is signed
- The name of the person who is signing the document
- The entity on whose behalf the person is signing
  (for example: a corporation, partnership, etc.)
- The name of the notary public (or similar official)
- The county in which the notary is registered to act
- The state in which the notary is authorized to perform
- The date on which the notary's commission will expire

In addition, many states require that the notary place an embossed seal on the document to authenticate the notarization process. The notary who completes the acknowledgment will know the correct procedure and if there are any other state-specific notary acknowledgement language requirements for your jurisdiction.

NOTE for residents of California: The state of California requires a different notary block than other states. If you intend any of the notarized forms in this book to be valid in California, you will need to use the California notary block that is provided on the accompanying Forms-on-CD.

A simple signature line merely serves to provide a place for a party to a document to sign his or her name. However, care must be taken to be sure that the type of signature line used corresponds exactly with the person or business entity who is joining in the signing of a document. If the entity is a partnership, the signature must be set up for a partner to sign and clearly state that the signature is for the partnership. The same holds true for the signature of a corporate officer.

Instructions

The following notary acknowledgments and signature lines are intended to be used for the specific purposes outlined below. When preparing a legal document, choose the correct version of these additions carefully. You may need to use the 'text' versions of a particular form in order to add the correct notary acknowledgment and/or signature lines to the document. The following are contained in this chapter:

Corporate Acknowledgment: This clause should be used on documents where a corporation is one of the parties who is to sign the document and the document needs to be notarized. The person signing the document on behalf of the corporation must be either an officer of the corporation or be specifically authorized by a resolution of the Board of Directors of the corporation to act on its behalf. See page 76.

Corporate Signature Line: This line should be inserted on all documents where a party that will sign the document is a corporation. This may be used regardless of whether the corporation is a corporation, an S-corporation, or a not-for-profit corporation. The person signing must have authority to bind the corporation. Again, it must either be an officer of the corporation or a person specifically authorized by a resolution of the Board of Directors of the corporation to act on its behalf. The state in which the corporation is registered to do business should be noted. See page 76.

Partnership Acknowledgment: This clause should be used on documents where one of the parties who is to sign the document is a standard partnership and the document needs to be notarized. Any partner in a partnership may have authority to act on behalf of the corporation. However, it may be wise to request a copy of the partnership agreement which authorizes the partner to bind the partnership. See page 77.

Partnership Signature Line: This line should be inserted on all documents where one of the parties that will sign the document is a partnership. This may be used if the entity is a partnership. Any partner may bind the partnership if authorized by the partnership agreement. The state in which the partnership is doing business should be noted. See page 77.

Limited Liability Company Acknowledgment: This clause should be used on documents where a limited liability company is one of the parties who is to sign the document and the document needs to be notarized. Any member of a limited liability company has authority to bind the limited liability company. See page 78.

Limited Liability Company Signature Line: This line should be inserted on all documents where one of the parties who will sign the document is a limited liability company. Any member may sign on behalf of a limited liability company. The state in which the limited liability company is doing business should be noted. See page 78.

Sole Proprietorship Acknowledgment: This clause should be used on documents where an individual who owns a sole proprietorship is one of the parties who is to sign the document and the document needs to be notarized. Many sole proprietorships are designated as persons "doing business as." This is abbreviated as "DBA." For example: "John Smith, DBA Blue Plate Restaurant" indicates that John Smith is operating the Blue Plate Restaurant as a sole proprietorship. The owner of the sole proprietorship is the person who should sign all documents for this type of business. See page 79.

Sole Proprietorship Signature Line: This line should be inserted on all documents where a party that will sign the document is an individual that owns a sole proprietorship. Only the owner of a sole proprietorship has authority to bind such a business. The state in which the sole proprietorship is doing business should be noted. See page 79.

Power of Attorney Acknowledgment: This clause should be used on documents where an individual acting under a power of attorney is one of the parties who is to sign the document and the document needs to be notarized. As noted in Chapter 4 an attorney-in-fact is a person who is authorized to act for another person by virtue of a document entitled a "power of attorney," also found in Chapter 4. See page 80.

Power of Attorney Signature Line: This line should be inserted on all documents where a party that will sign the document is an individual acting under a power of attorney. The person signing must have the specific authority to act for another person under some form of Power of Attorney. The date of the Power of Attorney form should be noted. See page 80.

Individual Acknowledgment: This clause should be used on documents where an individual is one of the parties who is to sign the document and the document needs to be notarized. However, if the document is to be signed by a husband and wife together, use the appropriate acknowledgment form which follows on page 81.

Individual Signature Line: This line should be inserted on all documents where a party that will sign the document is an individual. Again, however, if the document is to be signed by a husband and wife together, use the appropriate signature line which follows on page 81.

Husband and Wife Acknowledgment: This clause should be used on documents where both a husband and wife are to sign the document and the document needs to be notarized. See page 82.

Husband and Wife Signature Line: This line should be inserted on all documents where both a husband and wife are intended to sign the document. See page 82.

Corporate Signature Line

_____ (name of corporation), a(n)
_____ (state of incorporation) corporation

By:
_____
Signature of Corporate Officer

_____
Printed Name of Corporate Officer

The _____ (*title of corporate officer*) of the corporation

Corporate Acknowledgment

State of _____
County of _____

On _____ , 20 _____ , _____
personally came before me and, being duly sworn, did state that he or she is the
_____ of the corporation described in the above docu-
ment; that he or she signed the above document in my presence on behalf of this
corporation; and that he or she had full authority to do so.

_____
Signature of Notary Public

Notary Public, In and for the County of _____
State of _____
My commission expires: _____   Notary Seal

Partnership Acknowledgment

State of _____

County of _____

On _____ , 20 _____ , _____
personally came before me and, being duly sworn, did state that he or she is a
partner of the partnership described in the above document; that he or she signed
the above document in my presence on behalf of this partnership; and that he or
she had full authority to do so.

_____
Signature of Notary Public

Notary Public, In and for the County of _____
State of _____

My commission expires: _____   Notary Seal

Partnership Signature Line

_____ (*name of partnership*), a(n)
_____ (*state of operation*) partnership

By:

_____
Signature of Partner

_____
Printed Name of Partner

A Partner of the Partnership

Limited Liability Company Acknowledgment

State of _____

County of _____

On _____ , 20 _____ , _____
personally came before me and, being duly sworn, did state that he or she is a
member of the limited liability company described in the above document; that
he or she signed the above document in my presence on behalf of this limited
liability company; and that he or she had full authority to do so.

_____
Signature of Notary Public

Notary Public, In and for the County of _____
State of _____

My commission expires: _____   Notary Seal

Limited Liability Company Signature Line

_____ (*name of limited liability company*), a(n)
_____ (*state of operation*) limited liability company

By:

_____
Signature of Member

_____
Printed Name of Member

A Member of the Limited Liability Company

Sole Proprietorship Acknowledgment

State of _____

County of _____

On _____ , 20 _____ , _____

personally came before me and, being duly sworn, did state that he or she is the person who owns the sole proprietorship described in the above document and that he or she signed the above document in my presence on behalf of the sole proprietorship and on his or her own behalf.

_____

Signature of Notary Public

Notary Public, In and for the County of _____

State of _____

My commission expires: _____   Notary Seal

Sole Proprietorship Signature Line

_____

Signature of Sole Proprietor

_____

Printed Name of Sole Proprietor

DBA _____ (name of business), a(n)

_____ (state of operation) sole proprietorship

Power of Attorney Acknowledgment

State of _____

County of _____

On _____ , 20 _____ , _____

personally came before me and, being duly sworn, did state that he or she is the attorney-in-fact of _____ described in the above document; that he or she signed the above document in my presence as attorney-in-fact on behalf of this person; and that he or she had full authority to do so under Power of Attorney dated _____ , 20 _____ .

_____

Signature of Notary Public

Notary Public, In and for the County of _____

State of _____

My commission expires: _____   Notary Seal

Power of Attorney Signature Line

_____

Signature of Person Holding Power of Attorney

_____

Printed Name of Person Holding Power of Attorney

As attorney-in-fact for _____

(name of person granting power of attorney)

Under Power of Attorney dated _____ , 20 _____

Individual Acknowledgment

State of _____
County of _____

On _____ , 20 _____ , _____
personally came before me and, being duly sworn, did state that he or she is the
person described in the above document and that he or she signed the above
document in my presence as a free and voluntary act for the purposes stated.

_____
Signature of Notary Public

Notary Public, In and for the County of _____
State of _____

My commission expires: _____   Notary Seal

Individual Signature Line

_____
Signature

_____
Printed Name

Husband and Wife Acknowledgment

State of _____

County of _____

On _____ , 20 _____ , _____

and _____ personally came before me and, being duly sworn, did state that they are the husband and wife described in the above document and that they signed the above document in my presence as a free and voluntary act for the purposes stated.

_____

Signature of Notary Public

Notary Public, In and for the County of _____
State of _____

My commission expires: _____   Notary Seal

Husband and Wife Signature Line

_____

Signature of Husband

_____

Printed Name of Husband

_____

Signature of Wife

_____

Printed Name of Wife

Chapter 4

Powers of Attorney

A power of attorney is simply a document that is used to allow one person to give authority to another person to act on their behalf. The person signing the power of attorney (generally referred to as the *principal*) grants legal authority to another to "stand in their shoes" and act legally for them. The person who receives the such authority is called an *attorney-in-fact*. This title and the power of attorney form *does not* mean that the person receiving the power has to be a lawyer. If you appoint your spouse or a trusted relative or friend, then that person is your "attorney-in-fact". Think of the term "attorney-in-fact" as actually meaning "agent." Using a power of attorney, you will be appointing an "agent" to act in your place for some activities, perhaps relating to financial actions or perhaps relating to health care decisions, or any of a number of other possible actions that your "agent" may perform. The word 'attorney' in the context of a power of attorney or an attorney-in-fact is *not* related to the generally accepted notion of an 'attorney' as a lawyer.

Types of Powers of Attorney

Let's take a look at the various different types of powers of attorney. (Note that the plural for power of attorney is "powers of attorney" and not "power of attorneys." That is because the legal document is actually creating a "power," the ability for someone else to act on your behalf. The legal document provides them with the "power" to do so.) The following will be a very brief explanation of the types of powers of attorney. Each specific section of this chapter will contain a more detailed description of each type of power of attorney. You should read through this list carefully to determine which type of power of attorney is most appropriate in your particular circumstances. Here are the various types of powers of attorney that are included in this book:

General Power of Attorney

A general power of attorney allows you to authorize your agent (your "attorney in fact") to handle a few or all of your financial and/or business transactions. With this form, you are giving another person the right to manage your financial and/or business matters on your behalf. They are given the power to act exactly as you could. This, of course, is a very powerful grant of authority to someone else to act on your behalf. The person appointed must be someone that you fully trust to handle your affairs. The authority granted by this power of attorney may be revoked by you at any time and is automatically revoked if you die or become incapacitated or incompetent. If there is anything about this form that you do not understand, you should ask a lawyer to explain it to you. This power of attorney contains an important notice prior to the form itself. Please read this notice carefully before you complete this form.

When You Should Use a General Power of Attorney

A general power of attorney allows you to select any or all of a range of powers that you wish for your agent (attorney-in-fact) to have. This type of power of attorney can be used to authorize someone else to sign certain documents if you can not be present when the signatures are necessary. They can be used to authorize someone to handle any or all of the following possible matters:

> Real estate transactions; goods and services transactions; stock, bond, share and commodity transactions; banking transactions; business operating transactions; insurance transactions; estate transactions; legal claims and litigation; personal relationships and affairs; benefits from military service; records, reports and statements; retirement benefit transactions; making gifts to a spouse, children, parents and other descendants; and tax matters.

Additionally, you may also authorize your attorney-in-fact to delegate any or all of the above powers to someone that your appointed attorney-in-fact selects. This option should only be taken if you trust your appointed attorney-in-fact totally to make such a decision only with your best interests in mind.

A general power of attorney is most useful if you wish to grant your agent some, but not all of the possible powers available to an agent. If you wish to grant full and complete authority to your agent, you should use an *unlimited power of attorney* instead. An unlimited power of attorney provides that your agent will have total authority to act on your behalf for all financial and/or business matters (but not for health care decisions). If you wish to provide a very limited power to your agent, you may wish to use a *limited power of attorney* instead of a general power of attorney. A limited power of attorney allows you to limit the power granted to a specific action or a specific date range. A general power of attorney is not valid if you become disabled or incapacitated. You must use a *'durable' power of attorney* for that purpose. In addition, a general power of attorney also can *not* be used for health care decisions. You must use a *durable health care power of attorney* for that purpose. (This form is not provided; please see Nova's *Powers of Attorney Simplified*.)

Unlimited Power of Attorney

An unlimited power of attorney should be used only in situations where you desire to authorize another person to act for you in *any and all* transactions. The grant of power under this document is unlimited. However, the powers you grant with this document cease to be effective should you become disabled or incompetent. This form gives the person whom you designate as your "attorney-in-fact" extremely broad powers to handle your property during your lifetime, which may include powers to mortgage, sell, or otherwise dispose of any real or personal property without advance notice to you or approval by you. This document does not authorize anyone to make medical or other health care decisions. You must execute a durable health care power of attorney to do this. The authority granted by this power of attorney may be revoked by you at any time and is automatically revoked if you die or become incapacitated or incompetent. If there is anything about this form that you do not understand, you should ask a lawyer to explain it to you. This power of attorney contains an important notice prior to the form itself.

When You Should Use an Unlimited Power of Attorney

An unlimited power of attorney authorizes your agent to handle *any and all* of your financial and business affairs, including all of the following possible matters:

Real estate transactions; personal property and goods and services transactions; stock, bond, share and commodity transactions; banking and financial institution transactions; business operating transactions; insurance and annuity transactions; estate, trust, and other transactions where the principal is a beneficiary; legal claims and litigation; personal and family maintenance; benefits from social security, medicare, medicaid, or civil or military service; records, reports and statements; retirement benefit transactions; tax matters; delegation of the agent's authority to others; and any and all other matters except health care decisions.

All of the above mentioned powers that are granted to your agent are spelled out in great detail in this particular power of attorney form. This is the most extensive and detailed power of attorney form that is provided. It should only be used if you are absolutely certain that the agent you choose is fully and totally trustworthy and able to exercise these broad powers in your best interest. The detailed powers that are listed in this form are taken from the Uniform Power of Attorney Act that has been legislatively adopted by many states.

Please note that the "delegation of the agent's authority to others" provision in this document grants your chosen agent the power to delegate any of his or her powers to another person of his or her own choosing. If you do not wish your agent to have this authority, or you wish to limit your agent's power under any of the other powers which are enumerated in this document, you should use instead a *general power of attorney*. A general power of attorney will allow you to pick and choose which of these powers you wish to grant to your agent. If you wish to provide a very limited power to your agent, you may wish to use a *limited power of attorney* instead of an unlimited power of attorney. A limited power of attorney allows you to limit the power granted to a specific action or a specific date range. An unlimited power of attorney is not valid if you become disabled or incapacitated. You must use a *'durable' power of attorney* for that purpose. In addition, an unlimited power of attorney also can *not* be used for health care decisions. You must use a *durable health care power of attorney* for that purpose. (This form is not provided; please see Nova's *Powers of Attorney Simplified.*)

Limited Power of Attorney

This document provides for a *limited* grant of authority to another person. It should be used in those situations when you need to authorize another person to act for you in a specific transaction or transactions. The type of acts that you authorize the other person to perform should be spelled out in detail to avoid confusion (for example, to sign any necessary forms to open a bank account). If desired, the dates when the power of attorney will be valid may also be specified. The authority that you grant with a limited power of attorney may be revoked by you at any time and is automatically revoked if you die or become incapacitated or incompetent. This document does not authorize the appointed attorney-in-fact to make any decisions relating to medical or health care. If there is anything about these forms that you do not understand, you should ask a lawyer to explain it to you. These powers of attorney contain an important notice prior to the form itself.

When You Should Use a Limited Power of Attorney

A limited power of attorney allows you to select a specific power that you wish for your agent (attorney-in-fact) to have. This type of power of attorney can be used to authorize someone else to sign certain documents if you can not be present when the signatures are necessary. They can be used to authorize someone to handle any of the following possible matters:

Real estate transactions; goods and services transactions; stock, bond, share and commodity transactions; banking transactions; business operating transactions; insurance transactions; estate transactions; legal claims and litigation; personal relationships and affairs; benefits from military service; records, reports and statements; retirement benefit transactions; making gifts to a spouse, children, parents and other descendants; tax matters; and certain child care decisions, such as consent to emergency medical care.

A limited power of attorney is most useful if you wish to grant your agent only some, but not all of the possible powers available to an agent. If you wish to grant full and complete authority to your agent, you may wish to use an *unlimited power of attorney* instead. An unlimited power of attorney provides that your agent will have total authority to act on your behalf for all financial and/or business matters (but not for health care decisions). If you wish to provide a range of powers to your agent, you may wish to use a *general power of attorney* instead of a limited power of attorney. A limited power of attorney allows you to limit the power granted to a specific action or a specific date range. A limited power of attorney is not valid if you become disabled or incapacitated. You must use a *'durable' power of attorney* for that purpose (Note: you can prepare a *'durable' limited power of attorney*). In addition, a limited power of attorney also can *not* be used for health care decisions. You must use a *durable health care power of attorney* for that purpose.

Revocation of Powers of Attorney

This document may be used with any of the previous power of attorney forms. The revocation is used to terminate the original authority that was granted to the other person in the first place. Some limited powers of attorney specify that the powers that are granted will end on a specific date. If that is the case, you will not need a revocation unless you wish the powers to end sooner than the date specified. If the grant of power was for a limited purpose and that purpose is complete but no date for the power to end was specified, this revocation should be used as soon after the transaction as possible. In any event, if you choose to revoke a power of attorney, a copy of this revocation should be provided to the person to whom the power was given. Copies should also be given to any party that may have had dealings with the attorney-in-fact before the revocation and to any party with whom the attorney-in-fact may be expected to attempt to deal with after the revocation. If you feel that it is important to verify the revocation of your power of attorney, you should have any third party that you supply with a copy of the revocation sign another copy for you to keep. If that is not possible, you should mail a copy of the revocation to that person or institution by first class mail, with a return receipt requested that requires a signature to verify delivery.

Instructions for Powers of Attorney

General Power of Attorney: To complete this form, please provide the following information. A sample numbered version of this form is found on page 90.

① Name and address of person granting power (principal)
② Name and address of person granted power (attorney-in-fact)
③ Initial each of the specific powers that you wish your attorney-in-fact to have. If you wish your attorney-in-fact to have full authority to do anything that you yourself could do, simply initial line (q). (Note: if you wish to have your attorney-in-fact to have full authority, you may wish to use the *unlimited power of attorney* form instead).
④ Name and address of successor to person originally granted power (successor attorney-in-fact) (optional-if not used, write n/a in this space)
⑤ Date
⑥ Printed name of principal, date of signing of power of attorney, and signature of principal (signed in front of notary public)
⑦ Printed names and signatures of witnesses (signed in front of notary public)
⑧ Notary acknowledgement should be completed by the notary public
⑨ Printed name, date, and signature of attorney-in-fact (need not be witnessed or notarized)
⑩ Printed name, date, and signature of successor attorney-in-fact (optional-if not used, write N/A in this space)(need not be witnessed or notarized)

Unlimited Power of Attorney: To complete this form, please provide the following information. A sample numbered version of this form is found on page 95.

① Name and address of person granting power (principal)
② Name and address of person granted power (attorney-in-fact)
③ Name and address of successor to person originally granted power (successor attorney-in-fact) (optional-if not used, write N/A in this space)

④ Date
⑤ Printed name of principal, date of signing of power of attorney, and signature of principal (signed in front of notary public)
⑥ Printed names and signatures of witnesses (signed in front of notary public)
⑦ Notary acknowledgement should be completed by the notary public
⑧ Printed name, date, and signature of attorney-in-fact (need not be witnessed or notarized)
⑨ Printed name, date, and signature of successor attorney-in-fact (optional-if not used, write N/A in this space) (need not be witnessed or notarized)

Limited Power of Attorney: To complete this form, please provide the following information. A sample numbered version of this form is found on page 107.

① Name and address of person granting power (principal)
② Name and address of person granted power (attorney-in-fact)
③ List specific acts that you want your attorney-in-fact to perform (be as detailed as possible)
④ Name and address of successor to person originally granted power (successor attorney-in-fact) (optional-if not used, write N/A in this space.)
⑤ Date
⑥ Printed name of principal, date of signing of power of attorney, and signature of principal (signed in front of notary public)
⑦ Printed names and signatures of witnesses (signed in front of notary public)
⑧ Notary acknowledgement should be completed by the notary public
⑨ Printed name, date, and signature of attorney-in-fact (need not be witnessed or notarized)
⑩ Printed name, date, and signature of successor attorney-in-fact (optional-if not used, write N/A in this space) (need not be witnessed or notarized)

Revocation of Powers of Attorney: To complete this form, please provide the following information. A sample numbered version of this form is found on page 111.

① Printed name and address of person who originally granted power (principal)
② Date of original power of attorney
③ Printed name and address of person granted power (attorney-in-fact)
④ Date of revocation of power of attorney
⑤ Signature of person revoking power of attorney (principal) (signed in front of notary)
⑥ Notary to complete the notary acknowledgment

General Power of Attorney

Notice: This is an important document. Before signing this document, you should know these important facts. By signing this document, you are not giving up any powers or rights to control your finances and property yourself. In addition to your own powers and rights, you may be giving another person, your attorney-in-fact, broad powers to handle your finances and property. This general power of attorney may give the person whom you designate (your "attorney-in-fact") broad powers to handle your finances and property, which may include powers to encumber, sell or otherwise dispose of any real or personal property without advance notice to you or approval by you. THE POWERS GRANTED WILL NOT EXIST AFTER YOU BECOME DISABLED, OR INCAPACITATED. This document does not authorize anyone to make medical or other health care decisions for you. If you own complex or special assets such as a business, or if there is anything about this form that you do not understand, you should ask a lawyer to explain this form to you before you sign it. If you wish to change your general power of attorney, you must complete a new document and revoke this one. You may revoke this document at any time by destroying it, by directing another person to destroy it in your presence or by signing a written and dated statement expressing your intent to revoke this document. If you revoke this document, you should notify your attorney-in-fact and any other person to whom you have given a copy of the form. You also should notify all parties having custody of your assets. These parties have no responsibility to you unless you actually notify them of the revocation. If your attorney-in-fact is your spouse and your marriage is annulled, or you are divorced after signing this document, this document is invalid. Since some 3rd parties or some transactions may not permit use of this document, it is advisable to check in advance, if possible, for any special requirements that may be imposed. You should sign this form only if the attorney-in-fact you name is reliable, trustworthy and competent to manage your affairs. This form must be signed by the Principal (the person appointing the attorney-in-fact), witnessed by two persons other than the notary public, and acknowledged by a notary public.

① I, _____(printed name), of
(address)_____,

as principal, to grant a general power of attorney to, and do hereby appoint:

②_____ (printed name), of

(address)_____,

my attorney-in-fact to act in my name, place and stead in any way which I myself could do, if I were personally present, with respect to the following matters to the extent that I am permitted by law to act through an agent. The powers chosen below shall have the full force and effect given to them by their full enumeration as laid out in the text of the Power of Attorney Act of the laws of the State of _____:

(Place your initials before each item that you select and cross out each item that you do not select) ③

_____ (a) real estate transactions;

_____ (b) goods and services transactions;

_____ (c) bond, share and commodity transactions;

_____ (d) banking transactions;

_____ (e) business operating transactions;

_____ (f) insurance transactions;

_____ (g) estate transactions;

_____ (h) claims and litigation;

_____ (i) personal relationships and affairs;

_____ (j) benefits from military service;

_____ (k) records, reports and statements;

_____ (l) retirement benefit transactions;

_____ (m) making gifts to my spouse, children and more remote descendants, and parents;

_____ (n) tax matters;

_____ (o) all other matters;

_____ (p) full and unqualified authority to my attorney-in-fact to delegate any or all of the foregoing powers to any person or persons whom my attorney-in-fact shall select;

_____ (q) unlimited power and authority to act in all of the above situations (a) through (p)

If the attorney-in-fact named above is unable or unwilling to serve, I appoint ④ _____(printed name), of (address) _____ , to be my attorney-in-fact for all purposes hereunder.

To induce any third party to rely upon this power of attorney, I agree that any third party receiving a signed copy or facsimile of this power of attorney may rely upon such copy, and that revocation or termination of this power of attorney shall be ineffective as to such third party until actual notice or knowledge of such revocation or termination shall have been received by such third party. I, for myself and for my heirs, executors, legal representatives and assigns, agree to indemnify and hold harmless any such third party from any and all claims that may arise against such third party by reason of such third party having relied on the provisions of this power of attorney. **THIS POWER OF ATTORNEY SHALL NOT BE EFFECTIVE IN THE EVENT OF MY FUTURE DISABILITY OR INCAPACITY.** This power of attorney may be revoked by me at any time and is automatically revoked upon my death. My attorney-in-fact shall no be compensated for his or her services nor shall my attorney-in-fact be liable to me, my estate, heirs, successors, or assigns for acting or refraining from acting under this document, except for willful misconduct or gross negligence.

Dated: ⑤_____

Signature and Declaration of Principal ⑥

I, _____ (printed name), the principal, sign my name to this power of attorney this _____day of _____ and, being first duly sworn, do declare to the undersigned authority that I sign and execute this instrument as my power of attorney and that I sign it willingly, or willingly direct another to sign for me, that I execute it as my free and voluntary act for the purposes expressed in the power of attorney and that I am eighteen years of age or older, of sound mind and under no constraint or undue influence.

_____
Signature of Principal

Witness Attestation ⑦

I, _____ (printed name), the first witness, and I, _____ (printed name), the second witness, sign my name to the foregoing power of attorney being first duly sworn and do declare to the undersigned authority that the principal signs and executes this instrument as his/her power of attorney and that he\she signs it willingly, or willingly directs another to sign for him/her, and that I, in the presence and hearing of the principal, sign this power of attorney as witness to the principal's signing and that to the best of my knowledge the principal is eighteen years of age or older, of sound mind and under no constraint or undue influence.

_____
Signature of First Witness

_____
Signature of Second Witness

Notary Acknowledgment ⑧

State of _____
County of _____
Subscribed, sworn to and acknowledged before me by

_____,
the Principal, and subscribed and sworn to before me by

_____
and _____, the
witnesses, this _____ day of _____ .

_____
Notary Signature
Notary Public,
In and for the County of _____
State of _____
My commission expires: _____   Seal

Acknowledgment and Acceptance of Appointment as Attorney-in-Fact ⑨

I, _____, (printed name) have read the attached power of attorney and am the person identified as the attorney-in-fact for the principal. I hereby acknowledge that I accept my appointment as attorney-in-fact and that when I act as agent I shall exercise the powers for the benefit of the principal; I shall keep the assets of the principal separate from my assets; I shall exercise reasonable caution and prudence; and I shall keep a full and accurate record of all actions, receipts and disbursements on behalf of the principal.

_____   _____
Signature of Attorney-in-Fact   Date

Acknowledgment and Acceptance of Appointment as Successor Attorney-in-Fact ⑩

I, _____, (printed name) have read the attached power of attorney and am the person identified as the successor attorney-in-fact for the principal. I hereby acknowledge that I accept my appointment as successor attorney-in-fact and that, in the absence of a specific provision to the contrary in the power of attorney, when I act as agent I shall exercise the powers for the benefit of the principal; I shall keep the assets of the principal separate from my assets; I shall exercise reasonable caution and prudence; and I shall keep a full and accurate record of all actions, receipts and disbursements on behalf of the principal.

_____   _____
Signature of Successor Attorney-in-Fact   Date

Unlimited Power of Attorney

Notice: This is an important document. Before signing this document, you should know these important facts. By signing this document, you are not giving up any powers or rights to control your finances and property yourself. In addition to your own powers and rights, you are giving another person, your attorney-in-fact, broad powers to handle your finances and property. This unlimited power of attorney will give the person whom you designate (your "attorney-in-fact") broad powers to handle your finances and property, which includes powers to encumber, sell or otherwise dispose of any real or personal property without advance notice to you or approval by you. THE POWERS GRANTED WILL NOT EXIST AFTER YOU BECOME DISABLED, OR INCAPACITATED. This document does not authorize anyone to make medical or other health care decisions for you. If you own complex or special assets such as a business, or if there is anything about this form that you do not understand, you should ask a lawyer to explain this form to you before you sign it. If you wish to change your unlimited power of attorney, you must complete a new document and revoke this one. You may revoke this document at any time by destroying it, by directing another person to destroy it in your presence or by signing a written and dated statement expressing your intent to revoke this document. If you revoke this document, you should notify your attorney-in-fact and any other person to whom you have given a copy of the form. You also should notify all parties having custody of your assets. These parties have no responsibility to you unless you actually notify them of the revocation. If your attorney-in-fact is your spouse and your marriage is annulled, or you are divorced after signing this document, this document is invalid. Since some 3rd parties or some transactions may not permit use of this document, it is advisable to check in advance, if possible, for any special requirements that may be imposed. You should sign this form only if the attorney-in-fact you name is reliable, trustworthy and competent to manage your affairs. This form must be signed by the Principal (the person appointing the attorney-in-fact), witnessed by two persons other than the notary public, and acknowledged by a notary public.

① I, _____(printed name),
of   (address)_____,   as
principal, do grant an unlimited power of attorney to, and do hereby appoint: ②
_____(printed name), of
(address)_____,

my attorney-in-fact and do grant him or her unlimited power and authority to act in my name, place and stead in any way which I myself could do, if I were personally present, with respect to all of the following matters to the extent that I am permitted by law to act through an agent:

IN GENERAL, the principal authorizes the agent to: (1) demand, receive, and obtain by litigation or otherwise, money or other thing of value to which the principal is, may become, or claims to be entitled, and conserve, invest, disburse, or use anything so received for the purposes intended; (2) contract in any manner with any person, on terms agreeable to the agent, to accomplish a purpose of a transaction, and perform, rescind, reform, release, or modify the contract or another contract made by or on behalf of the principal; (3) execute, acknowledge, seal, and deliver a deed, revocation, mortgage, security agreement, lease, notice, check, promissory note, electronic funds transfer, release, or other instrument or communication the agent considers desirable to accomplish a purpose of a transaction, including creating a schedule of the principal's property and attaching it to the power of attorney; (4) prosecute, defend, submit to arbitration or mediation, settle, and propose or accept a compromise with respect to, a claim existing in favor of or against the principal or intervene in litigation relating to the claim; (5) seek on the principal's behalf the assistance of a court to carry out an act authorized by the principal in the power of attorney; (6) engage, compensate, and discharge an attorney, accountant, expert witness, or other assistant; (7) keep appropriate records of each transaction, including an accounting of receipts and disbursements; (8) prepare, execute, and file a record, report, or other document the agent considers desirable to safeguard or promote the principal's interest under a statute or governmental regulation; (9) reimburse the agent for expenditures properly made by the agent in exercising the powers granted by the power of attorney; and (10) in general, do any other lawful act with respect to the power and all property related to the power.

WITH RESPECT TO REAL PROPERTY, the principal authorizes the agent to: (1) accept as a gift or as security for an extension of credit, reject, demand, buy, lease, receive, or otherwise acquire, an interest in real property or a right incident to real property; (2) sell, exchange, convey with or without covenants, quitclaim, release, surrender, mortgage, retain title for security, encumber, partition, consent to partitioning, subdivide, apply for zoning, rezoning, or other governmental permits, plat or consent to platting, develop, grant options concerning, lease, sublease, or otherwise dispose of, an interest in real property or a right incident to real property; (3) release, assign, satisfy, or enforce by litigation or otherwise, a mortgage, deed of trust, conditional sale contract, encumbrance, lien, or other claim to real property which exists or is asserted; (4) manage or conserve an interest in real property or a right incident to real property, owned or claimed to be owned by the principal, including: (a) insuring against a casualty, liability, or loss; (b) obtaining or regaining possession, or protecting the interest or right, by litigation or otherwise; (c) paying, compromising, or contesting taxes or assessments, or applying for and receiving refunds in connection with them; and (d) purchasing supplies, hiring assistance or labor, and making repairs or alterations to the real property; (5) use, develop, alter, replace, remove, erect, or install structures or other improvements upon real property in or incident to which the principal has, or claims to have, an interest or right; (6) participate in a reorganization with respect to real property or a legal entity that owns an interest in or right incident to real property and receive and hold, directly or indirectly, shares of stock or obligations, or other evidences of ownership or debt, received in a plan of reorganization, and act with respect to them, including: (a) selling or otherwise disposing of them; (b) exercising or selling an option, conversion, or similar right with respect to them; and (c) voting them in person or by proxy; (7) change the form of title of an interest in or right incident to real property, and (8) dedicate to public use, with or without consideration, easements or other real property in which the principal has, or claims to have, an interest.

WITH RESPECT TO TANGIBLE PERSONAL PROPERTY, the principal authorizes the agent to: (1) accept as a gift or as security for an extension of credit, reject, demand, buy, receive, or otherwise acquire ownership or possession of tangible personal property or an interest in tangible personal property; (2) sell, exchange, convey with or without covenants, release, surrender, create a security interest in, grant options concerning, lease, sublease to others, or otherwise dispose of tangible personal property or an interest in tangible personal property; (3) release, assign, satisfy, or enforce by litigation or otherwise, a security interest, lien, or other claim on behalf of the principal, with respect to tangible personal property or an interest in tangible personal property; (4) manage or conserve tangible personal property or an interest in tangible personal property on behalf of the principal, including: (a) insuring against casualty, liability, or loss; (b) obtaining or regaining possession, or protecting the property or interest, by litigation or otherwise; (c) paying, compromising, or contesting taxes or assessments or applying for and receiving refunds in connection with taxes or assessments; (d) moving from place to place; (e) storing for hire or on a gratuitous bailment; and (f) using, altering, and making repairs or alterations; and (5) change the form of title of an interest in tangible personal property.

WITH RESPECT TO TRANSACTIONS CONCERNING STOCKS AND BONDS, the principal authorizes the agent to: (1) buy, sell, and exchange stocks, bonds, mutual funds, and all other types of securities and financial instruments, whether held directly or indirectly, except commodity futures contracts and call and put options on stocks and stock indexes, (2) receive certificates and other evidences of ownership with respect to securities, (3) exercise voting rights with respect to securities in person or by proxy, enter into voting trusts, and consent to limitations on the right to vote.

WITH RESPECT TO TRANSACTIONS CONCERNING COMMODITIES AND OPTIONS, the principal authorizes the agent to: (1) buy, sell, exchange, assign, settle, and exercise commodity futures contracts and call and put options on stocks and stock indexes traded on a regulated option exchange, and (2) establish, continue, modify, and terminate option accounts with a broker.

WITH RESPECT TO TRANSACTIONS CONCERNING BANKS AND OTHER FINANCIAL INSTITUTIONS, the principal authorizes the agent to: (1) continue, modify, and terminate an account or other banking arrangement made by or on behalf of the principal; (2) establish, modify, and terminate an account or other banking arrangement with a bank, trust company, savings and loan association, credit union, thrift company, brokerage firm, or other financial institution selected by the agent; (3) rent a safe deposit box or space in a vault; (4) contract for other services available from a financial institution as the agent considers desirable; (5) withdraw by check, order, or otherwise money or property of the principal deposited with or left in the custody of a financial institution; 6) receive bank statements, vouchers, notices, and similar documents from a financial institution and act with respect to them; (7) enter a safe deposit box or vault and withdraw or add to the contents; (8) borrow money at an interest rate agreeable to the agent and pledge as security personal property of the principal necessary in order to borrow, pay, renew, or extend the time of payment of a debt of the principal; (9) make, assign, draw, endorse, discount, guarantee, and negotiate promissory notes, checks, drafts, and other negotiable or nonnegotiable paper of the principal, or payable to the principal or the principal's order, transfer money, receive the cash or other proceeds of those transactions, accept a draft drawn by a person upon the principal, and pay it when due; (10) receive for the principal and act upon a sight draft, warehouse receipt, or other negotiable or nonnegotiable instrument; (11) apply for, receive, and use letters of credit, credit and debit cards, and traveler's checks from a financial institution and give an indemnity or other agreement in connection with letters of credit; and (12) consent to an extension of the time of payment with respect to commercial paper or a financial transaction with a financial institution.

WITH RESPECT TO OPERATING A BUSINESS, the principal authorizes the agent to: (1) operate, buy, sell, enlarge, reduce, and terminate a business interest; (2) act for a principal, subject to the terms of a partnership agreement or operating agreement, to: (a) perform a duty or discharge a liability and exercise a right, power, privilege, or option that the principal has, may have, or claims to have, under the partnership agreement or operating agreement, whether or not the principal is a partner in a partnership or member of a limited liability company; (b) enforce the terms of the partnership agreement or operating agreement by litigation or otherwise; and (c) defend, submit to arbitration, settle, or compromise litigation to which the principal is a party because of membership in a partnership or limited liability company; (3) exercise in person or by proxy, or enforce by litigation or otherwise, a right, power, privilege, or option the principal has or claims to have as the holder of a bond, share, or other instrument of similar character and defend, submit to arbitration or mediation, settle, or compromise litigation to which the principal is a party because of a bond, share, or similar instrument; (4) with respect to a business controlled by the principal: (a) continue, modify, renegotiate, extend, and terminate a contract made by or on behalf of the principal with respect to the business before execution of the power of attorney; (b) determine: (i) the location of its operation; (ii) the nature and extent of its business; (iii) the methods of manufacturing, selling, merchandising, financing, accounting, and advertising employed in its operation; (iv) the amount and types of insurance carried; and (v) the mode of engaging, compensating, and dealing with its accountants, attorneys, other agents, and employees; (c) change the name or form of organization under which the business is operated and enter into a partnership agreement or operating agreement with other persons or organize a corporation or other business entity to take over all or part of the operation of the business; and (d) demand and receive money due or claimed by the principal or on the principal's behalf in the operation of the business, and control and disburse the money in the operation of the business; (5) put additional capital into a business in which the principal has an interest; (6) join in a plan of reorganization, consolidation, or merger of the business; (7) sell or liquidate a business or part of it at the time and upon the terms the agent considers desirable; (8) establish the value of a business under a buy-out agreement to which the principal is a party; (9) prepare, sign, file, and deliver reports, compilations of information, returns, or other papers with respect to a business which are required by a governmental agency or instrumentality or which the agent considers desirable, and make related payments; and (10) pay, compromise, or contest taxes or assessments and perform any other act that the agent considers desirable to protect the principal from illegal or unnecessary taxation, fines, penalties, or assessments with respect to a business, including attempts to recover, in any manner permitted by law, money paid before or after the execution of the power of attorney.

WITH RESPECT TO INSURANCE AND ANNUITIES, the principal authorizes the agent to: (1) continue, pay the premium or assessment on, modify, rescind, release, or terminate a contract procured by or on behalf of the principal which insures or provides an annuity to either the principal or another person, whether or not the principal is a beneficiary under the contract; (2) procure new, different, and additional contracts of insurance and annuities for the principal and the principal's spouse, children, and other dependents, and select the amount, type of insurance or annuity, and mode of payment; (3) pay the premium or assessment on, modify, rescind, release, or terminate a contract of insurance or annuity procured by the agent; (4) apply for and receive a loan on the security of a contract of insurance or annuity; (5) surrender and receive the cash surrender value; (6) exercise an election; (7) change the manner of paying premiums; (8) change or convert the type of insurance or annuity, with respect to which the principal has or claims to have a power described in this section; (9) apply for and procure government aid to guarantee or pay premiums of a contract of insurance on the life of the principal; (10) collect, sell, assign, hypothecate, borrow upon, or pledge the interest of the principal in a contract of insurance or annuity; and (11) pay from proceeds or otherwise, compromise or contest, and apply for refunds in connection with, a tax or assessment levied by a taxing authority with respect to a contract of insurance or annuity or its proceeds or liability accruing by reason of the tax or assessment.

WITH RESPECT TO ESTATES, TRUSTS, AND OTHER RELATIONSHIPS IN WHICH THE PRINCIPAL IS A BENEFICIARY, the principal authorizes the agent to act for the principal in all matters that affect a trust, probate estate, guardianship, conservatorship, escrow, custodianship, or other fund from which the principal is, may become, or claims to be entitled, as a beneficiary, to a share or payment, including to: (1) accept, reject, disclaim, receive, receipt for, sell, assign, release, pledge, exchange, or consent to a reduction in or modification of a share in or payment from the fund; (2) demand or obtain by litigation or otherwise money or other thing of value to which the principal is, may become, or claims to be entitled by reason of the fund; (3) initiate, participate in, and oppose litigation to ascertain the meaning, validity, or effect of a deed, will, declaration of trust, or other instrument or transaction affecting the interest of the principal; (4) initiate, participate in, and oppose litigation to remove, substitute, or surcharge a fiduciary; (5) conserve, invest, disburse, and use anything received for an authorized purpose; and (6) transfer an interest of the principal in real property, stocks, bonds, accounts with financial institutions or securities intermediaries, insurance, annuities, and other property, to the trustee of a revocable trust created by the principal as settlor.

WITH RESPECT TO CLAIMS AND LITIGATION, the principal authorizes the agent to: (1) assert and prosecute before a court or administrative agency a claim, a claim for relief, cause of action, counterclaim, offset, or defense against an individual, organization, or government, including actions to recover property or other thing of value, to recover damages sustained by the principal, to eliminate or modify tax liability, or to seek an injunction, specific performance, or other relief; (2) bring an action to determine adverse claims, intervene in litigation, and act as amicus curiae; (3) in connection with litigation, procure an attachment, garnishment, libel, order of arrest, or other preliminary, provisional, or intermediate relief and use an available procedure to effect or satisfy a judgment, order, or decree; (4) in connection with litigation, perform any lawful act, including acceptance of tender, offer of judgment, admission of facts, submission of a controversy on an agreed statement of facts, consent to examination before trial, and binding the principal in litigation; (5) submit to arbitration or mediation, settle, and propose or accept a compromise with respect to a claim or litigation; (6) waive the issuance and service of process upon the principal, accept service of process, appear for the principal, designate persons upon whom process directed to the principal may be served, execute and file or deliver stipulations on the principal's behalf, verify pleadings, seek appellate review, procure and give surety and indemnity bonds, contract and pay for the preparation and printing of records and briefs, receive and execute and file or deliver a consent, waiver, release, confession of judgment, satisfaction of judgment, notice, agreement, or other instrument in connection with the prosecution, settlement, or defense of a claim or litigation; (7) act for the principal with respect to bankruptcy or insolvency, whether voluntary or involuntary, concerning the principal or some other person, or with respect to a reorganization, receivership, or application for the appointment of a receiver or trustee which affects an interest of the principal in property or other thing of value; and (8) pay a judgment against the principal or a settlement made in connection with litigation and receive and conserve money or other thing of value paid in settlement of or as proceeds of a claim or litigation.

WITH RESPECT TO PERSONAL AND FAMILY MAINTENANCE, the principal authorizes the agent to: (1) perform the acts necessary to maintain the customary standard of living of the principal, the principal's spouse, children, and other individuals customarily or legally entitled to be supported by the principal, including providing living quarters by purchase, lease, or other contract, or paying the operating costs, including interest, amortization payments, repairs, and taxes, on premises owned by the principal and occupied by those individuals; (2) provide for the individuals described under (1) normal domestic help, usual vacations and travel expenses, and funds for shelter, clothing, food, appropriate education, and other current living costs; (3) pay on behalf of the individuals described under (1) expenses for necessary medical, dental, and surgical care, hospitalization, and custodial care; (4) act as the principal's personal representative pursuant to sections 1171 through 1179 of the Social Security Act, 42 U.S.C. Section 1320d (sections 262 and 264 of Public Law 104-191) [or successor provisions] and applicable regulations, in making decisions related to the past, present, or future payment for the provision of health care consented to by the principal or anyone authorized under the law of this state to consent to health care on behalf of the principal; (5) continue any provision made by the principal, for the individuals described under (1), for automobiles or other means of transportation, including registering, licensing, insuring, and replacing them; (6) maintain or open charge accounts for the convenience of the individuals described under (1) and open new accounts the agent considers desirable to accomplish a lawful purpose; and (7) continue payments incidental to the membership or affiliation of the principal in a church, club, society, order, or other organization or to continue contributions to those organizations.

WITH RESPECT TO BENEFITS FROM SOCIAL SECURITY, MEDICARE, MEDICAID, OTHER GOVERNMENTAL PROGRAMS, OR CIVIL OR MILITARY SERVICE, the principal authorizes the agent to: (1) execute vouchers in the name of the principal for allowances and reimbursements payable by the United States or a foreign government or by a state or subdivision of a state to the principal, including allowances and reimbursements for transportation of the individuals described in Section 212(1), and for shipment of their household effects; (2) take possession and order the removal and shipment of property of the principal from a post, warehouse, depot, dock, or other place of storage or safekeeping, either governmental or private, and execute and deliver a release, voucher, receipt, bill of lading, shipping ticket, certificate, or other instrument for that purpose; (3) prepare, file, and prosecute a claim of the principal to a benefit or assistance, financial or otherwise, to which the principal claims to be entitled under a statute or governmental regulation; (4) prosecute, defend, submit to arbitration or mediation, settle, and propose or accept a compromise with respect to any benefit or assistance the principal may be entitled to receive under a statute or governmental regulation; and (5) receive the financial proceeds of a claim of the type described in paragraph (3) and conserve, invest, disburse, or use anything so received for a lawful purpose.

WITH RESPECT TO RETIREMENT PLANS, the principal authorizes the agent to: (1) select a payment option under a retirement plan in which the principal participates, including a plan for a self-employed individual; (2) make voluntary contributions to those plans; (3) exercise the investment powers available under a self-directed retirement plan; (4) make a rollover of benefits into another retirement plan; (5) if authorized by the plan, borrow from, sell assets to, purchase assets from, or request distributions from the plan; and (6) waive the right of the principal to be a beneficiary of a joint or survivor annuity if the principal is a spouse who is not employed.

WITH RESPECT TO TAX MATTERS, the principal authorizes the agent to: (1) prepare, sign, and file federal, state, local, and foreign income, gift, payroll, Federal Insurance Contributions Act, and other tax returns, claims for refunds, requests for extension of time, petitions regarding tax matters, and any other tax-related documents, including receipts, offers, waivers, consents, including consents and agreements under the Internal Revenue Code, 26 U.S.C. Section 2032A [or successor provisions], closing agreements, and any power of attorney required by the Internal Revenue Service or other taxing authority with respect to a tax year upon which the statute of limitations has not run and the following 25 tax years; (2) pay taxes due, collect refunds, post bonds, receive confidential information, and contest deficiencies determined by the Internal Revenue Service or other taxing authority; (3) exercise any election available to the principal under federal, state, local, or foreign tax law; and (4) act for the principal in all tax matters for all periods before the Internal Revenue Service, and any other taxing authority.

WITH RESPECT TO GIFTS, the principal authorizes the agent to make gifts of any of the principal's property to individuals or organizations within the limits of the annual exclusion under the Internal Revenue Code, 26 U.S.C. Section 2503(b) [or successor provisions], as the agent determines to be in the principal's best interest based on all relevant factors, including: (1) the value and nature of the principal's property; (2) the principal's foreseeable obligations and need for maintenance; 3) minimization of income, estate, inheritance, generation-skipping transfer or gift taxes; (4) eligibility for public benefits or assistance under a statute or governmental regulation; and (5) the principal's personal history of making or joining in making gifts.

WITH RESPECT TO DELEGATION OF AGENCY AUTHORITY, the principal authorizes the agent to delegate revocably by writing or other record to one or more persons a power granted to the agent by the principal.

If the attorney-in-fact named above is unable or unwilling to serve, I appoint
③ _____ (printed name), of (address) _____ , to be my attorney-in-fact for all purposes hereunder.

To induce any third party to rely upon this power of attorney, I agree that any third party receiving a signed copy or facsimile of this power of attorney may rely upon such copy, and that revocation or termination of this power of attorney shall be ineffective as to such third party until actual notice or knowledge of such revocation or termination shall have been received by such third party. I, for myself and for my heirs, executors, legal representatives and assigns, agree to indemnify and hold harmless any such third party from any and all claims that may arise against such third party by reason of such third party having relied on the provisions of this power of attorney. **THIS POWER OF ATTORNEY SHALL NOT BE EFFECTIVE IN THE EVENT OF MY FUTURE DISABILITY OR INCAPACITY.** This power of attorney may be revoked by me at any time and is automatically revoked upon my death. My attorney-in-fact shall no be compensated for his or her services nor shall my attorney-in-fact be liable to me, my estate, heirs, successors, or assigns for acting or refraining from acting under this document, except for willful misconduct or gross negligence.

Dated: ④ _____

Signature and Declaration of Principal ⑤

I, _____ (printed name), the principal, sign my name to this power of attorney this _____day of _____ and, being first duly sworn, do declare to the undersigned authority that I sign and execute this instrument as my power of attorney and that I sign it willingly, or willingly direct another to sign for me, that I execute it as my free and voluntary act for the purposes expressed in the power of attorney and that I am eighteen years of age or older, of sound mind and under no constraint or undue influence.

_____
Signature of Principal

Witness Attestation ⑥

I, _____ (printed name), the first witness, and I, _____ (printed name), the second witness, sign my name to the foregoing power of attorney being first duly sworn and do declare to the undersigned authority that the principal signs and executes this instrument as his/her power of attorney and that he\she signs it willingly, or willingly directs another to sign for him/her, and that I, in the presence and hearing of the principal, sign this power of attorney as witness to the principal's signing and that to the best of my knowledge the principal is eighteen years of age or older, of sound mind and under no constraint or undue influence.

_____
Signature of First Witness

_____
Signature of Second Witness

Notary Acknowledgment ⑦

State of _____
County of _____
Subscribed, sworn to and acknowledged before me by _____,
the Principal, and subscribed and sworn to before me by _____,
and _____, the witnesses, this _____ day of _____ .

_____
Notary Signature
Notary Public, In and for the County of _____
State of _____
My commission expires: _____   Seal

Acknowledgment and Acceptance of Appointment as Attorney-in-Fact ⑧

I, _____, (printed name) have read the attached power of attorney and am the person identified as the attorney-in-fact for the principal. I hereby acknowledge that I accept my appointment as attorney-in-fact and that when I act as agent I shall exercise the powers for the benefit of the principal; I shall keep the assets of the principal separate from my assets; I shall exercise reasonable caution and prudence; and I shall keep a full and accurate record of all actions, receipts and disbursements on behalf of the principal.

_____   _____
Signature of Attorney-in-Fact   Date

Acknowledgment and Acceptance of Appointment as Successor Attorney-in-Fact ⑨

I, _____, (printed name)
have read the attached power of attorney and am the person identified as the
successor attorney-in-fact for the principal. I hereby acknowledge that I accept
my appointment as successor attorney-in-fact and that, in the absence of a
specific provision to the contrary in the power of attorney, when I act as agent I
shall exercise the powers for the benefit of the principal; I shall keep the assets
of the principal separate from my assets; I shall exercise reasonable caution and
prudence; and I shall keep a full and accurate record of all actions, receipts and
disbursements on behalf of the principal.

_____   _____

Signature of Successor Attorney-in-Fact   Date

Limited Power of Attorney

Notice: This is an important document. Before signing this document, you should know these important facts. By signing this document, you are not giving up any powers or rights to control your finances and property yourself. In addition to your own powers and rights, you may be giving another person, your attorney-in-fact, broad powers to handle your finances and property. This limited power of attorney may give the person whom you designate (your "attorney-in-fact") broad powers to handle your finances and property, which may include powers to encumber, sell or otherwise dispose of any real or personal property without advance notice to you or approval by you. THE POWERS GRANTED WILL NOT EXIST AFTER YOU BECOME DISABLED, OR INCAPACITATED. This document does not authorize anyone to make medical or other health care decisions for you. If you own complex or special assets such as a business, or if there is anything about this form that you do not understand, you should ask a lawyer to explain this form to you before you sign it. If you wish to change your limited power of attorney, you must complete a new document and revoke this one. You may revoke this document at any time by destroying it, by directing another person to destroy it in your presence or by signing a written and dated statement expressing your intent to revoke this document. If you revoke this document, you should notify your attorney-in-fact and any other person to whom you have given a copy of the form. You also should notify all parties having custody of your assets. These parties have no responsibility to you unless you actually notify them of the revocation. If your attorney-in-fact is your spouse and your marriage is annulled, or you are divorced after signing this document, this document is invalid. Since some 3rd parties or some transactions may not permit use of this document, it is advisable to check in advance, if possible, for any special requirements that may be imposed. You should sign this form only if the attorney-in-fact that you appoint is reliable, trustworthy and competent to manage your affairs. This form must be signed by the Principal (the person appointing the attorney-in-fact), witnessed by two persons other than the notary public, and acknowledged by a notary public.

① I, _____ (printed name),
of (address)_____,
as principal, do grant a limited and specific power of attorney to, and do hereby

appoint ② _____ (printed name),
of (address) _____ to act
as my attorney-in-fact and to have the full power and authority to perform only
the following acts on my behalf to the same extent that I could do so personally
if I were personally present, with respect to the following matter to the extent
that I am permitted by law to act through an agent: (list specific acts and/or
restrictions) ③

If the attorney-in-fact named above is unable or unwilling to serve, I appoint ④
_____ (printed name),
of (address) _____ ,
to be my attorney-in-fact for all purposes hereunder.

To induce any third party to rely upon this power of attorney, I agree that any
third party receiving a signed copy or facsimile of this power of attorney may
rely upon such copy, and that revocation or termination of this power of attorney
shall be ineffective as to such third party until actual notice or knowledge of such
revocation or termination shall have been received by such third party. I, for
myself and for my heirs, executors, legal representatives and assigns, agree to
indemnify and hold harmless any such third party from any and all claims that
may arise against such third party by reason of such third party having relied on
the provisions of this power of attorney.

This power of attorney shall not be effective in the event of my future disability
or incapacity. This limited grant of authority does not authorize my attorney-in-
fact to make any decisions regarding my medical or health care. This power of
attorney may be revoked by me at any time and is automatically revoked upon
my death. My attorney-in-fact shall not be compensated for his or her services
nor shall my attorney-in-fact be liable to me, my estate, heirs, successors, or
assigns for acting or refraining from acting under this document, except for willful
misconduct or gross negligence. My attorney-in-fact accepts this appointment
and agrees to act in my best interest as he or she considers advisable. This
grant of authority shall include the power and authority to perform any incidental
acts which may be reasonably required in order to perform the specific acts
stated above.

Dated: ⑤ _____

Signature and Declaration of Principal ⑥

I, _____ (printed name), the principal, sign my name to this power of attorney this _____day of _____ and, being first duly sworn, do declare to the undersigned authority that I sign and execute this instrument as my power of attorney and that I sign it willingly, or willingly direct another to sign for me, that I execute it as my free and voluntary act for the purposes expressed in the power of attorney and that I am eighteen years of age or older, of sound mind and under no constraint or undue influence.

_____
Signature of Principal

Witness Attestation ⑦

I, _____ (printed name), the first witness, and I, _____ (printed name), the second witness, sign my name to the foregoing power of attorney being first duly sworn and do declare to the undersigned authority that the principal signs and executes this instrument as his/her power of attorney and that he\she signs it willingly, or willingly directs another to sign for him/her, and that I, in the presence and hearing of the principal, sign this power of attorney as witness to the principal's signing and that to the best of my knowledge the principal is eighteen years of age or older, of sound mind and under no constraint or undue influence.

_____
Signature of First Witness

_____
Signature of Second Witness

Notary Acknowledgment ⑧

State of _____
County of _____
Subscribed, sworn to and acknowledged before me by _____,
the Principal, and subscribed and sworn to before me by _____,
and _____, the witnesses, this
_____ day of _____ .

_____

Notary Signature
Notary Public,
In and for the County of _____
State of _____
My commission expires: _____ Seal

Acknowledgment and Acceptance of Appointment as Attorney-in-Fact ⑨

I, _____, (printed name)
have read the attached power of attorney and am the person identified as
the attorney-in-fact for the principal. I hereby acknowledge that I accept my
appointment as attorney-in-fact and that when I act as agent I shall exercise
the powers for the benefit of the principal; I shall keep the assets of the principal
separate from my assets; I shall exercise reasonable caution and prudence; and
I shall keep a full and accurate record of all actions, receipts and disbursements
on behalf of the principal.

_____   _____
Signature of Attorney-in-Fact   Date

Acknowledgment and Acceptance of Appointment as Successor Attorney-in-Fact ⑩

I, _____, (printed
name) have read the attached power of attorney and am the person identified
as the successor attorney-in-fact for the principal. I hereby acknowledge that I
accept my appointment as successor attorney-in-fact and that, in the absence of
a specific provision to the contrary in the power of attorney, when I act as agent
I shall exercise the powers for the benefit of the principal; I shall keep the assets
of the principal separate from my assets; I shall exercise reasonable caution and
prudence; and I shall keep a full and accurate record of all actions, receipts and
disbursements on behalf of the principal.

_____   _____
Signature of Successor Attorney-in-Fact   Date

Revocation of Power of Attorney

I, ① _____(printed name) ,
address: _____
do revoke the power of attorney dated ② _____ , 20 _____ ,
which was granted to ③ _____ (printed name),
address:_____,
to act as my attorney-in-fact.

This Revocation is dated ④ _____ , 20 _____

⑤_____
Signature of Person Revoking Power of Attorney

⑥ **Notary Acknowledgement**

State of _____
County of _____

On _____ , 20 _____ , _____
personally came before me and, being duly sworn, did state that he or she is
the person described in the above document and that he or she signed the
above document in my presence.

_____
Signature of Notary Public

Notary Public, In and for the County of _____
State of _____

My commission expires: _____   Notary Seal

Chapter 5

Releases

Releases are a method of acknowledging the satisfaction of an obligation or of releasing parties from liability or claims. Releases are used in various situations in the business world, from releasing a person or company from liability after an accident to a release of liens or claims against property. Releases can be very powerful documents. The various releases contained in this chapter are tailored to meet the most common situations in which a release is used. For a release to be valid, there must be some type of consideration received by the person who is granting the release. Releases should be used carefully as they may prevent any future claims against the party to whom it is granted. In general, a release from claims relating to an accident which causes personal injury should not be signed without a prior examination by a doctor. Also note that a release relating to damage to community property in a "community property" state must be signed by both spouses. Study the various forms provided to determine which one is proper for the use intended. Note: Chapter 7 provides a Waiver and Release of Lien; Chapter 15 provides a Release of Security Interest and a Release of U.C.C. Financing Statement; and Chapter 16 provides a Release of Promissory Note.

Instructions for Releases

General Release: This release serves as a full blanket-release from one party to another. It should only be used when all obligations of one party are to be released. The party signing this release is discharging the other party from all of their obligations to the other party stemming from a specific incident or transaction. This form can be used when one party has a claim against another and the other agrees to waive the claim for payment. A sample numbered version of this form is found on page 114. To complete this form, fill in the following information:

① Name of person granting release
② Address of person granting release
③ Name of person granted release
④ Address of person granted release
⑤ Transaction or incident for which release is being granted
⑥ Date of release
⑦ Signature of person granting release
⑧ Printed name of person granting release

Mutual Release: The mutual release form provides a method for two parties to jointly release each other from their mutual obligations or claims. This form should be used when both parties intend to discharge each other from all of their mutual obligations. It essentially serves the purpose of two reciprocal General Releases. A sample numbered version of this form is found on page 115.

① Name of first person granting release
② Address of first person granting release
③ Name of second person granting release
④ Address of second person granting release
⑤ Transaction or incident for which release is being granted
⑥ Date of release
⑦ Signature of first person granting release
⑧ Printed name of first person granting release
⑨ Signature of second person granting release
⑩ Printed name of second person granting release

Specific Release: This release form should be used only when a particular claim or obligation is being released, while allowing other liabilities to continue. The obligation being released should be spelled out in careful and precise terms to prevent confusion with any other obligation or claim. In addition, the liabilities or obligations which are not being released, but will continue, should also be carefully noted. A sample numbered version of this form is found on page 116.

① Name of person granting release
② Address of person granting release
③ Name of person granted release
④ Address of person granted release
⑤ Claim or obligation for which release is being granted (Also note any claims,liabilities, or obligations that are not being released)
⑥ Transaction or incident for which release is being granted
⑦ Date of release
⑧ Signature of person granting release
⑨ Printed name of person granting release

General Release

For consideration, I, ①_____ ,
address: ②

release ③_____ ,
address: ④

from all claims and obligations, known or unknown, to this date arising from the
following transaction or incident: ⑤

The party signing this release has not assigned any claims or obligations
covered by this release to any other party.

The party signing this release intends that it both bind and benefit itself and any
successors.

Dated ⑥_____ , 20 _____

⑦_____
Signature of person granting release

⑧_____
Printed name of person granting release

Mutual Release

For consideration, ①_____ ,
address: ②

and ③_____ ,
address: ④

release each other from all claims and obligations, known or unknown, that they may have against each other arising from the following transaction or incident:
⑤

Neither party has assigned any claims or obligations covered by this release to any other party. Both parties signing this release intend that it both bind and benefit themselves and any successors.

Dated ⑥_____ , 20 _____

⑦_____   ⑨_____
Signature of 1st person   Signature of 2nd person

⑧_____   ⑩_____
Printed name of 1st person   Printed name of 2nd person

Specific Release

For consideration, I, ①_____ ,
address: ②

release ③_____ ,
address: ④

from the following specific claims and obligations: ⑤

arising from the following transaction or incident: ⑥

Any claims or obligations that are not specifically mentioned are not released by this Specific Release.

The party signing this release has not assigned any claims or obligations covered by this release to any other party.

The party signing this release intends that it both bind and benefit itself and any successors.

Dated ⑦_____ , 20 _____

⑧_____
Signature of person granting release

⑨_____
Printed name of person granting release

Chapter 6

Receipts

In this chapter, various receipt forms are provided. In general, receipts are a formal acknowledgment of having received something, whether it is money or property. These forms do not have to be notarized. Please note that Chapter 8 *Leases of Real Estate* contains both a Receipt for Lease Security Deposit and a Rent Receipt to be used in conjunction with leases of real estate. Additionally, Chapter 15 contains a Receipt for Collateral. The following receipt forms are included in this chapter:

Instructions for Receipts

Receipt in Full: This form should be used as a receipt for a payment that completely pays off a debt. You will need to include the amount paid, the name of the person who paid it, the date when paid, and a description of the obligation that is paid off (for example: an invoice, statement, or bill of sale). The original receipt should go to the person making the payment, but a copy should be retained. A sample numbered version of this form is found on page 119. To complete this form, fill in the following information:

① Amount paid
② Name of person paying
③ Identify what is being paid for
④ Date
⑤ Signature
⑥ Printed name

Receipt on Account: This form should be used as a receipt for a payment that does not fully pay off a debt, but, rather, is a payment on account and is credited to the total balance due. You will need to include the amount paid, the name of the person who paid it, the date when paid, and a description of the account to which the payment is to be applied. The original receipt should go to the person making the payment, but a copy should be kept by you. A sample numbered version of this form is found on page 120. To complete this form, fill in the following information:

① Amount paid
② Name of person paying
③ Identify what account
④ Date
⑤ Signature
⑥ Printed name

Receipt for Goods: This form should be used as a receipt for the acceptance of goods. It is intended to be used in conjunction with a delivery order or purchase order. It also states that the goods have been inspected and found to be in conformance with the order. The original of this receipt should be retained by the person delivering the goods and a copy should go to the person accepting delivery. A sample numbered version of this form is found on page 121. To complete this form, fill in the following information:

① Date
② Signature
③ Printed name

Receipt in Full

The undersigned acknowledges receipt of the sum of $ ①_____ paid
by ②_____ .

This payment constitutes full payment and satisfaction of the following obligation:
③

Dated ④_____ , 20 _____

⑤_____
Signature of Person Receiving Payment

⑥_____
Printed Name of Person Receiving Payment

Receipt on Account

The undersigned acknowledges receipt of the sum of $ ①_____ paid
by ②_____ .

This payment will be applied and credited to the following account: ③

Dated ④_____ , 20 _____

⑤_____
Signature of Person Receiving Payment

⑥_____
Printed Name of Person Receiving Payment

Receipt for Goods

The undersigned acknowledges receipt of the goods which are described on the attached purchase order. The undersigned also acknowledges that these goods have been inspected and found to be in conformance with the purchase order specifications.

Dated ①_____ , 20 _____

②_____
Signature of Person Receiving Goods

③_____
Printed Name of Person Receiving Goods

Chapter 7

Liens

The documents in this chapter are all related to the use of liens. Liens are a charge or a claim upon a piece of property that makes that property act as the security for the payment of a debt. For example, a mortgage is a lien against a house. If the mortgage is not paid on time, the house can be seized to satisfy the lien. Liens are thus legal claims against a piece of property. When a property which has an outstanding lien is sold, the lien holder is then generally paid the amount that is owed under the lien out of the proceeds of the sale of the property. There are two documents relating to liens included in this chapter. A Claim of Lien is used to impose a lien or obligation on a piece of property based on labor and/or materials provided for work on the property. A Waiver and Release of Lien is used to release such a lien. **Important Note:** Before relying on the Claim of Lien in this chapter, you should always check the Real Estate Law Appendix and consult an attorney to determine if there are any other requirements, deadlines, or state-specific language that may be required for the Claim of Lien to be effective in your jurisdiction.

Claim of Lien: This form is used to assert a claim of lien against a particular piece of real estate, for money owed by the owner of the real estate for labor or materials that were provided for improvements to that particular piece of property. A lien is claim against a piece of real estate that must be paid off prior to the property being transferred or sold. This type of lien is often referred to as a mechanic's lien and may, generally, be filed by anyone who has supplied labor and/or materials for the improvement of a piece of real estate. This form must be signed in front of a notary public and then must be filed in the recorder's office of the county in which the property is located. Finally, at the time that you record this Claim of Lien, you will need to make two (2) copies of the Claim of Lien with the recorder's file stamp on them. Keep one copy for your records and mail one copy (on the same day that it was recorded) to the owner of the property, by USPS certified mail, with a return receipt requested. (Note: separate forms for Florida and Georgia are included on the Forms-on-CD). A sample numbered version of this form is found on page 125. To complete this form, fill in the following information:

1. Name of person requesting recording of this claim (you)
2. Name of person to whom the recorded claim should be mailed by the recorder's office (generally, you)
3. Street address where claim should be mailed
4. City where claim should be mailed
5. State and Zip Code where claim should be mailed
6. Name of who prepared document (usually you)
7. Address of who prepared document (usually you)
8. State and Zip Code of who prepared document (usually you)
9. State in which Notary is located
10. County in which Notary is located
11. Name of person claiming lien (you)
12. Description of labor and/or materials provided
13. County where labor or materials were provided
14. State where labor or materials were provided
15. Street address where labor or materials were provided
16. Legal description of property (obtain from recorder's office or county tax office)
17. Owner of property
18. Address of owner of property
19. Total value of all labor and/or materials provided
20. Value of labor and/or materials that remain unpaid
21. Date on which first labor and/or materials were provided
22. Date on which last labor and/or materials were provided
23. State in which property is located
24. Signature of person claiming lien (you)
25. Name of person claiming lien
26. Address of person claiming lien
27. The following section should be completed by a notary public (You should always check with an attorney to be certain that this notary language is sufficient in your jurisdiction)
28. Name of person mailing copy of claim of lien (generally, you)
29. Date of mailing of claim of lien
30. Name of owner of property
31. Address of owner of property
32. Date of signing of form
33. Signature of person mailing claim of lien
34. Name of person mailing claim of lien
35. *Note: California residents must use this California Notary box.

Waiver and Release of Lien: This form is used to waive or release a claim of lien against a particular piece of real estate, for money owed by the owner of the real estate for labor or materials that were provided for improvements to that particular piece of property. This form is used to *waive* a future lien (give up the right to assert a lien), or to *release* a lien (state that the reasons for the lien have now been satisfied). It may be used by a homeowner to make certain that any contractors or subcontractors who have been paid in full will not, in the future, attempt to file a lien against a piece of property. It may also be used by a contractor or subcontractor to release a lien that they, themselves, have filed against a particular piece of real estate. To effectively release a lien, this form must be signed in front of a notary public and then must be filed in the recorder's office of the county in which the property is located. A sample numbered version of this form is found on page 126. To complete this form, fill in the following information:

① Name of person requesting recording of this waiver and release
② Name of person to whom the recorded waiver and release should be mailed to by the recorder's office
③ Street address where waiver and release should be mailed
④ City where waiver and release should be mailed
⑤ State and Zip Code where waiver and release should be mailed
⑥ Name of person preparing document
⑦ Address of who prepared document (usually you)
⑧ State and Zip Code of who prepared document (usually you)
⑨ State in which Notary is located
⑩ County in which Notary is located
⑪ Name of person waiving and releasing lien
⑫ Name of employer
⑬ Address of employer (your address if self-employed)
⑭ Description of labor and/or materials provided
⑮ Street address where labor or materials were provided
⑯ Legal description of property (obtain from recorder's office or county tax office)
⑰ Owner of property
⑱ Address of owner of property
⑲ Signature of person waiving and releasing lien
⑳ Name of person waiving and releasing lien
㉑ Address of person waiving and releasing lien
㉒ The following section should be completed by a notary public. (You should always check with an attorney to be certain that this notary language is sufficient in your jurisdiction)
㉓ *Note: California residents must use this California Notary box

Recording requested by: ① _____
When recorded, mail to:

Name: ② _____

Address: ③ _____

City: ④ _____

State/Zip: ⑤ _____

Space above reserved for use by Recorder's Office

Document prepared by:

Name ⑥ _____

Address ⑦ _____

City/State/Zip ⑧ _____

Claim of Lien

State of ⑨ _____

County of ⑩ _____

I, ⑪ _____ , being duly sworn, state the following:
In accordance with an agreement to provide labor and/or material, I did furnish the following labor and/or materials: ⑫

on the following described real property located in ⑬ _____ County,
State of ⑭ _____ , commonly known as: ⑮

and legally described as: ⑯

which property is owned by ⑰ _____ , whose address is
⑱ _____ , of a total value of $ ⑲ _____ ,
of which there remains unpaid $ ⑳ _____ , and I further state that I furnished the first of
the items on the date of ㉑ _____ , and the last of the items on the date of
㉒ _____ .

I hereby, under the laws of the State of ㉓ _____ , claim a lien against the
above-described property in the amount of money, stated above, which remains unpaid to me.

㉔ _____   ㉕ _____
Signature of Person Claiming Lien   Name of Person Claiming Lien

Address of person claiming lien: ㉖

㉗ On _____ , _____ came before
me personally and, under oath, stated that he/she is the person described in the above document and that
he/she signed the above document in my presence.

_____
Notary Signature
Notary Public,
In and for the County of _____ State of _____
My commission expires: _____   Seal

CERTIFICATE OF MAILING

I, ㉘ _____ , certify that on this date, ㉙ _____ , I have mailed a
copy of this Claim of Lien by USPS certified mail, return receipt requested, in accordance with the law, to:
Name: ㉚ _____
Address: ㉛ _____
Date: ㉜ _____

㉝ _____   ㉞ _____
Signature of Person Mailing Claim of Lien   Name of Person Mailing Claim of Lien

㉟ *California residents or persons intending that this document be valid in the*
State of California should use the following California Notary Acknowledgment form:

State of California

County of _____ } S.S.

On _____ , before me, _____

(name and title of notary), personally appeared _____ , who
proved to me on the basis of satisfactory evidence to be the person(s) whose name(s) is/are subscribed to
the above instrument and acknowledged to me that they/he/she executed the instrument in their/his/her
authorized capacity. I certify under penalty of perjury under the laws of the State of California that the
foregoing is true and correct. Witness my hand and official seal.

_____   Seal
Notary Signature

Recording requested by: ① _____
When recorded, mail to:

Name: ② _____

Address: ③ _____

City: ④ _____

State/Zip: ⑤ _____

Space above reserved for use by Recorder's Office

Document prepared by:

Name ⑥ _____

Address ⑦ _____

City/State/Zip ⑧ _____

Waiver & Release of Lien

State of ⑨ _____

County of ⑩ _____

I, ⑪ _____ , being duly sworn, state the following:
I am employed by ⑫ _____ , whose address is ⑬ _____
_____ , I have furnished labor and/or materials described as:
⑭

for work done at the address of ⑮ _____ ,
the legal property description of which is: ⑯

and which is owned by ⑰ _____ , whose address is ⑱ _____
_____ , and I do hereby state I have been paid in
full for the above-mentioned labor and/or materials and I do unconditionally waive all liens or claims of
liens relating to this labor and/or materials that I have or had on the foregoing real property.

⑲ _____

Signature of Person Waiving Lien

⑳ _____

Name of Person Waiving Lien

Address of person waiving lien: ㉑

㉒ On _____ , _____ ,

came before me personally and, under oath, stated that he/she is the person described in the above docu-

ment and that he/she signed the above document in my presence.

_____

Notary Signature

Notary Public,

In and for the County of _____ State of _____

My commission expires: _____   Seal

㉓ *California residents or persons intending that this document be valid in the*
State of California should use the following California Notary Acknowledgment form:

State of California

County of _____ } S.S.

On _____ , before me, _____

__ (name and title of notary), personally appeared _____ ,

who

proved to me on the basis of satisfactory evidence to be the person(s) whose name(s) is/are subscribed to

the above instrument and acknowledged to me that they/he/she executed the instrument in their/his/her

authorized capacity. I certify under penalty of perjury under the laws of the State of California that the

foregoing is true and correct. Witness my hand and official seal.

_____   Seal

Notary Signature

Chapter 8

Leases of Real Estate

A lease of real estate is simply a written contract for one party to rent a specific property from another for a certain amount and certain time period. As such, all of the general legal ramifications that relate to contracts also relate to leases. However, all states have additional requirements which pertain only to leases. If the rental period is to be for one year or more, most states require that leases be in writing. Leases can be prepared for *periodic tenancies* (that is, for example, month-to-month or week-to-week) or they can be for a fixed period. There are leases contained in this chapter that provide for both fixed-period tenancies and for month-to-month tenancies.

There are also general guidelines for security deposits in most states. These most often follow a reasonable pattern and should be adhered to. Most states provide for the following with regard to lease security deposits:

- Should be no greater than one month's rent and should be fully refundable
- Should be used for the repair of damages only, and not applied for the nonpayment of rent (an additional month's rent may be requested to cover potential nonpayment of rent situations)
- Should be kept in a separate, interest-bearing account and returned, with interest, to the tenant within 10 days of termination of a lease (minus, of course, any deductions for damages)

In addition to state laws regarding security deposits, many states have requirements relating to the time periods required prior to terminating a lease. These rules have evolved over time to prevent both the landlord or the tenant from being harmed by early termination of a lease. In general, if the lease is for a fixed time period, the termination of the lease is governed by the lease itself. Early termination of a fixed-period lease may, however, be governed by individual state law. For periodic leases (month-to-month, etc.), there are normally state rules as to how much advance notice must be given prior to termination of a lease. A Real Estate Law Appendix provides a state-by-state listing of the main provisions of landlord-tenant law for all 50 states and Washington D.C., including details of state laws regarding security deposits, entry into leased premises, and other rental issues. Please see the Real Estate Appendix on the CD for information on the requirements in your state. In addition, be advised that there may also be specific local laws that pertain to landlord and tenant relationships that may be applicable. You are advised to check any local ordinances or state laws for any possible additional requirements. You will also need to supply your tenant with a copy of the enclosed federal form: "Protect Your Family from Lead in Your Home," if the rental unit was built before 1978. This form is included on the CD.

Instructions for Leases of Real Estate

Credit/Rental Application: This form is the basis of a check into the credit history of a potential tenant (or customer). With this form, an applicant furnishes various information which may be checked further to ascertain the reliability and background of the credit or tenant applicant. The applicant is requested to furnish personal information, two credit references, two bank references, two personal references, and answer a few basic questions. The form also provides for information to be entered regarding the verification of the references. A sample numbered version of this form is found on page 147. The Applicant will furnish the following information:

1. Name, address, phone number, fax number, and e-mail address of applicant
2. Creditor #1- Name, account number, phone, and address of creditor #1
3. Creditor #2- Name, account number, phone, and address of creditor #2
4. Bank #1- Name, account number, phone, and address of bank #1
5. Bank #2- Name, account number, phone, and address of bank #2
6. Personal Reference #1- Name, relationship, phone, and address of personal reference #1
7. Personal Reference #2- Name, relationship, phone, and address of personal reference #2
8. Other informations (bankruptcy, felony, eviction, etc.)
9. Applicant's driver's license number and state issuing driver's license
10. Date of Application
11. Signature of Applicant
12. Printed Name of Applicant

Landlord (or Creditor) to fill in the following information:

⑬ Person at Credit reference #1 contacted
⑭ Remarks
⑮ Person at Credit reference #2 contacted
⑯ Remarks
⑰ Person at Bank reference #1 contacted
⑱ Remarks
⑲ Person at Bank reference #2 contacted
⑳ Remarks
㉑ Person at Personal reference #1 contacted
㉒ Remarks
㉓ Person at Personal reference #2 contacted
㉔ Remarks
㉕ Person contacting references
㉖ Date references contacted
㉗ Applicant approval
㉘ Person making approval
㉙ Date of approval

Move-in/Move-out Checklist and Acknowledgment: This form is to be used to catalog and note the condition of all of the furniture, furnishings, appliances, and personal property that are present at the leased property. The tenant is responsible for returning all of the following property in as good a condition as is noted on the Move-in section of this form, except for normal wear and tear. Landlord should complete this form prior to move-in and Tenant should check this form upon move-in, noting any disagreements with landlord's assessment. Both Tenant and Landlord should sign the form at move-in. When the Tenant moves out, the Landlord should again check the presence and condition of the items listed on this form and note the condition of such items on the form. The Tenant should then check the items and note any disagreements with the Landlord's assessment of the condition or presence of any of the items listed. Both the Tenant and Landlord should sign this form again at the moving out of the Tenant. This form may be used to determine any deductions from the security deposit of the Tenant. Both the Landlord and the Tenant should get a copy of this form. A sample numbered version of this form is found on page 150. To complete this form, enter the following information:

① Name of landlord
② Name of tenant
③ Address of leased property
④ Term of the lease
⑤ Date tenant moves into property

⑥ Date tenant moves out of property
⑦ Listing of all items and their condition (Complete at time of move-in and again at move-out)
⑧ Date of landlord signature for move-in condition
⑨ Signature of landlord for move-in condition
⑩ Date of tenant signature for move-in condition
⑪ Signature of tenant for move-in condition
⑫ Date of landlord signature for move-out condition
⑬ Signature of landlord for move-out condition
⑭ Date of tenant signature for move-out condition
⑮ Signature of tenant for move-out condition

Residential Lease: This form should be used when renting a residential property for a fixed period. Although the landlord and tenant can agree to any terms they desire, this particular lease provides for the following basic terms to be included:

- A fixed-period term for the lease
- A security deposit for damages, which will be returned within 10 days after the termination of the lease, but without interest unless required by state law
- An additional month's rent as security for payment of the rent, which will be returned within 10 days after the termination of the lease, but without interest unless required by state law
- That the tenant agrees to keep the property in good repair and not make any alterations without consent
- Tenant agrees not to conduct any business without permission of the landlord
- Tenant agrees not to have any pets without permission of the landlord
- That landlord and tenant agree on who will pay utilities
- That the tenant agrees not to assign the lease or sublet the property without the landlord's consent
- That the landlord has the right to inspect the property on a reasonable basis, and that the tenant has already inspected it and found it satisfactory
- That the landlord has the right to re-enter and take possession upon breach of the lease (as long as it is in accordance with state law)
- Once the lease term has expired, any continued occupancy will be as a month-to month tenancy
- That the landlord will provide tenant with the U.S. EPA lead pamphlet: "Protect Your Family from Lead in Your Home." *Note:* This document is provided on the Forms-on-CD (under 'Sale of Real Estate') and is necessary *only* if the rental dwelling was built prior to 1978
- Any other additional terms that the parties agree upon

(Note: Residents of California will need to include the California Addendum to

Lease form that is included on the Forms-on-CD. Residents of Chicago will need to include the Chicago Addendum to Lease and other required Chicago forms that are included on the Forms-on-CD). A sample numbered version of this form is found on page 152. To prepare this form, fill in the following information:

① Date of lease
② Name of landlord
③ Address of landlord
④ Name of tenant
⑤ Address of tenant
⑥ Complete address of leased property
⑦ Beginning date of lease
⑧ End date of lease
⑨ Amount of the rental payment
⑩ Day of the period when rent will be due and length of period (usually, month)
⑪ Due date of first rental payment
⑫ Amount of security deposit for damages
⑬ Which state's laws will be used
⑭ Amount of additional rent held as rental default deposit
⑮ Which state's laws will be used
⑯ Maximum number of tenants
⑰ Which state's laws will be used
⑱ Utilities that landlord will supply
⑲ Utilities that tenant will provide
⑳ Which state's laws will be used
㉑ Landlord's initials on presence of lead paint disclosure
㉒ Landlord's initials on records and/or reports of lead paint
㉓ Tenant's initials on lead paint acknowledgment
㉔ Any other additional terms
㉕ Which state's laws will be used to interpret lease
㉖ Signature of landlord
㉗ Printed name of landlord
㉘ Signature of tenant
㉙ Printed name of tenant

Month-to-Month Rental Agreement: This rental agreement provides for a month-to-month tenancy: one that continues each month indefinitely or until terminated by either party. For a fixed tenancy lease, please see the Residential Lease, explained above. Although the landlord and tenant can agree to any terms they desire, this particular lease provides for the following basic terms to be included:

• A month-to-month tenancy for the agreement
• A security deposit for damages, to be returned within 10 days after the termina-

tion of the agreement, but without interest unless required by state law
- An additional month's rent as security for payment of the rent, which will be returned within 10 days after the termination of the agreement, but without interest unless required by state law
- That the tenant agrees to keep the property in good repair and not make any alterations without consent
- Tenant agrees not to conduct any business without permission of the landlord
- Tenant agrees not to have any pets without permission of the landlord
- That landlord and tenant agree on who will pay utilities
- That the tenant agrees not to assign or sublet the property without the landlord's consent
- That the landlord has the right to inspect the property on a reasonable basis, and that the tenant has already inspected it and found it satisfactory
- That the landlord has the right to re-enter and take possession upon breach of the agreement (as long as it is in accordance with state law)
- That the landlord will provide tenant with the U.S. EPA lead pamphlet: "Protect Your Family from Lead in Your Home." *Note*: This document is provided on the Forms-on-CD (under 'Sale of Real Estate') and is necessary *only* if the rental dwelling was built prior to 1978
- Any other additional terms that the parties agree upon

(Note: Residents of California will need to include the California Addendum to Lease form that is included on the Forms-on-CD. Residents of Chicago will need to include the Chicago Addendum to Lease and other required Chicago forms that are included on the Forms-on-CD). A sample numbered version of this form is found on page 156. To complete this form, fill in the following information:

① Date of rental agreement
② Name of landlord
③ Address of landlord
④ Name of tenant
⑤ Address of tenant
⑥ Complete address of rental property
⑦ Beginning date of rental agreement
⑧ Number of days required for termination of rental agreement
⑨ Amount of rental payment
⑩ Day of the month when rent will be due and period of tenancy
⑪ Due date of first rent payment
⑫ Amount of security deposit for damages
⑬ Which state's laws will be used
⑭ Amount of additional rent held as rental default deposit
⑮ Which state's laws will be used

⑯ Maximum number of tenants
⑰ Which state's laws will be used
⑱ Utilities that landlord will supply
⑲ Utilities that tenant will provide
⑳ Which state's laws will be used
㉑ Landlord's initials on presence of lead paint disclosure
㉒ Tenant's initials on lead paint acknowledgment
㉓ Any other additional terms
㉔ Which state's laws will be used to interpret agreement
㉕ Signature of landlord
㉖ Printed name of landlord
㉗ Signature of tenant
㉘ Printed name of tenant

Commercial Lease: This form should be used when renting a commercial property. Although the landlord and tenant can agree to any terms they desire, this particular lease provides for the following basic terms to be included:

- An initial fixed-period term for the lease, with the lease continuing on after this term as a month-to-month lease
- A five percent late charge for rent payments over five days late
- A limitation on what business the tenant may conduct on the property
- A security deposit for damages, which will be returned within 10 days after the termination of the lease
- An additional month's rent as security for payment of the rent, which will be returned within 10 days after the termination of the lease
- That the tenant agrees to keep the property in good repair and not make any alterations without consent
- That the tenant agrees not to assign the lease or sublet the property without the landlord's consent
- That the landlord has the right to inspect the property on a reasonable basis, and that the tenant has already inspected it and found it satisfactory
- That the landlord has the right to re-enter and take possession upon breach of the lease (as long as it is in accordance with state law)
- That the landlord is responsible for the upkeep of the exterior and the tenant for the upkeep of the interior of the property
- That the landlord will carry fire and casualty insurance on the property, and that the tenant will carry casualty insurance on their own equipment and fixtures and also carry general business liability insurance
- That the lease is subject to any mortgage or deed of trust and that the tenant agrees to sign any future subordination documents
- Any other additional terms that the parties agree upon

A sample numbered version of this form is found on page 160. To prepare this form, fill in the following information:

1. Date of lease
2. Name of landlord
3. Address of landlord
4. City of landlord
5. State of landlord
6. Name of tenant
7. Address of tenant
8. City of tenant
9. State of tenant
10. Complete address and description of leased property
11. Amount of rental payment
12. Day of the month when rent will be due
13. Due date of first rent payment
14. Beginning date of lease
15. End date of lease
16. Additional lease term upon renewal of lease
17. Amount of rent upon renewal
18. Amount of rent if tenancy is extended as month-to-month
19. Amount of security deposit for damages
20. Amount of additional rent held as rental default deposit
21. Description of tenant's business
22. Description of equipment or fixtures tenant will install
23. Number of days tenant allowed to correct violation or rent default
24. Number of days required for termination of lease if violation or default
25. Minimum amount of business liability insurance tenant will carry
26. Number of days required for termination of lease for other than violation or default
27. Any other additional terms
28. Any attachments to lease
29. Which state's laws will be used to interpret lease
30. Signature of landlord
31. Printed name of landlord
32. Signature of tenant
33. Printed name of tenant

Lease with Purchase Option: This lease provides for a fixed-period tenancy and contains a "purchase option" which offers the tenant a time period in which to have an exclusive option to purchase a parcel of real estate. Through the use of this agreement, the landlord can offer the tenant a time period with which to consider the purchase without concern of a sale to another party. This option provides that in exchange for a percentage of the rent (which will be applied to the purchase price if the option is exercised), the tenant is given a period of time to exercise the option and accept the terms of a completed real estate contract. If the tenant accepts the terms and exercises the option in writing, the landlord agrees to complete the sale. If the option is not exercised, the landlord is then free to sell the property on the market and retain the money paid for the option as rent. You will also need to supply your tenant with a copy of the enclosed federal form: "Protect Your Family from Lead in Your Home," if the rental unit was built before 1978. (Note: Residents of California will need to include the California Addendum to Lease form that is included on the Forms-on-CD. Residents of Chicago will need to include the Chicago Addendum to Lease and other required Chicago forms that are included on the Forms-on-CD). A sample numbered version of this form is found on page 164. To prepare this form, fill in the following information:

① Date of lease
② Name of landlord
③ Address of landlord
④ City of landlord
⑤ State of landlord
⑥ Name of tenant
⑦ Address of tenant
⑧ City of tenant
⑨ State of tenant
⑩ Complete address of leased property
⑪ Beginning date of lease
⑫ End date of lease
⑬ Amount of rental payment
⑭ Period of time between payments
⑮ Day of the month when rent will be due
⑯ Due date of first rental payment
⑰ Percentage of each rental payment which will be applied to purchase price if option exercised
⑱ Date option period expires
⑲ Anticipated purchase price of property
⑳ Anticipated rental payment deposit held in trust for option (use full term of lease amount)
㉑ Type of any other deposit
㉒ Amount of any other deposit
㉓ Balance of purchase price due at closing
㉔ Total purchase price
㉕ Amount of mortgage commitment required

㉖ Number of monthly payments of mortgage commitment
㉗ Annual interest rate of mortgage commitment
㉘ Amount of security deposit for damages
㉙ Amount of additional rent held as rental default deposit
㉚ Maximum number of tenants
㉛ Utilities that landlord will supply
㉜ Utilities that tenant will provide
㉝ Landlord's initials on presence of lead paint disclosure
㉞ Landlord's initials on records and/or reports of lead paint
㉟ Tenant's initials on lead paint acknowledgment
㊱ Any other additional terms
㊲ State where property is located
㊳ Signature of landlord
㊴ Printed name of landlord
㊵ Signature of tenant
㊶ Printed name of tenant

Amendment of Lease: Use this form to modify any terms of a lease. A copy of the original lease should be attached to this form. The amendment can be used to change any portion of the lease. Simply note what changes are being made in the appropriate place on this form. If a portion of the lease is being deleted, make note of the deletion. If certain language is being substituted, state the substitution clearly. If additional language is being added, make this clear. For example, you may wish to use language as follows:

"Paragraph _____ is deleted from this lease."

"Paragraph _____ is deleted from this lease and the following paragraph is substituted in its place:"

"The following new paragraph is added to this lease:"

A sample numbered version of this form is found on page 169. To prepare this form, fill in the following information:

① Date of amendment
② Name of landlord and address
③ Name of tenant and address
④ Description of original lease (including date of lease and description of property involved)
⑤ Terms of amendment
⑥ Signature of landlord

⑦ Printed name of landlord
⑧ Signature of tenant
⑨ Printed name of tenant

Extension of Lease: This document should be used to extend the effective time period during which a lease is in force. The use of this form allows the time limit to be extended without having to entirely re-draft the lease. Under this document, all of the other terms of the lease will remain the same, with only the expiration date changing. A copy of the original lease should be attached to this form. A sample numbered version of this form is found on page 170. To prepare this form, fill in the following information:

① Date of extension
② Name of landlord and address
③ Name of tenant and address
④ Description of original lease (including date of lease and description of property involved)
⑤ Date on which original lease will end
⑥ Date on which extension of lease will end
⑦ Signature of landlord
⑧ Printed name of landlord
⑨ Signature of tenant
⑩ Printed name of tenant

Mutual Termination of Lease: This form should be used when both the landlord and tenant desire to terminate a lease. This document releases both parties from any claims that the other may have against them for any actions under the lease. It also states that the landlord agrees that the rent has been paid in full and that the property has been delivered in good condition. A sample numbered version of this form is found on page 171. To prepare this form, fill in the following information:

① Date of termination
② Name of landlord and address
③ Name of tenant and address
④ Description of original lease (including date of lease and description of property involved)
⑤ Signature of landlord
⑥ Printed name of landlord
⑦ Signature of tenant
⑧ Printed name of tenant

Assignment of Lease: This form is for use if one party to a lease is assigning its full interest in the lease to another party. This effectively substitutes one party for another under a lease. This particular assignment form has both of the parties agreeing to indemnify and hold each other harmless for any failures to perform under the lease while they were the party liable under it. This Assignment of Lease may be used by a seller of real estate to assign their interest in any lease that covers the property for sale to the new buyer. This *indemnify and hold harmless* clause simply means that if a claim arises for failure to perform, each party agrees to be responsible for the period of their own performance obligations. A description of the lease which is assigned should include the parties to the lease, a description of the property, and the date of the lease. Other information that is necessary to complete the assignment is the name and address of the *assignor* (the party who is assigning the lease), the name and address of the *assignee* (the party to whom the lease is being assigned), and the date of the assignment. A copy of the original lease should be attached to this form. A sample numbered version of this form is found on page 172. To prepare this Assignment, please fill in the following:

① Date of assignment
② Name of assignor
③ Address of assignor
④ Name of assignee
⑤ Address of assignee
⑥ Description of original lease (including date of lease and description of property involved)
⑦ Signature of assignor
⑧ Printed name of assignor
⑨ Signature of assignee
⑩ Printed name of assignee

Consent to Assignment of Lease: This form is used if the original lease states that the consent of the landlord is necessary for the assignment of the lease to be valid. A landlord may wish to supply a copy of this form to a tenant if a tenant requests the landlord's consent for an assignment of the lease to another party. A copy of the original lease should be attached to this form. A sample numbered version of this form is found on page 173. To complete this form, the following information is needed:

① Date of consent to assignment
② Name of tenant requesting consent
③ Address of tenant requesting consent
④ Name of tenant requesting consent
⑤ Description of lease, including date of lease and location of leased premises

⑥ Signature of landlord
⑦ Printed name of landlord

Sublease: This form is used if the tenant subleases the property covered by an original lease. This particular sublease form has both of the parties agreeing to indemnify and hold each other harmless for any failures to perform under the lease while they were the party liable under it. This *indemnify and hold harmless* clause simply means that if a claim arises for failure to perform, each party agrees to be responsible for the period of their own performance obligations. A description of the lease which is subleased should include the parties to the lease, a description of the property, and the date of the lease. Note that the *subtenant* is the party to whom the property is being subleased. A copy of the original lease should be attached to this form. A copy of a Consent to Sublease of Lease should also be attached, if necessary. A sample numbered version of this form is found on page 174. To complete this form, enter the following information:

① Date of sublease
② Name of tenant
③ Address of tenant
④ Name of subtenant
⑤ Address of subtenant
⑥ Description of property covered by lease
⑦ Description of original lease (including date of lease and name and address of landlord)
⑧ Beginning date of sublease
⑨ Ending date of sublease
⑩ Amount of subrental payments
⑪ Period for each subrental payment (generally, per month)
⑫ Day of month each subrental payment is due
⑬ Beginning date for first subrental payment
⑭ Any additional terms of sublease
⑮ State law which will govern the sublease
⑯ Signature of tenant
⑰ Printed name of tenant
⑱ Signature of subtenant
⑲ Printed name of subtenant

Consent to Sublease: This form is used if the original lease states that the consent of the landlord is necessary for a sublease to be valid. A landlord may wish to supply a copy of this form to a tenant if a tenant requests the landlord's consent for a sublease of the lease to another party. A copy of the original lease should be attached to this form and a copy should be attached to any sublease of a property.

A sample numbered version of this form is found on page 176. To complete this form, the following information is needed:

① Date of consent to sublease
② Name of tenant requesting consent
③ Address of tenant requesting consent
④ Name of tenant requesting consent
⑤ Description of lease, including date of lease and location of leased premises
⑥ Signature of landlord
⑦ Printed name of landlord

Notice of Rent Default: This form allows for notice to a tenant of default in the payment of rent. It provides for the amount of the defaulted payments to be specified and for a time limit to be placed on payment before further action is taken. Most states have laws relating to the time limits that must be allowed to a tenant to pay the late rent after the landlord's notice of a rent default. You should check your state's listing in the Real Estate Appendix on the CD for the time limit that you should use in this form. If the breach is not taken care of within the time period allowed, you may send the tenant a Notice to Pay Rent or Vacate (shown later in this kit). In addition, a lawyer should be consulted for further action, which may involve a lawsuit to enforce the lease terms. A copy of the original lease should be attached to this form. A sample numbered version of this form is found on page 177. To complete this form, fill in the following information:

① Date of notice
② Name of tenant
③ Address of tenant
④ Name of tenant
⑤ Description of lease (address of property, dates covered, etc.)
⑥ Date of this notice
⑦ Exact amount of rent past due
⑧ Number of days allowed to pay rent (Check the Appendix for your state's requirements)
⑨ Signature of landlord
⑩ Printed Name of landlord

Notice of Breach of Lease: This form should be used to notify a party to a lease of the violation of a term of the lease or of an instance of failure to perform a required duty under the lease, other than the failure to pay rent. Such violation might be having a pet if the lease prohibits this, or perhaps having too many people living in the rental property, or any other violation of the terms of the lease. This notice provides for a description of the alleged violation of the lease and for a time period in which the party is instructed to cure the breach of the lease. If the breach is not taken care of within the time period allowed, you may send the tenant a Final Notice Before Legal Action. In any event, a lawyer should be consulted for further action, which may entail a lawsuit to enforce the lease terms. A copy of the original lease should be attached to this form. A sample numbered version of this form is found on page 178. To complete this form, fill in the following information:

① Date of notice
② Name of tenant
③ Address of tenant
④ Name of tenant
⑤ Description of lease (address of property, dates covered, etc.)
⑥ Date of this notice
⑦ Exact description of breach of lease
⑧ Number of days allowed to correct the breach
⑨ Signature of landlord
⑩ Printed Name of landlord

Notice to Pay Rent or Vacate: This form allows for notice to be given to a tenant who is in default of the payment of rent. It provides for the amount of the defaulted payments to be specified and for a time limit to be placed on payment before further action is taken. It provides notice to either pay the rent or to vacate the property by a certain date. *This notice is not an eviction notice.* If the defaulted rent is not paid or the property is not vacated by the tenant within the time period allowed, a Landlord's Notice to Terminate Lease may be delivered to the tenant which demands that possession of the property be relinquished. Most states have laws relating to the time limits that must be allowed to a tenant to pay the late rent after the landlord's notice of a rent default. You should check your state's listing in the Appendix of this book for the time limit that you should use in this form. A lawyer should be consulted for further action, which may involve a lawsuit to enforce the lease terms, a lawsuit for collection of the past due rent, or legal proceedings for eviction of the tenant. A copy of the original lease should be attached to this form. A sample numbered version of this form is found on page 179. To complete this form, fill in the following information:

① Date of notice
② Name of tenant
③ Address of tenant
④ Name of tenant
⑤ Description of lease (address of property, dates covered, etc.)
⑥ Date of this notice
⑦ Exact amount of rent past due

⑧ Date on which tenant must pay rent or vacate the property (Check state's listing in the Appendix)
⑨ Signature of landlord
⑩ Printed Name of landlord

Landlord's Notice to Terminate Lease: By this notice, a landlord may inform a tenant of the termination of a lease for breach of the lease. This action may be taken under a lease, provided that there are specific lease provisions that allow this action and the tenant has agreed to these provisions by signing the lease. This notice is generally sent to a tenant after the tenant has first been notified that the rent is past due or that the lease has been breached for other reasons and the tenant has been given a time period in which to pay. *This notice is not an eviction notice.* It is a notice to demand that the tenant surrender possession of the property back to the landlord. Some states have time limits that must be complied with before a lease can be terminated and you should check your state's listing in the Appendix to determine if your state has such requirements. A lawyer should be consulted for further action, which may involve a lawsuit to enforce the lease terms, a lawsuit for collection of the past-due rent, or legal proceedings for eviction of the tenant. A copy of the original lease should be attached to this form. This form should be delivered to the tenant by certified first-class mail and the Proof of Service portion of this form should be completed by the person actually mailing the notice. A sample numbered version of this form is found on page 180. To complete this form, fill in the following information:

① Date of notice
② Name and address of tenant
③ Name of tenant
④ Description of lease (address of property, dates covered, etc.)
⑤ Date of this Notice
⑥ Exact nature of breach of lease (amount rent past due, etc.)
⑦ Date of the original Notice to Pay Rent or Vacate or Notice of Breach of Lease
⑧ Number of days allowed in original Notice to Pay Rent or Vacate or Notice of Breach of Lease
⑨ Date on which possession of property is demanded
⑩ Signature of landlord
⑪ Printed Name of landlord
⑫ Address of landlord
⑬ City, state, and zip code of landlord
⑭ Date of mailing of Notice
⑮ Date of signature on Proof of Service
⑯ Signature of person mailing Notice
⑰ Name of person mailing Notice

Final Notice Before Legal Action: This form allows for a final notice to be given to a person who is in default with a rent payment or other breach of a lease. It provides for the amount of the defaulted payments to be specified and for a time limit to be placed on payment before immediate legal action is taken. If the defaulted amount is not paid within the time period allowed, a lawyer should be consulted for further action, Further action may involve a lawsuit for collection of the past due amount, a lawsuit for possession of any collateral (if involved) or other legal proceedings. A copy of the original account statement or invoice should be attached to this form. A sample numbered version of this form is found on page 182. To complete this form, fill in the following information:

① Date of notice
② Name of person in default
③ Address of person in default
④ Description of lease which has been breached
⑤ Date of this notice
⑥ Exact amount of past due rent
⑦ Date on which payment must be made
⑧ Date of this notice
⑨ Signature of landlord
⑩ Printed name of landlord
⑪ Address of landlord
⑫ City, state, and zip code of landlord

Notice of Lease: This document should be used to record notice that a parcel of real estate has a current lease in effect on it. This may be necessary if the property is on the market for sale or it may be required by a bank or mortgage company at the closing of a real estate sale in order for the seller to verify to the buyer the existence of a lease covering the property. This form should be notarized. A sample numbered version of this form is found on page 183. In order to complete this document, the following information is required:

① Description of lease
② Name of landlord
③ Address of landlord
④ Name of tenant
⑤ Address of tenant
⑥ Description of property leased
⑦ Term of lease
⑧ Any extensions of lease
⑨ Signature of landlord
⑩ Printed name of landlord
⑪ The following should be completed by a notary public:

145

Receipt for Lease Security Deposit: This form is to be used for receipt of a lease security deposit. A sample numbered version of this form is found on page 184. To complete this form, insert the following information:

1. Amount of security deposit paid
2. Description of lease
3. Date of receipt
4. Signature of landlord
5. Printed name of landlord

Rent Receipt: This form may be used as a receipt for the periodic payment of rent. A sample numbered version of this form is found on page 184. To complete this form, insert the following information:

1. Amount of rent paid
2. Name of Tenant
3. Time period
4. Description of property for which rent is due
5. Date of receipt
6. Signature of landlord
7. Printed Name of landlord

CREDIT/RENTAL APPLICATION

Name ①
Address
City
State   Zip
Phone
Fax
e-mail Address

CREDIT REFERENCES

Creditor Name ②
Account Number
Phone
Address
City
State   Zip

Creditor Name ③
Account Number
Phone
Address
City
State   Zip

BANK REFERENCES

Bank Name ④
Account Number
Phone
Address
City
State   Zip

Bank Name ⑤
Account Number
Phone

Address
City
State   Zip

PERSONAL REFERENCES

Name ⑥
Relationship
Phone
Address
City
State   Zip

Name ⑦
Relationship
Phone
Address
City
State   Zip

OTHER INFORMATION ⑧

Have you ever filed for bankruptcy?
Have you ever been convicted of a felony?
Have you ever been evicted from or asked to leave a property you were renting?
Have you ever intentionally refused to pay rent when due?
How were you referred to us?

Driver's License Number: ⑨ State:

The Applicant accepts the above terms and states that all information contained in this application is true and correct. Applicant authorizes creditor to contact all references, inquire as to credit information, and receive any confidential information relevant to approving credit.

Dated: ⑩_____

⑪_____
Signature of Applicant

⑫_____
Printed Name of Applicant

FOR OFFICE USE ONLY

References Contacted	Person Contacted	
Remarks		
Creditor #1	⑬	⑭
Creditor #2	⑮	⑯
Bank #1	⑰	⑱
Bank #2	⑲	⑳
Personal #1	㉑	㉒
Personal #2	㉓	㉔

References Contacted by: ㉕
Date References Contacted: ㉖
Applicant Approved: ㉗
Approval by: ㉘
Date Approved: ㉙

Move-in/Move-out Checklist and Acknowledgment

Landlord Name: ①

Tenant Name: ②

Address of leased property: ③

Term of Lease: ④

Date of Move-in: ⑤

Date of Move-out: ⑥

This form is to catalog and note the condition of all of the furniture, furnishing, appliances, and personal property that is present at the leased property. The tenant is responsible for returning all of the following property upon moving out in as good a condition as is noted on the Move-in section of this form, except for normal wear and tear. Landlord should complete this form prior to move-in and Tenant should check this form upon move-in, noting any disagreements with landlord's assessment.

Item Description	Move-in Condition	Landlord Comments	Tenant Comments	Move-out Condition	Landlord Comments	Tenant Comments
⑦						

Move-in Acknowledgment

Landlord has reviewed this document and agrees with the items listed and their condition on the date of the Tenant's moving into the leased property.
Date: ⑧_____

⑨_____
Landlord Signature

Tenant has inspected all of the listed items and found them to be present on the leased property and to be in the condition indicated on the date of the Tenant's moving in to the leased property (or else has noted any discrepancy on this form). Tenant agrees to return all of the listed property on the date of moving out of the leased property in the same condition as indicated on this form, except for normal wear and tear. By signing this form, Tenant agrees with Landlord's assessment or notes his or her disagreement with the Landlord.
Date: ⑩_____

⑪_____
Tenant Signature

Move-out Acknowledgment

Landlord has inspected the listed items and compared them to the move-in condition. If any property differs from its move-in condition, other than normal wear and tear, any differences have been listed on this form.

Date:⑫_____
⑬_____
Landlord Signature

Tenant has inspected the listed items and compared them to the move-in condition. If any property differs from its move-in condition, other than normal wear and tear, any differences have been listed on this form. If Tenant disagrees with Landlord's assessment of any differences in condition upon moving out, those discrepancies have been listed on this form. By signing this form, Tenant agrees with Landlord's assessment or notes his or her disagreement with the Landlord.

Date: ⑭_____
⑮_____
Tenant Signature

RESIDENTIAL LEASE

This lease is made on ①_____ , 20 _____ , between
②_____ , landlord,
address: ③_____
and ④_____ , tenant,
address: ⑤

1. The landlord agrees to rent to the tenant and the tenant agrees to rent from the landlord the following residence:
⑥

2. The term of this lease will be from ⑦_____ , 20 _____ ,
until ⑧_____ , 20 _____ .

3. The rental payments will be $ ⑨_____ per ⑩_____
and will be payable by the tenant to the landlord on the ⑪_____
day of each month, beginning on _____ , 20 _____ .

4. The tenant has paid the landlord a security deposit of $ ⑫_____ .
This security deposit will be held as security for the repair of any damages to the residence by the tenant. This deposit will be returned to the tenant within ten (10) days of the termination of this lease, minus any amounts needed to repair the residence, but without interest, except as required by law in the State of
⑬_____ .

5. The Tenant has paid the Landlord an additional month's rent in the amount of $ ⑭_____ . This rent deposit will be held as security for the payment of rent by the tenant. This rent payment deposit will be returned to the tenant within ten (10) days of the termination of this lease, minus any rent still due upon termination but without interest, except as required by law in the State of ⑮_____ .

6. Tenant agrees to maintain the residence in a clean and sanitary manner and not to make any alterations to the residence without the landlord's written consent. Tenant also agrees not to conduct any business in the residence. At the termination of this lease, the tenant agrees to leave the residence in the same condition as when it was received, except for normal wear and tear.

7. Tenant also agrees not to conduct any type of business in the residence,

nor store or use any dangerous or hazardous materials. Tenant agrees that the residence is to be used only as a single family residence, with a maximum of ⑯_____ tenants. Tenant also agrees to comply with all rules, laws, and ordinances affecting the residence, including all laws of the State of ⑰_____. Tenant agrees that no pets or other animals are allowed in the residence without the written permission of the Landlord.

8. The landlord agrees to supply the following utilities to the tenant: ⑱

9. The tenant agrees to obtain and pay for the following utilities: ⑲

10. Tenant agrees not to sublet the residence or assign this lease without the landlord's written consent. Tenant agrees to allow the landlord reasonable access to the residence for inspection and repair. Landlord agrees to enter the residence only after notifying the tenant in advance, except in an emergency, and according to the laws of the State of _____.

11. The tenant has inspected the residence and has found it satisfactory.

12. If the tenant fails to pay the rent on time or violates any other terms of this lease, the landlord will have the right to terminate this lease in accordance with state law. The landlord will also have the right to re-enter the residence and take possession of it and to take advantage of any other legal remedies available under the laws of the State of ⑳_____.

13. If the Tenant remains as tenant after the expiration of this lease without signing a new lease, a month-to-month tenancy will be created with the same terms and conditions as this lease, except that such new tenancy may be terminated by thirty (30) days written notice from either the Tenant or the Landlord.

14. As required by law, the landlord makes the following statement: "Radon gas is a naturally occurring radioactive gas that, when accumulated in sufficient quantities in a building, may present health risks to persons exposed to it. Levels of radon gas that exceed federal and state guidelines have been found in buildings in this state. Additional information regarding radon gas and radon gas testing may be obtained from your county health department."

15. As required by law, the landlord makes the following LEAD WARNING STATEMENT:
"Every purchaser or lessee of any interest in residential real property on which a residential dwelling was built prior to 1978 is notified that such property

may present exposure to lead from lead-based paint that may place young children at risk of developing lead poisoning. Lead poisoning in young children may produce permanent neurological damage, including learning disabilities, reduced intelligence quotient, behavioral problems, and impaired memory. Lead poisoning also poses a particular threat to pregnant women. The seller or lessor of any interest in residential real estate is required to provide the buyer with any information on lead-based paint hazards from risk assessments or inspection in the seller's or lessor's possession and notify the buyer or lessee of any known lead-based paint hazards. A risk assessment or inspection for possible lead-based paint hazards is recommended prior to purchase."

Landlord's Disclosure

Presence of lead-based paint and/or lead-based paint hazards: (Landlord to initial one).㉑

_____ Known lead-based paint and/or lead-based paint hazards are present in building (explain):
_____ Landlord has no knowledge of lead-based paint and/or lead-based paint hazards in building.
Records and reports available to landlord: (Landlord to initial one). ㉒
_____ Landlord has provided tenant with all available records and reports pertaining to lead-based paint and/or lead-based paint hazards are present in building (list documents):
_____ Landlord has no records and reports pertaining to lead-based paint and/or lead-based paint hazards in building.

Tenant's Acknowledgment

(Tenant to initial all applicable).㉓
_____ Tenant has received copies of all information listed above.
_____ Tenant has received the pamphlet "Protect Your Family from Lead in Your Home."
_____ Tenant has received a ten (10)-day opportunity (or mutually agreed on period) to conduct a risk assessment or inspection for the presence of lead-based paint and/or lead-based paint hazards in building.
_____ Tenant has waived the opportunity to conduct a risk assessment or inspection for the presence of lead-based paint and/or lead-based paint hazards in building.
The landlord and tenant have reviewed the information above and certify, by their signatures at the end of this lease, to the best of their knowledge, that the

information they have provided is true and accurate.

16. The following are additional terms of this lease: ㉔

17. The parties agree that this lease is the entire agreement between them. This lease binds and benefits both the landlord and tenant and any successors. This Lease is governed by the laws of the State of ㉕_____ .

㉖_____ ㉘_____
Signature of Landlord   Signature of Tenant

㉗_____ ㉙_____
Printed Name of Landlord   Printed Name of Tenant

MONTH TO MONTH RENTAL AGREEMENT

This Agreement is made on ①_____ , 20 _____ , between
②_____ , landlord,
address: ③_____
and④_____ , tenant,
address: ⑤_____

1. The Landlord agrees to rent to the Tenant and the Tenant agrees to rent from the Landlord on a month-to-month basis, the following residence: ⑥

2. This Agreement will begin on ⑦_____ and will continue on a month-to-month basis until terminated. This agreement may only be terminated by ⑧_____ days written notice from either party.

3. The rental payments will be $ ⑨_____ per ⑩_____ and will be payable by the tenant to the landlord on the ⑪_____ day of each month, beginning on _____ , 20 _____ .

4. The tenant has paid the landlord a security deposit of $ ⑫_____ . This security deposit will be held as security for the repair of any damages to the residence by the tenant. This deposit will be returned to the tenant within ten (10) days of the termination of this agreement, minus any amounts needed to repair the residence, but without interest, except as required by law in the State of ⑬_____ .

5. The Tenant has paid the Landlord an additional month's rent in the amount of $ ⑭_____ . This rent deposit will be held as security for the payment of rent by the tenant. This rent payment deposit will be returned to the tenant within ten (10) days of the termination of this agreement, minus any rent still due upon termination but without interest, except as required by law in the State of ⑮_____ .

6. Tenant agrees to maintain the residence in a clean and sanitary manner and not to make any alterations to the residence without the landlord's written consent. Tenant also agrees not to conduct any business in the residence. At the termination of this agreement, the tenant agrees to leave the residence in the same condition as when it was received, except for normal wear and tear.

7. Tenant also agrees not to conduct any type of business in the residence,

nor store or use any dangerous or hazardous materials. Tenant agrees that the residence is to be used only as a single family residence, with a maximum of ⑯_____ tenants. Tenant also agrees to comply with all rules, laws, and ordinances affecting the residence, including all the laws of the State of ⑰____ _____. Tenant agrees that no pets or other animals are allowed in the residence without the written permission of the Landlord.

8. The landlord agrees to supply the following utilities to the tenant: ⑱

9. The tenant agrees to obtain and pay for the following utilities: ⑲

10. Tenant agrees not to sublet the residence or assign this agreement without the landlord's written consent. Tenant agrees to allow the landlord reasonable access to the residence for inspection and repair. Landlord agrees to enter the residence only after notifying the tenant in advance, except in an emergency, and according to the laws of the State of ⑳_____.

11. The tenant has inspected the residence and has found it satisfactory.

12. If the tenant fails to pay the rent on time or violates any other terms of this agreement, the landlord will have the right to terminate this agreement in accordance with state law. The landlord will also have the right to re-enter the residence and take possession of it and to take advantage of any other legal remedies available.

13. As required by law, the landlord makes the following statement: "Radon gas is a naturally occurring radioactive gas that, when accumulated in sufficient quantities in a building, may present health risks to persons exposed to it. Levels of radon gas that exceed federal and state guidelines have been found in buildings in this state. Additional information regarding radon gas and radon gas testing may be obtained from your county health department."

14. As required by law, the landlord makes the following LEAD WARNING STATEMENT: "Every purchaser or lessee of any interest in residential real property on which a residential dwelling was built prior to 1978 is notified that such property may present exposure to lead from lead-based paint that may place young children at risk of developing lead poisoning. Lead poisoning in young children may produce permanent neurological damage, including learning disabilities, reduced intelligence quotient, behavioral problems, and impaired memory. Lead poisoning also poses a particular threat to pregnant women. The seller or lessor of any interest in residential real estate is required to provide

the buyer or lessee with any information on lead-based paint hazards from risk assessments or inspection in the seller's or lessor's possession and notify the buyer or lessee of any known lead-based paint hazards. A risk assessment or inspection for possible lead-based paint hazards is recommended prior to purchase."

Landlord's Disclosure

Presence of lead-based paint and/or lead-based paint hazards: (Landlord to initial one). ㉑

_____ Known lead-based paint and/or lead-based paint hazards are present in building (explain):

_____ Landlord has no knowledge of lead-based paint and/or lead-based paint hazards in building.

Records and reports available to landlord: (Landlord to initial one).

_____ Landlord has provided tenant with all available records and reports pertaining to lead-based paint and/or lead-based paint hazards are present in building (list documents):

_____ Landlord has no records and reports pertaining to lead-based paint and/or lead-based paint hazards in building.

Tenant's Acknowledgment

(Tenant to initial all applicable) ㉒

_____ Tenant has received copies of all information listed above.

_____ Tenant has received the pamphlet "Protect Your Family from Lead in Your Home."

_____ Tenant has received a ten (10)-day opportunity (or mutually agreed on period) to conduct a risk assessment or inspection for the presence of lead-based paint and/or lead-based paint hazards in building.

_____ Tenant has waived the opportunity to conduct a risk assessment or inspection for the presence of lead-based paint and/or lead-based paint hazards in building.

The landlord and tenant have reviewed the information above and certify, by their signatures at the end of this agreement, to the best of their knowledge, that the information they have provided is true and accurate.

15. The following are additional terms of this agreement: ㉓

16. The parties agree that this agreement is the entire agreement between them. This Agreement binds and benefits both the landlord and tenant and any

successors. This Agreement is governed by the laws of the State of ㉔ _____ .

㉕_____
Signature of Landlord

㉗_____
Signature of Tenant

㉖_____
Printed Name of Landlord

㉘_____
Printed Name of Tenant

COMMERCIAL LEASE

This lease is made on ①_____ , 20 _____ , between
②_____ , landlord,
address: ③④⑤_____
and ⑥_____ , tenant,
address: ⑦⑧⑨_____

1. The Landlord agrees to rent to the Tenant and the Tenant agrees to rent from the Landlord the following property: ⑩

2. The rental payments will be $ ⑪ _____ per month and will be payable by the Tenant to the Landlord on the ⑫_____ day of each month, beginning on ⑬_____. If any rental payment is not paid within 5 (five) days of its due date, the Tenant agrees to pay an additional late charge of 5% (five percent) of the rental due.

3. The term of this Lease will be from ⑭ _____,
until ⑮_____. If Tenant is in full compliance with all of the terms of this Lease at the expiration of this term, Tenant shall have the option to renew this Lease for an additional term of ⑯ _____, with all terms and conditions of this Lease remaining the same, except that the rent shall be ⑰_____
If the Tenant remains as tenant after the expiration of this Lease with the consent of the Landlord but without signing a new lease, a month-to-month tenancy will be created with the same terms and conditions as this Lease, except that such new tenancy may be terminated by ninety (90) days written notice from either the Tenant or the Landlord, and that the rent shall be $ ⑱_____.

4. The Tenant has paid the Landlord a security deposit of $ ⑲ _____ .
This security deposit will be held as security for the repair of any damages to the property by the Tenant. This deposit will be returned to the Tenant within 10 (ten) days of the termination of this Lease, minus any amounts needed to repair the property, but without interest., unless required by state law.

5. The Tenant has paid the Landlord an additional month's rent in the amount of $ ⑳_____ . This rent deposit will be held as security for the payment of rent by the Tenant. This rent payment deposit will be returned to the Tenant within 10 (ten) days of the termination of this Lease, minus any rent still due upon termination, but without interest, unless required by state law.

6. The Tenant agrees to use the property only for the purpose of carrying on the following lawful business: ㉑

7. The Landlord agrees that the Tenant may install the following equipment and fixtures for the purpose of operating the Tenant's business and that such equipment and fixtures shall remain the property of the Tenant: ㉒

8. The Tenant has inspected the property and has found it satisfactory for its intended purposes. The Landlord shall be responsible for the repair and upkeep of the exterior of the property, including the roof, exterior walls, parking areas, landscaping, and building foundation. The Tenant shall be responsible for the repair and upkeep of the interior of the property, including all electrical, mechanical, plumbing, heating, cooling, or any other system or equipment on the property. Tenant agrees to maintain the interior of the property and the surrounding outside area in a clean, safe, and sanitary manner and not to make any alterations to the property without the Landlord's written consent. At the termination of this Lease, the Tenant agrees to leave the property in the same condition as when it was received, except for normal wear and tear. Tenant also agrees to comply with all rules, laws, regulations, and ordinances affecting the property or the business activities of the Tenant.

9. The Tenant agrees to obtain and pay for all necessary utilities for the property.

10. The Tenant agrees not to sub-let the property or assign this Lease without the Landlord's written consent, which shall not be unreasonably withheld. Tenant agrees to allow the Landlord reasonable access to the property for inspection and repair. Landlord agrees to enter the property only after notifying the Tenant in advance, except in an emergency.

11. If the Tenant fails to pay the rent on time or violates any other terms of this Lease, the Landlord will provide written notice of the violation or default, allowing ㉓ _____ days to correct the violation or default. If the violation or default is not completely corrected within the time prescribed, the Landlord will have the right to terminate this Lease with ㉔ _____ days notice and in accordance with state law. Upon termination of this Lease, the Tenant agrees to surrender possession of the property. The Landlord will also have the right to re-enter the property and take possession of it, remove Tenant and any equipment or possessions of Tenant, and to take advantage of any other legal remedies available.

12. The Landlord agrees to carry fire and casualty insurance on the property, but shall have no liability for the operation of the Tenant's business. The Tenant agrees not to do anything that will increase the Landlord's insurance premiums and, further agrees to indemnify and hold the Landlord harmless from any liability or damage, whether caused by Tenant's operations or otherwise. The Tenant agrees to carry and pay all premiums for casualty insurance on any equipment or fixtures that Tenant installs at the property. In addition, the Tenant agrees to carry business liability insurance, including bodily injury and property damage coverage, covering all Tenant's business operations in the amount of $ ㉕ _____ with the Landlord named as a co-insured party. Tenant agrees to furnish Landlord copies of the insurance policies and to not cancel the policies without notifying the Landlord in advance. Tenant agrees to provide Landlord with a Certificate of Insurance which indicates that Landlord is a co-insured party and that Landlord shall be provided with a minimum of ten (10) days written notice prior to cancellation or change of coverage.

13. This Lease is subject to any mortgage or deed of trust currently on the property or which may be made against the property at any time in the future. The Tenant agrees to sign any documents necessary to subordinate this Lease to a mortgage or deed of trust for the Landlord.

14. This Lease may only be terminated by ㉖_____ days written notice from either party, except in the event of a violation of any terms or default of any payments or responsibilities due under this Lease, which are governed by the terms in Paragraph 11 of this Lease.

15. Tenant agrees that if any legal action is necessary to recover the property, collect any amounts due under this Lease, or correct a violation of any term of this Lease, Tenant shall be responsible for all costs incurred by Landlord in connection with such action, including any reasonable attorney's fees.

16. As required by law, the Landlord makes the following statement: "Radon gas is a naturally-occurring radioactive gas that, when accumulated in sufficient quantities in a building, may present health risks to persons exposed to it. Levels of radon gas that exceed federal and state guidelines have been found in buildings in this state. Additional information regarding radon gas and radon gas testing may be obtained from your county health department."

17. The following are additional terms of this Lease: ㉗

18. The parties agree that this Lease, including the following attachments: ㉘

is the entire agreement between them and that no terms of this Lease may be changed except by written agreement of both parties. This Lease is intended to comply with any and all applicable laws relating to landlord and tenant relationships in this state. This Lease binds and benefits both the Landlord and Tenant and any heirs, successors, representatives, or assigns. This Lease is governed by the laws of the State of ㉙_____ .

㉚_____
Signature of Landlord
㉛_____
Printed Name of Landlord
㉜_____
Signature of Tenant
㉝_____
Printed Name of Tenant

LEASE WITH PURCHASE OPTION

This lease is made on ①_____ , 20 _____ , between
②_____ , landlord,
address: ③④⑤
and ⑥_____ , tenant,
address: ⑦⑧⑨

1. The Landlord agrees to rent to the Tenant and the Tenant agrees to rent from the Landlord the following residence: ⑩

2. The term of this lease will be from ⑪_____ , until ⑫_____ .

3. The rental payments will be $ ⑬_____ per ⑭_____ and will be payable by the Tenant to the Landlord on the ⑮_____ day of each month, beginning on ⑯_____ .

4. The Landlord agrees to give the Tenant an exclusive option to buy this property for the following price and terms:

A. ⑰_____ percent of the amount that the Tenant pays the Landlord as rent under this Lease will be held as a deposit and credited against the purchase price of this property if this option is exercised by the Tenant. If the option is not exercised, the Seller will retain all of these payments as rent under this Lease.

B. The option period will be from the beginning date of this Lease until ⑱_____ _____ , at which time it will expire unless exercised.

C. During this period, the Tenant has the exclusive option and right to buy the leased property for the purchase price of $ ⑲_____ .
The Tenant must notify the Landlord, in writing, of the decision to exercise this option. The purchase price will be paid as follows:
Rental payment deposit, to be held in trust by Landlord $ ⑳_____
Other deposit: ㉑_____ $ ㉒_____
Cash or certified check for balance on closing $㉓_____
(subject to any adjustments or prorations on closing)
Total Purchase Price $ ㉔_____

D. Should the Tenant exercise this Option in writing, Landlord and Tenant agree to enter into a standard Agreement for the Sale of Real Estate. The Agreement will be conditional upon the Tenant being able to arrange suitable financing on the following terms at least thirty (30) days prior to the closing date specified in the Agreement for the Sale of Real Estate: a mortgage in the amount of ㉕_____ _____ , payable in ㉖ _____ monthly payments, with an annual interest rate of ㉗_____ percent.

5. The Tenant has paid the Landlord a security deposit of $ ㉘_____ . This security deposit will be held as security for the repair of any damages to the residence by the Tenant. This deposit will be returned to the Tenant within ten (10) days of the termination of this lease, minus any amounts needed to repair the residence, but without interest, unless required by state law.

6. The Tenant has paid the Landlord an additional month's rent in the amount of $ ㉙_____ . This rent deposit will be held as security for the payment of rent by the Tenant. This rent payment deposit will be returned to the Tenant within ten (10) days of the termination of this lease, minus any rent still due upon termination, but without interest unless required by state law.

7. The Tenant has inspected the residence and has found it satisfactory. Tenant agrees to maintain the residence and the surrounding outside area in a clean and sanitary manner and not to make any alterations to the residence without the Landlord's written consent. At the termination of this lease, the Tenant agrees to leave the residence in the same condition as when it was received, except for normal wear and tear.

8. Tenant also agrees not to conduct any type of business in the residence, nor store or use any dangerous or hazardous materials. Tenant agrees that the residence is to be used only as a single family residence, with a maximum of ㉚_____ tenants. Tenant also agrees to comply with all rules, laws, and ordinances affecting the residence. Tenant agrees that no pets or other animals are allowed in the residence without the written permission of the Landlord.

9. The Landlord agrees to supply the following utilities to the Tenant: ㉛

10. The Tenant agrees to obtain and pay for the following utilities: ㉜

11. Tenant agrees not to sub-let the residence or assign this lease without the Landlord's written consent. Tenant agrees to allow the Landlord reasonable access to the residence for inspection and repair. Landlord agrees to enter the

residence only after notifying the Tenant in advance, except in an emergency.

12. If the Tenant fails to pay the rent on time or violates any other terms of this lease, the Landlord will provide written notice of the violation or default. If the violation or default is not corrected, the Landlord will have the right to terminate this lease in accordance with state law. The Landlord will also have the right to re-enter the residence and take possession of it and to take advantage of any other legal remedies available.

13. If the Tenant remains as tenant after the expiration of this lease without signing a new lease, a month-to-month tenancy will be created with the same terms and conditions as this lease, except that such new tenancy may be terminated by thirty (30) days written notice from either the Tenant or the Landlord.

14. As required by law, the Landlord makes the following statement: "Radon gas is a naturally-occurring radioactive gas that, when accumulated in sufficient quantities in a building, may present health risks to persons exposed to it. Levels of radon gas that exceed federal and state guidelines have been found in buildings in this state. Additional information regarding radon gas and radon gas testing may be obtained from your county health department."

15. As required by law, the Landlord makes the following LEAD WARNING STATEMENT: "Every purchaser or lessee of any interest in residential real property on which a residential dwelling was built prior to 1978 is notified that such property may present exposure to lead from lead-based paint that may place young children at risk of developing lead poisoning. Lead poisoning in young children may produce permanent neurological damage, including learning disabilities, reduced intelligence quotient, behavioral problems, and impaired memory. Lead poisoning also poses a particular threat to pregnant women. The seller of any interest in residential real estate is required to provide the buyer with any information on lead-based paint hazards from risk assessments or inspection in the seller's possession and notify the buyer of any known lead-based paint hazards. A risk assessment or inspection for possible lead-based paint hazards is recommended prior to purchase."

LANDLORD'S DISCLOSURE

Presence of lead-based paint and/or lead-based paint hazards: (Landlord to initial one). ③③

_____ Known lead-based paint and/or lead-based paint hazards are present in building (explain).

_____ Landlord has no knowledge of lead-based paint and/or lead-based paint hazards in building.

RECORDS AND REPORTS AVAILABLE TO LANDLORD: (Landlord to initial one). ㉞

_____ Landlord has provided Tenant with all available records and reports pertaining to lead-based paint and/or lead-based paint hazards are present in building (list documents).

_____ Landlord has no records and reports pertaining to lead-based paint and/or lead-based paint hazards in building.

TENANT'S ACKNOWLEDGMENT (Tenant to initial all applicable). ㉟

_____ Tenant has received copies of all information listed above.

_____ Tenant has received the pamphlet "Protect Your Family from Lead in Your Home."

_____ Tenant has received a 10-day opportunity (or mutually-agreed on period) to conduct a risk assessment or inspection for the presence of lead-based paint and/or lead-based paint hazards in building.

_____ Tenant has waived the opportunity to conduct a risk assessment or inspection for the presence of lead-based paint and/or lead-based paint hazards in building.

The Landlord and Tenant have reviewed the information above and certify, by their signatures at the end of this Lease, to the best of their knowledge, that the information they have provided is true and accurate.

16. The following are additional terms of this Lease: ㊱

17. The parties agree that this Lease with Option is the entire agreement between them and that no terms of this Lease with Option may be changed except by written agreement of both parties. This Lease is intended to comply with any and all applicable laws relating to landlord and tenant relationships in this state. This Lease binds and benefits both the Landlord and Tenant and any successors, representatives, or assigns. Time is of the essence of this agreement. This Lease is governed by the laws of the State of ㊲_____ .

㊳_____
Signature of Landlord

㊴_____
Printed Name of Landlord

㊵_____
Signature of Tenant

㊶_____
Printed Name of Tenant

AMENDMENT OF LEASE

This amendment of lease is made on ①_____ , 20 _____ , between ②_____ , landlord, address:

and ③_____ , tenant, address:

For valuable consideration, the parties agree as follows:

1. The following described lease is attached to this amendment and is made a part of this amendment: ④

2. The parties agree to amend this lease as follows: ⑤

3. All other terms and conditions of the original lease remain in effect without modification. This amendment binds and benefits both parties and any successors. This document, including the attached lease, is the entire agreement between the parties.

The parties have signed this amendment on the date specified at the beginning of this amendment.

⑥_____
Signature of Landlord
⑦_____
Printed Name of Landlord

⑧_____
Signature of Tenant
⑨_____
Printed Name of Tenant

EXTENSION OF LEASE

This extension of lease is made on ①_____ , 20 _____ ,
between
②_____ , landlord,
address:

and ③_____ , tenant,
address:

For valuable consideration, the parties agree as follows: ④

1. The following described lease will end on ⑤_____ , 20 _____ :
This lease is attached to this extension and is a part of this extension.

2. The parties agree to extend this lease for an additional period, which will begin
immediately on the expiration of the original time period and will end on
⑥_____ , 20 _____ .

3. The extension of this lease will be on the same terms and conditions as the
original lease. This extension binds and benefits both parties and any successors.
This document, including the attached lease, is the entire agreement between
the parties.

The parties have signed this extension on the date specified at the beginning of
this extension.

⑦_____   ⑨_____
Signature of Landlord   Signature of Tenant
⑧_____   ⑩_____
Printed Name of Landlord   Printed Name of Tenant

MUTUAL TERMINATION OF LEASE

This termination of lease is made on ①_____ , 20 _____ , between
②_____ , landlord,
address:

and ③_____ , tenant,
address:

For valuable consideration, the parties agree as follows:

1. The parties are currently bound under the terms of the following described lease: ④

2. They agree to mutually terminate and cancel this lease effective on this date. This termination agreement will act as a mutual release of all obligations under this lease for both parties, as if the lease has not been entered into in the first place. Landlord agrees that all rent due has been paid and that the possession of the property has been returned in satisfactory condition.

3. This termination binds and benefits both parties and any successors. This document, including the attached lease being terminated, is the entire agreement between the parties.

The parties have signed this termination on the date specified at the beginning of this termination.

⑤_____   ⑦_____
Signature of Landlord   Signature of Tenant
⑥_____   ⑧_____
Printed Name of Landlord   Printed Name of Tenant

ASSIGNMENT OF LEASE

This assignment is made on ① _____ , 20 _____ , between
② _____ , assignor,
address: ③ _____

and ④ _____ , assignee,
address: ⑤ _____

For valuable consideration, the parties agree to the following terms and conditions:

1. The assignor assigns all interest, burdens, and benefits in the following described lease to the assignee: ⑥

This lease is attached to this assignment and is a part of this assignment.

2. The assignor warrants that this lease is in effect, has not been modified, and is fully assignable. If the consent of the landlord is necessary for this assignment to be effective, such consent is attached to this assignment and is a part of this assignment. Assignor agrees to indemnify and hold the assignee harmless from any claim which may result from the assignor's failure to perform under this lease prior to the date of this assignment.

3. The assignee agrees to perform all of the obligations of the assignor and receive all of the benefits of the assignor under this lease. Assignee agrees to indemnify and hold the assignor harmless from any claim which may result from the assignee's failure to perform under this lease after the date of this assignment.

4. This assignment binds and benefits both parties and any successors. This document, including any attachments, is the entire agreement between the parties.

⑦ _____   ⑨ _____
Signature of Assignor   Signature of Assignee

⑧ _____   ⑩ _____
Printed Name of Assignor   Printed Name of Assignee

CONSENT TO ASSIGNMENT OF LEASE

Date: ①_____ , 20 _____

To: ②③

RE: Assignment of Lease

Dear ④_____ :

I am the landlord under the following described lease: ⑤

This lease is the subject of the attached assignment of lease.

I consent to the assignment of this lease as described in the attached assignment, which provides that the assignee is fully substituted for the assignor.

⑥_____
Signature of Landlord

⑦_____
Printed Name of Landlord

SUBLEASE

This sublease is made on ① _____ , 20 _____ , between
② _____ , tenant,
address: ③

and ④ _____ , subtenant,
address: ⑤

For valuable consideration, the parties agree to the following terms and conditions:

1. The tenant subleases to the subtenant the following described property: ⑥

2. This property is currently leased to the tenant under the terms of the following described lease: ⑦
This lease is attached to this sublease and is a part of this sublease.

3. This sublease will be for the period from ⑧ _____ , 20 _____ , to
⑨ _____ , 20 _____ .

4. The subrental payments will be $ ⑩ _____ per ⑪ _____
and will be payable by the subtenant to the landlord on the ⑫ _____ day of each month, beginning on ⑬ _____ , 20 _____ .

5. The tenant warrants that the underlying lease is in effect, has not been modified, and that the property may be sublet. If the consent of the landlord is necessary for his sublease to be effective, such consent is attached to this sublease and is a part of this sublease. Tenant agrees to indemnify and hold the subtenant harmless from any claim which may result from the tenant's failure to perform under this lease prior to the date of this sublease.

6. The subtenant agrees to perform all of the obligations of the tenant under the original lease and receive all of the benefits of the tenant under this lease. Subtenant agrees to indemnify and hold the tenant harmless from any claim which may result from the subtenant's failure to perform under this lease after the date of this sublease.

7. The tenant agrees to remain primarily liable to the landlord for the obligations under the lease.

8. The parties agree to the following additional terms: ⑭

9. This sublease binds and benefits both parties and any successors. This document, including any attachments, is the entire agreement between the parties. This sublease is subject to the laws of the State of ⑮_____.

⑯_____
Signature of Tenant

⑱_____
Signature of Subtenant

⑰_____
Printed Name of Tenant

⑲_____
Printed Name of Subtenant

CONSENT TO SUBLEASE

Date: ①_____ , 20 _____

To: ②③

RE: Sublease of Lease

Dear ④_____ :

I am the landlord under the following described lease: ⑤

This lease is the subject of the attached sublease.

I consent to the sublease of this lease as described in the attached sublease, which provides that the subtenant is substituted for the tenant for the period indicated in the sublease. This consent does not release the tenant from any obligations under the lease and the tenant remains fully bound under the lease.

⑥_____
Signature of Landlord

⑦_____
Printed Name of Landlord

NOTICE OF RENT DEFAULT

Date: ①_____ , 20 _____

To: ②③

RE: Notice of Rent Default

Dear ④_____ :

This notice is in reference to the following described lease: ⑤

Please be advised that as of ⑥_____ , 20 _____ , you are in DEFAULT IN YOUR PAYMENT OF RENT in the amount of $ ⑦ _____ .

If this breach of lease is not corrected within ⑧_____ days of this notice, we will take further action to protect our rights, which may include termination of this lease and collection proceedings. This notice is made under all applicable laws. All of our rights are reserved under this notice.

⑨_____
Signature of Landlord

⑩_____
Printed Name of Landlord

NOTICE OF BREACH OF LEASE

Date: ①_____ , 20 _____

To: ②③

RE: Breach of Lease

Dear ④_____ :

This notice is in reference to the following described lease: ⑤

Please be advised that as of ⑥_____ , 20 _____ , we are holding you in BREACH OF LEASE for the following reasons: ⑦

If this breach of lease is not corrected within ⑧_____ days of this notice, we will take further action to protect our rights, which may include termination of this lease. This notice is made under all applicable laws. All of our rights are reserved under this notice.

⑨_____
Signature of Landlord

⑩_____
Printed Name of Landlord

NOTICE TO PAY RENT OR VACATE

Date: ①_____ , 20 _____

To: ②③

RE: Notice to Vacate Property

Dear ④_____ :

This notice is in reference to the following described lease: ⑤

Please be advised that as of ⑥_____ , you are in DEFAULT OF YOUR PAYMENT OF RENT in the amount of $ ⑦_____ , which is immediately payable.

THEREFORE, YOU ARE HEREBY GIVEN NOTICE:

To immediately pay the amount of rent that is in default as noted above or to immediately vacate the property and deliver possession to the Landlord on or before ⑧_____ . If you fail to pay the rent in default or vacate the property by this date, we will take further action to protect our rights, which may include termination of this lease, collection, and eviction proceedings. Be also advised that any legal costs involved in the collection of rent in default or in obtaining possession of this property will also be recovered from you as may be allowed by law. This notice is made under all applicable laws of this state. All of our rights are reserved under this notice. Regardless of your vacating the property, you are still responsible for all rent due under the lease.

THIS IS NOT AN EVICTION NOTICE.

⑨_____
Signature of Landlord

⑩_____
Printed Name of Landlord

LANDLORD'S NOTICE TO TERMINATE LEASE

Date: ①_____ , 20 _____

To: ②

RE: Notice to Terminate Lease

Dear ③_____ :

This notice is in reference to the following described lease: ④

Please be advised that as of ⑤_____ , 20 _____ , you have been in BREACH OF LEASE for the following reasons: ⑥

You were previously notified of this breach in the NOTICE dated ⑦_____, 20 _____ . At that time you were given ⑧_____ days to correct the breach of the lease and you have not complied.

THEREFORE, YOU ARE HEREBY GIVEN NOTICE:
The lease is immediately terminated and you are directed to deliver possession of the property to the landlord on or before ⑨_____ , 20 _____ .
If you fail to deliver the property by this date, legal action to evict you from the property will be taken. Regardless of your deliverance of the property, you are still responsible for all rent due under the lease.

THIS IS NOT AN EVICTION NOTICE.

⑩_____
Signature of Landlord

⑪_____
Printed Name of Landlord

⑫_____
Address of Landlord

⑬_____
City, State, Zip code of Landlord

PROOF OF SERVICE

I, the undersigned, being of legal age, declare under penalty of perjury that I served the above Notice to Terminate Lease on the above-named tenant by mailing an exact copy to the tenant by certified mail on ⑭_____.

Signed on: ⑮_____

By: ⑯_____
           Signature of person mailing notice
   ⑰_____
           Printed name of person mailing notice

FINAL NOTICE BEFORE LEGAL ACTION

Date: ① _____ , 20 _____

To: ②③

This notice is in reference to the following Lease: ④

Please be advised that as of ⑤ _____ ,
you are in DEFAULT ON THIS LEASE in the amount of $ ⑥ _____ , which
is immediately due and payable. You have previously been repeatedly notified of
your delinquency regarding this Lease.

THEREFORE, YOU ARE HEREBY GIVEN FINAL NOTICE:

That you must immediately pay the full amount that is in default as noted above
on or before ⑦ _____ . If you fail to pay the full amount in default
by this date, we will take immediate action to protect our rights by proceeding
with legal action. Be also advised that any and all legal costs associated with
such legal action will also be recovered from you to the fullest extent allowed by
law and that such legal proceedings may impair your credit rating. This notice is
made under all applicable laws of this state. All of our rights are reserved under
this notice.

THIS IS YOUR FINAL OPPORTUNITY TO RESOLVE MATTERS WITHOUT
THE EXPENSE OF COURT PROCEEDINGS.

Dated: ⑧ _____

⑨ _____
Signature of Landlord

⑩ _____
Printed Name of Landlord

⑪ _____
Address of Landlord

⑫ _____
City, State, Zip Code of Landlord

NOTICE OF LEASE

NOTICE is given of the existence of the following lease: ①

Name of landlord: ②
Address: ③

Name of tenant: ④
Address: ⑤

Description of property leased: ⑥

Term of lease: From ⑦_____ , 20 _____ , to _____ , 20 _____ .

Any options to extend lease: ⑧

⑨_____   ⑩_____
Signature of Landlord   Printed Name of Landlord

⑪
State of _____
County of _____

On _____ , 20 _____ , _____ personally came
before me and, being duly sworn, did state that he or she is the person described
in the above document and that he or she signed the above document in my
presence.

_____
Signature of Notary Public

Notary Public, In and for the County of _____
State of _____

My commission expires: _____   Notary Seal

RECEIPT FOR LEASE SECURITY DEPOSIT

The landlord acknowledges receipt of the sum of $ ①_____
paid by the tenant under the following described lease: ②

This security deposit payment will be held by the landlord under the terms of this lease, and unless required by law, will not bear any interest. This security deposit will be repaid when due under the terms of the lease.

Dated: ③_____ , 20 _____

④_____
Signature of Landlord

⑤_____
Printed Name of Landlord

RENT RECEIPT

The landlord acknowledges receipt of the sum of $ ① _____ paid by ②_____ , the tenant, for rent during the time period of ③_____ to _____ for the property located at: ④_____.

Dated: ⑤_____ , 20 _____

⑥_____
Signature of Landlord

⑦_____
Printed Name of Landlord

Chapter 9

Rental and Sale of Personal Property

Instructions for Rental of Personal Property

Personal Property Rental Agreement: Leases of personal property are often undertaken for the use of tools, equipment, or property necessary to perform a certain task. Other situations where such an agreement is often used is in the rental of property for recreational purposes. The needs of the parties for a personal property rental agreement depend a great deal on the type of property involved and the value of the property.

A sample numbered version of this form is found on page 189. To prepare this form, fill in the following information:

① Date of rental agreement
② Name of Owner
③ Address of Owner
④ Name of Renter
⑤ Address of Renter
⑥ Complete description of rental property
⑦ Beginning and ending date and time of rental agreement
⑧ Amount being charged for rental
⑨ Period of time for payment (usually a month or day)
⑩ Describe payment details
⑪ Amount of late fee
⑫ Number of days the rental not paid to make it in default
⑬ Amount of security deposit
⑭ Amount of insurance coverage required

⑮ Additional terms
⑯ Which state's laws will be used
⑰ Signature of Owner
⑱ Printed name of Owner
⑲ Signature of Renter
⑳ Printed name of Renter

Instructions for Sale of Personal Property

Contract for Sale of Personal Property: This form may be used for documenting the sale of any type of personal property. It may be used for vehicles, business assets, or any other personal property. The information necessary to complete this form are the names and addresses of the seller and the buyer, a complete description of the property being sold, the total purchase price, and the terms of the payment of this price.

A sample numbered version of this form is found on page 191. To prepare this form, fill in the following information:

① Date of Contract
② Name of Seller
③ Address of Seller
④ Name of Buyer
⑤ Address of Buyer
⑥ Describe personal property being sold
⑦ Amount personal property being sold for
⑧ Payment description
⑨ The date that the buyer takes ownership of property
⑩ State where transaction occurs
⑪ Signature of Seller
⑫ Printed name of Seller
⑬ Signature of Buyer
⑭ Printed name of Buyer

Bill of Sale, with Warranties: This document is used as a receipt of the sale of personal property. It is, in many respects, often used to operate as a *title* (or ownership document) to items of personal property. It verifies that the person noted in the bill of sale has obtained legal title to the property from the previous owner. This particular version also provides that the seller *warrants* (or guarantees) that he or she has the authority to transfer legal title to the buyer and that there are no outstanding debts or liabilities for the property. In addition, this form provides that the seller warrants that the property is in good working condition on the date of the sale. To complete this form, simply fill in the names and addresses of the seller and buyer, the purchase price of the item, and a description of the property.

A sample numbered version of this form is found on page 192. To prepare this form, fill in the following information:

① Date of Bill of Sale
② Name of Seller
③ Address of Seller
④ Name of Buyer
⑤ Address of Buyer
⑥ Amount received for property
⑦ Describe property being purchased
⑧ Signature of Seller
⑨ Printed name of Seller

Bill of Sale, without Warranties: This form also provides a receipt to the buyer for the purchase of an item of personal property. However, in this form, the seller makes no warranties at all, either regarding the authority to sell the item or the condition of the item. It is sold to the buyer in "as is" condition. The buyer takes it regardless of any defects. To complete this form, fill in the names and addresses of the seller and buyer, the purchase price of the item, and a description of the property.

A sample numbered version of this form is found on page 193. To prepare this form, fill in the following information:

① Date of Bill of Sale
② Name of Seller
③ Address of Seller
④ Name of Buyer
⑤ Address of Buyer
⑥ Amount received for property
⑦ Describe property being purchased
⑧ Signature of Seller
⑨ Printed name of Seller

Bill of Sale, Subject to Debt: This form also provides a receipt to the buyer for the purchase of an item of personal property. This form, however, provides that the property sold is subject to a certain prior debt. It verifies that the seller has obtained legal title to the property from the previous owner, but that the seller specifies that the property is sold subject to a certain debt which the buyer is to pay off. In addition, the buyer agrees to indemnify the seller regarding any liability on the debt.

This particular bill of sale version also provides that the seller warrants that he or she has authority to transfer legal title to the buyer. In addition, this form provides that the owner warrants that the property is in good working condition on the date of the sale. To complete this form, fill in the names and addresses of the seller and buyer, the purchase price of the item, a description of the property, and a description of the debt.

A sample numbered version of this form is found on page 194. To prepare this form, fill in the following information:

① Date of Bill of Sale
② Name of Seller
③ Address of Seller
④ Name of Buyer
⑤ Address of Buyer
⑥ Amount received for property
⑦ Describe property being purchased
⑧ Describe debt
⑨ Signature of Seller
⑩ Printed name of Seller
⑪ Signature of Buyer
⑫ Printed name of Buyer

PERSONAL PROPERTY RENTAL AGREEMENT

This Agreement is made on ①_____ , 20 _____ ,
between ②_____ , Owner,
address: ③

and ④_____ , Renter,
address: ⑤

1. The Owner agrees to rent to the Renter and the Renter agrees to rent from the Owner the following property: ⑥

2. The term of this agreement will be from ⑦_____ o'clock ____ . m., _____ ,
20 _____ , until _____ o'clock ____ . m., _____ , 20 _____ .

3. The rental payments will be $ ⑧_____ per ⑨_____ and will be payable by the Renter to the Owner as follows: ⑩

4. The Renter agrees to pay a late fee of $ ⑪_____ per day that the rental payment is late. If the rental payments are in default for over ⑫_____ days, the Owner may immediately demand possession of the property without advance notice to the Renter.

5. The Owner warrants that the property is free of any known faults which would affect its safe operation under normal usage and is in good working condition.

6. The Renter states that the property has been inspected and is in good working condition. The Renter agrees to use the property in a safe manner and in normal usage and to maintain the property in good repair. The Renter further agrees not to use the property in a negligent manner or for any illegal purpose.

7. The Renter agrees to fully indemnify the Owner for any damage to or loss of the property during the term of this agreement, unless such loss or damage is caused by a defect of the rented property.

8. The Owner shall not be liable for any injury, loss, or damage caused by any use of the property.

9. The Renter has paid the Owner a security deposit of $ ⑬_____ . This security deposit will be held as security for payments of the rent and for the repair

of any damages to the property by the Renter. This deposit will be returned to the Renter upon the termination of this agreement, minus any rent still owed to the Owner and minus any amounts needed to repair the property, beyond normal wear and tear.

10. The Renter may not assign or transfer any rights under this agreement to any other person, nor allow the property to be used by any other person, without the written consent of the Owner.

11. Renter agrees to obtain insurance coverage for the property during the term of this rental agreement in the amount of $ ⑭_____ . Renter agrees to provide the Owner with a copy of the insurance policy and to not cancel the policy during the term of this rental agreement.

12. This agreement may be terminated by either party by giving twenty-four (24) hours written notice to the other party.

13. Any dispute related to this agreement will be settled by voluntary mediation. If mediation is unsuccessful, the dispute will be settled by binding arbitration using an arbitrator of the American Arbitration Association.

14. The following are additional terms of this agreement: ⑮

15. The parties agree that this agreement is the entire agreement between them. This agreement binds and benefits both the Owner and Renter and any successors. Time is of the essence of this agreement.

16. This agreement is governed by the laws of the State of ⑯_____ .

⑰_____   ⑲_____
Signature of Owner   Signature of Renter

⑱_____   ⑳_____
Printed Name of Owner   Printed Name of Renter

CONTRACT FOR SALE OF PERSONAL PROPERTY

This Contract is made on ① _____ , 20 _____ , between
② _____ , Seller,
address: ③

and ④ _____ , Buyer,
address: ⑤

1. The Seller agrees to sell to the Buyer, and the Buyer agrees to buy the following personal property: ⑥

2. The Buyer agrees to pay the Seller $ ⑦ _____ for the property. The Buyer agrees to pay this purchase price in the following manner: ⑧

3. The Buyer will be entitled to possession of this property on
⑨ _____ , 20 _____ .

4. The Seller represents that it has legal title to the property and full authority to sell the property. Seller also represents that the property is sold free and clear of all liens, indebtedness, or liabilities. Seller agrees to provide Buyer with a Bill of Sale for the property.

5. This Contract binds and benefits both the Buyer and Seller and any successors. This document, including any attachments, is the entire agreement between the Buyer and Seller. This agreement is governed by the laws of the State of ⑩ _____ .

⑪ _____   ⑬ _____
Signature of Seller   Signature of Buyer

⑫ _____   ⑭ _____
Printed Name of Seller   Printed Name of Buyer

BILL OF SALE, WITH WARRANTIES

This Bill of Sale is made on ①_____ , 20 _____ , between
②_____ , Seller,
address: ③

and ④_____ , Buyer,
address: ⑤

In exchange for the payment of $ ⑥_____ , received from the Buyer, the Seller sells and transfers possession of the following property to the Buyer: ⑦

The Seller warrants that it owns this property and that it has the authority to sell the property to the Buyer. Seller also warrants that the property is sold free and clear of all liens, indebtedness, or liabilities.

The Seller also warrants that the property is in good working condition as of this date.

Signed and delivered to the Buyer on the above date.

⑧_____
Signature of Seller

⑨_____
Printed Name of Seller

BILL OF SALE, WITHOUT WARRANTIES

This Bill of Sale is made on ①_____ , 20 _____ , between
②_____ , Seller,
address: ③

and ④_____ , Buyer,
address: ⑤

In exchange for the payment of $ ⑥ _____ , received from the Buyer, the
Seller sells and transfers possession of the following property to the Buyer: ⑦

The Seller disclaims any implied warranty of merchantability or fitness and the
property is sold in its present condition, "as is."

Signed and delivered to the Buyer on the above date.

⑧_____
Signature of Seller

⑨_____
Printed Name of Seller

BILL OF SALE, SUBJECT TO DEBT

This Bill of Sale is made on ①_____ , 20 _____ , between
②_____ , Seller,
address: ③

and ④_____ , Buyer,
address: ⑤

In exchange for the payment of $ ⑥_____ , received from the Buyer, the Seller sells and transfers possession of the following property to the Buyer: ⑦

The Seller warrants that it owns this property and that it has the authority to sell the property to the Buyer. Seller also states that the property is sold subject to the following debt: ⑧

The Buyer buys the property subject to the above debt and agrees to pay the debt. Buyer also agrees to indemnify and hold the Seller harmless from any claim based on failure to pay off this debt.

The Seller also warrants that the property is in good working condition as of this date.

Signed and delivered to the Buyer on the above date.

⑨_____
Signature of Seller

⑪_____
Signature of Buyer

⑩_____
Printed Name of Seller

⑫_____
Printed Name of Buyer

Chapter 10

Sale of Real Estate

In this chapter are various forms for the sale and transfer of real estate. Although most real estate sales today are handled by real estate professionals, it is still perfectly legal to buy and sell property without the use of a real estate broker or lawyer. The forms provided in this chapter allow anyone to prepare the necessary forms for many basic real estate transactions. Please note, however, that there may be various state and local variations on sales contracts, mortgages, or other real estate documents. Please check the Real Estate Laws Appendix on the CD for details of your own state's particular requirements. If in doubt, check with a local real estate professional or an attorney. Please read the description of what each form provides and also what information is necessary to complete each form. Also, carefully read through each form itself so that you understand the meaning of each of the terms of the document.

Instructions for Sale of Real Estate

Agreement to Sell Real Estate: This form can be used for setting down an agreement to buy and sell property. It contains the basic clauses to cover situations that will arise in most typical real estate transaction. The various items that are covered in this contract are

- That the sale is conditioned on the buyer being able to obtain financing 30 days prior to the closing
- That if the sale is not completed, the buyer will be given back the earnest money deposit, without interest or penalty
- That the seller will provide a Warranty Deed for the real estate and a Bill of Sale

for any personal property included in the sale
- That certain items will be pro-rated and adjusted as of the closing date
- That the buyer and the seller may split the various closing costs
- That the seller represents that it has good title to the property and that the personal property included is in good working order
- That the title to the property will be evidenced by either title insurance or an abstract of title
- That the buyer has the right to a termite inspection
- That the buyer has a right to a complete home inspection at least 30 days prior to closing
- That the seller provide a radon statement and lead paint disclosure
- That the seller will provide the buyer with the U.S. EPA pamphlet: "Protect Your Family from Lead in Your Home." *Note*: This document is necessary *only* if the residential dwelling was built prior to 1978 and is found on the CD.
- That the seller will provide a Real Estate Disclosure Statement to the buyer within 5 days and that the buyer has the right to rescind the agreement within 5 days after the receipt of the disclosure statement

A sample numbered version of this form is found on page 210. In order to prepare this agreement, please fill in the following information:

① Date of Agreement
② Name of seller
③ Address of seller
④ Name of buyer
⑤ Address of buyer
⑥ Address of property
⑦ City of property
⑧ State of property
⑨ A legal description of the property involved
⑩ A description of any personal property to be included in the sale
⑪ The purchase price of the property
⑫ The amount of any mortgage which will be arranged 30 days prior to closing
⑬ Number of monthly payments of this mortgage
⑭ Annual interest rate of this mortgage
⑮ Interest rate spelled out
⑯ Amount of earnest money deposit
⑰ Amount of any other deposits
⑱ Amount of balance due at closing
⑲ Total purchase price of the property
⑳ Amount of earnest money paid upon signing the contract
㉑ Date for closing sale

㉒ Time for closing
㉓ A.M or P.M.
㉔ Address of closing
㉕ City of closing
㉖ State of closing
㉗ Any other documents to be provided to buyer at closing
㉘ Any other items that will be adjusted and pro-rated at closing
㉙ Closing costs which will be paid for by seller
㉚ Closing costs which will be paid for by buyer
㉛ Whether there are any outstanding claims, liabilities, indebtedness and/or restrictions pertaining to the property
㉜ Seller's initials on 'presence of lead paint' disclosure
㉝ Seller's initials on records or reports of lead paint
㉞ Buyer's initials on lead paint acknowledgment
㉟ Whether there are any additional terms
㊱ Which state's laws will be used to interpret contract
㊲ Signature of seller
㊳ Printed Name of seller
㊴㊶ Signatures of witnesses for seller
㊵㊷ Printed names of witnesses for seller
㊸ Signature of buyer
㊹ Printed name of buyer
㊺㊼ Signatures of witnesses for buyer
㊻㊽ Printed names of witnesses for buyer

Title insurance or an abstract of title will need to be obtained from a local title company or attorney. A Bill of Sale for any personal property (Chapter 9) and a Warranty Deed (later in this chapter) will need to be prepared for use at the closing of the sale. Finally, a federal lead brochure will need to be provided to the buyer if the dwelling was built before 1978 (provided on the CD). Both the seller's and buyer's signatures should be witnessed by two witnesses. Note: California residents will need to include the California Addendum to Contract that is included on the Forms-on-CD as well as the appropriate disclosure forms.

Contract for Deed: This form is also known in some localities as an Installment Real Estate Sales Contract, a Land Contract, or a Conditional Sales Contract. This form is used in real estate situations where it is desired that the Buyer receives possession of the property, but does not receive actual title to the property until the entire sales price has been paid to the Seller. Under this type of contract, the Buyer agrees to make periodic installment payments until the sales price of the property has been paid in full. The reason that some real estate transactions are handled in this manner is that it is much easier for the property to be returned to the Seller in the case of a *default* (failure to make an installment payment when due) by the Buyer. Most Contracts for Deed (as does the one provided in this book) provide for the complete forfeiture of all money paid if the Buyer misses even one payment. This harsh remedy also precludes the need for any foreclosure proceedings against a defaulting Buyer in order to regain possession of the property, as the Buyer does not have legal title to the property until all payments have been made. This type of real estate transaction is generally only used for the sale of undeveloped vacant land. Although a Contract for Deed can be used for the sale of improved property as well, the lack of the legal protections that a mortgage provides make this type of real estate contract a bad choice for a Buyer of residential or commercial property that has a home or business already erected on the property.

This contract provides that a Buyer pay a down payment of some amount and that the remaining balance due for the sale of the real estate be paid in equal monthly installment payments, which include principal and interest at a certain percentage rate. The Buyer also has the right to pay off part of or the entire balance due at any time, without penalty. The Buyer and Seller will need to determine a sales price, what the annual interest rate will be, the amount of a down payment, and also how many monthly payments will be required. For example, the Buyer and Seller agree that the property will be sold for $50,000.00 and that this total amount includes an annual interest rate of 6%. They also agree that there will be 60 monthly payments (five years) and that the Buyer will make a $2,000.00 down payment, leaving $48,000.00 remaining to be paid. Thus, the Buyer will be required to make 60 monthly install-ment payments of $800.00 per payment for a total of $48,000.00.

The contract also provides that the Buyer agrees to forfeit all of the payments made if any payment has been missed for a period of 30 days and another 30-day period has elapsed after the Buyer has received from the Seller, via Certified U.S. Mail, a Declaration of Intent to Forfeit and Terminate Contact for Deed (explained below). The forfeited payments will be then retained by the Seller as accumulated rent for the property. The Buyer also agrees to immediately vacate the property if the Contract for Deed is terminated. The Buyer agrees to pay all real estate property taxes and assessments on the property when due. The contract allows for the Buyer to build new construction on the property as long as the building complies with all applicable zoning laws and health and building codes. Finally, the Buyer has the right, under this contract, to examine an abstract of title to the property to determine that the Seller actually has title to the property. If and when the Buyer has made all payments and is up-to-date on payment of all taxes and assessments on the property, the Seller agrees to transfer full title to the Buyer by the use of a Warranty Deed. A Bill of Sale for any personal property (Chapter 9) and a Warranty Deed (later in this chapter) will need to be prepared for use at the closing of the sale. Finally, a federal lead brochure will need to be provided to the buyer if the dwelling was built before 1978. Both the seller's and buyer's signatures should be witnessed by two witnesses. Note: California residents will need to include the California Addendum to Contract that is included on the Forms-on-CD as well as the appropriate state disclosure forms. A sample numbered version of this form is found on page 215. To complete this form, provide the following:

① Date of Contract for Deed
② Name of seller
③ Address of seller
④ Name of buyer
⑤ Address of buyer
⑥ Address of property
⑦ City of property
⑧ State of property
⑨ A legal description of the property involved
⑩ A description of any personal property to be included in the sale
⑪ The purchase price of the property
⑫ The total purchase price of the property
⑬ Amount of the down payment
⑭ Balance due from the buyer
⑮ Number of monthly payment
⑯ Amount of each monthly payments
⑰ Day of the month on which payment will be due
⑱ Due date of first monthly payment
⑲ Percent of interest rate
⑳ Amount of down payment paid upon signing the contract
㉑ Any other documents to be provided to buyer at closing
㉒ Tax year for which buyer will begin paying taxes
㉓ Whether there are any outstanding claims, liabilities, indebtedness and/or restrictions pertaining to the property
㉔ Seller's initials on presence of lead paint disclosure
㉕ Seller's initials on records or reports of lead paint
㉖ Buyer's initials on lead paint acknowledgment
㉗ Whether there are any additional terms
㉘ Which state's laws will be used to interpret contract
㉙ Signature of seller
㉚ Printed Name of seller
㉛㉝ Signatures of witnesses for seller
㉜㉞ Printed names of witnesses for seller
㉟ Signature of buyer
㊱ Printed name of buyer
㊲㊴ Signatures of witnesses for buyer
㊳㊵ Printed names of witnesses for buyer

Declaration of Intent to Forfeit and Terminate Contract for Deed: This form is to be used by a Seller under a Contract for Deed to notify the Buyer that they are in default of a term of the contract and that the Seller is declaring that the Buyer's payments under the contract thus far are forfeited and that the Contract will be terminated by the Seller for non-compliance by the Buyer. Under the terms of the above Contract for Deed, the Seller must provide this Declaration to the Buyer by Certified U.S. Mail. The Buyer then has 30 days to become current with their payments under the contract. If the Buyer does not make the past-due payments within 30 of receipt of this Declaration, the Buyer's prior payments will be forfeited to the Seller, the Contract for Deed will be terminated, and the Buyer will be required to vacate the property immediately. A sample numbered version of this form is found on page 220. To complete this document, you will need the following information:

① Date of original Contract for Deed
② Name of seller
③ Address of seller
④ Name of buyer
⑤ Address of buyer
⑥ Address of property
⑦ A legal description of the property involved
⑧ Date of Declaration
⑨ Reason buyer is in default on Contract for Deed (if buyer has missed a payment or payments, you will need to specify the due date of the payment(s) and the exact amount of any past due amounts)
⑩ Date of mailing of this Declaration
⑪ Date of this Declaration
⑫ Signature of seller
⑬ Printed name of seller

Option to Buy Real Estate: This form is designed to be used to offer an interested buyer a time period in which to have an exclusive option to purchase a parcel of real estate. It should be used in conjunction with a filled-in but unsigned copy of the above Agreement to Sell Real Estate. Through the use of this option agreement, the seller can offer the buyer a time during which he or she can consider the purchase without concern of a sale to another party.

This agreement provides that in exchange for a payment (which will be applied to the purchase price if the option is exercised), the buyer is given a period of time to accept the terms of a completed real estate contract. If the buyer accepts the terms and exercises the option in writing, the seller agrees to complete the sale. If the option is not exercised, the seller is then free to sell the property on the market and to retain the money that the potential buyer paid for the option. A sample numbered version of this form is found on page 221. To complete this form, please fill in the following information:

① Date of Option
② Name of seller
③ Address of seller
④ Name of buyer
⑤ Address of buyer
⑥ Address of property
⑦ City of property
⑧ State of property
⑨ Legal description of property
⑩ Price buyer will pay for option
⑪ Date that option period will end
⑫ Price buyer will pay seller for property if option is exercised
⑬ State whose laws will govern the agreement
⑭ Date of option agreement
⑮ Signature of seller
⑯ Printed name of seller
⑰ Signature of buyer
⑱ Printed name of buyer

In addition, an Agreement to Sell Real Estate covering the property subject to the option to buy should be completed and attached to the option agreement. This contract will provide all of the essential terms of the actual agreement to sell the property.

Offer to Purchase Real Estate: This document is used by a potential buyer of real estate to make an offer to purchase the property. It is *not* a contract or agreement for the purchase of the real estate. It is an offer to pay a certain price for a parcel of real estate, based on the meeting of certain conditions. The conditions that must be met are as follows: The buyer must be able to arrange for suitable financing prior to closing. The buyer must receive a satisfactory termite inspection report. The property to be purchased will be transferred to the buyer free of any debts or liabilities. The parties agree to sign a standard Agreement to Sell Real Estate. The date of the closing is set forth in the Offer. Any other terms that the buyer would like should be included. The Offer is only open for acceptance by the Owner until the time and date set in the Offer. A sample numbered version of this form is found on page 221. To complete this form, please fill in the following information:

① Date of Offer
② Name of buyer

③ Address of buyer
④ Name of owner
⑤ Address of owner
⑥ Address of property
⑦ City of property
⑧ State of property
⑨ Legal description of property
⑩ Purchase price offered for property
⑪ Escrow deposit included with Offer
⑫ Any additional deposit anticipated
⑬ Balance of price due to owner at closing
⑭ Total purchase price
⑮ Amount of mortgage commitment required within 90 days
⑯ Number of monthly payments of mortgage commitment
⑰ Annual interest rate percentage of mortgage commitment
⑱ Date for closing
⑲ Time for closing
⑳ Address for closing
㉑ City for closing
㉒ State for closing
㉓ Any other terms
㉔ Expiration time of Offer
㉕ Expiration date of Offer
㉖ Signature of buyer
㉗ Printed name of buyer
㉘ Date of buyer's signature
㉙ Signature of owner
㉚ Printed name of owner
㉛ Date of owner's signature

Lead Warning Statement: Under the Federal Real Estate Disclosure and Notification Rule, if you are a seller of a residential property that has a home built before 1978, you are required to notify the buyer of the risk of lead exposure and provide them with a copy of the enclosed brochure: "Protect Your Family from Lead in Your Home." In addition, you must disclose your knowledge of any risk of lead hazards in the home. Clauses in the Agreement to Purchase Real Estate, the Contract for Deed, and the Residential Lease forms that are included in this book satisfy the federal requirement. The Lead Warning Statement form explained in this chapter and included on the Forms-on-CD is for use in any real estate transaction for residential property built prior to 1978, for which the main sale or lease document does not already contain the required Lead Warning Statement. A sample numbered version of this form is found on page 224. To complete this form, the following must be done:

① Seller should initial the appropriate choices regarding knowledge of lead paint and/or hazards in the building

② If available, seller should also provide buyer with any records or reports pertaining to lead paint and/or hazards

③ Buyer should initial the appropriate choices regarding receipt of copies of any seller-provided information, receipt of the Federal Lead Brochure (Protect Your Family From Lead in Your Home).

④ Buyer either accepts or waives the right to conduct an inspection of the building within the following 10 days (or any other agreed upon period).

⑤ Date of signing of statement

⑥ Signature of seller (change to Landlord if using this Statement with a lease)

⑦ Printed name of seller (change to Landlord if using this Statement with a lease)

⑧ Signature of buyer (change to Tenant if using this Statement with a lease)

⑨ Printed name of buyer (change to Tenant if using this Statement with a lease)

Federal Lead Brochure: A PDF-format copy of the U.S. EPA's pamphlet, "Protect Your Family from Lead in Your Home," is provided *only* on the included Forms-on-CD. A copy of this brochure must be provided to every potential buyer (or renter) of any residential dwelling that was built prior to 1978.

Appraisal Report: An appraisal of real estate is an impartial evaluation of real estate by a knowledgeable and qualified person after they have performed a careful inspection and study of the property and have used certain techniques to compare the property to other properties. There are three generally-accepted approaches to estimating real estate values. The 'Cost' approach arrives at a value by estimating the replacement value of the property. The 'Market' approach compares the property with similar properties and uses the comparison to determine what the property would sell for on the open market. The 'Income' approach looks at what the net return for a piece of property would be. This approach is generally used for commercial property. Appraisers will use various combinations of these approaches to come to a reasonable estimate of a property's value. Real estate brokers are qualified to perform appraisals and there are professional appraisers who are also qualified. An appraisal report can range from a short 1 or 2 page opinion to a detailed bound document with a survey, photos, plot plans, etc.

The form provided is a simple version of an Appraisal Report and provides that the appraiser certifies that he or she has investigated a certain piece of property and has determined the market value of the property to be a certain amount. The report then provides a list of conditions which the appraiser has used to limit the market determination. A sample numbered version of this form is found on page 255. To complete this form, an appraiser will need to insert the following:

① Date of appraisal
② Name of appraiser
③ Address of appraiser
④ Name of person requesting appraisal
⑤ Address of property appraised
⑥ Legal description of property appraised
⑦ Market value of land only
⑧ Market value of improvements to land
⑨ Total market value
⑩ Qualifications of appraiser
⑪ Signature of appraiser
⑫ Printed name of appraiser

Appraisal Affidavit: An appraisal affidavit provides the basic details of an appraisal that is signed and sworn to before a notary public. This type of document is often required by financing institutions at the closing of a real estate transaction. This documents supplies essentially the same information as the basic Appraisal Report, but in a more formal affidavit. A sample numbered version of this form is found on page 216. To complete this form, the following needs to be completed:

① Date of appraisal
② Name of appraiser
③ Address of appraiser
④ Name of person requesting appraisal
⑤ Address of property appraised
⑥ Legal description of property appraised
⑦ Market value of land only
⑧ Market value of improvements to land
⑨ Total market value
⑩ Qualifications of appraiser
⑪ Signature of appraiser
⑫ Printed name of appraiser
⑬ The following must be completed by a Notary Public

Quitclaim Deed: This form is used to transfer property from the seller (called the *'grantor'* on the deed) to the buyer (called the *'grantee'* on the deed) without any warranties that he or she actually owns the property involved. Any transfers of real estate must be in writing. This type of Quitclaim Deed is intended to be used when the seller is merely selling whatever interest she or he may have in the property. By using a Quitclaim Deed, a seller is not, in any way, guaranteeing that she or he actually owns any interest in the property. This type of Deed may be used to settle any claims that a person may have to a piece of real estate, to settle disputes over property, or to transfer property between co-owners. For this deed form to be recorded, it must be properly notarized. A sample numbered version of this form is found on page 227. **Important Note:** Before relying on the Quitclaim Deed in this chapter, you should always consult an attorney to determine if there are any other requirements that may be required for the Quitclaim Deed to be effective in your jurisdiction. To prepare this Deed, simply fill in the following information:

① Name of person requesting recording of deed (generally, you)
② Name and address of person who prepared the deed
③ Name and address of person to whom the recorded deed should be mailed by the recorder's office (not necessary if you bring the deed to the recorder's office personally)
④ Property Tax Parcel number or Tax account number (generally found on latest tax bill)
⑤ Date of signing deed
⑥ Name of grantor (the one transferring the property)
⑦ Address of grantor
⑧ Name of grantee (the one receiving the property)
⑨ Address of grantee
⑩ Street address of property itself
⑪ Legal description of property (should be taken from current deed)
⑫ Current year for property taxes (taxes will be prorated between grantor and grantee for the portion of the tax year that each party owned the property)
⑬ Date of signing of deed by grantor
⑭ Signature of grantor (signed in the front of notary public)
⑮ Printed Name of grantor
⑯ Signatures and printed names of two witnesses (signed in front of notary public)
⑰ Notary Acknowledgement to be completed by notary public

Warranty Deed: This form is used to transfer property from the seller (called the *'grantor'* in the deed) to a buyer (called the *'grantee'* in the deed) with various standard warranties that he or she actually owns the property involved. Any transfers of real estate must be in writing. This type of Warranty Deed is intended to be used when the seller is selling his or her entire legal interest in the property. By using a Warranty Deed, a seller is guaranteeing that she or he actually owns any interest in the property. This type of deed is used in most real estate situations. It provides that the seller is conveying to the buyer a full and complete title to the land without any restrictions or debts. If the property will be subject to any restrictions or debts, these should be noted in the legal description area provided.

For the transfer to actually take place, the grantor must give the actual deed to the grantee. In addition, in order for this document to be recorded, this form should be properly notarized. A sample numbered version of this form is found on page 229. **Important Note:** Before relying on the Warranty Deed in this chapter, you should always consult an attorney to determine if there are any other requirements that may be required for the Warranty Deed to be effective in your jurisdiction. To prepare this Deed, simply fill in the following information:

① Name of person requesting recording of deed (generally, you)
② Name and address of person who prepared the deed
③ Name and address of person to whom the recorded deed should be mailed by the recorder's office (not necessary if you bring the deed to the recorder's office personally)
④ Property Tax Parcel number or Tax account number (generally found on latest tax bill)
⑤ Date of signing deed
⑥ Name of grantor (the one transferring the property)
⑦ Address of grantor
⑧ Name of grantee (the one receiving the property)
⑨ Address of grantee
⑩ Street address of property itself
⑪ Legal description of property (should be taken from current deed)
⑫ Current year for property taxes (taxes will be prorated between grantor and grantee for the portion of the tax year that each party owned the property)
⑬ Date of signing of deed by grantor
⑭ Signature of grantor (signed in the front of notary public)
⑮ Printed Name of grantor
⑯ Signatures and printed names of two witnesses (signed in front of notary public)
⑰ Notary Acknowledgment to be completed by notary public

Instructions for Disclosure Statements

In addition to the federal requirement to disclose information regarding lead in a home, many states have adopted laws requiring some form of disclosure regarding sales of residential real estate. In general, sales of commercial, industrial, or multi-family residences do not require disclosure statements. In addition, condominiums, vacation properties or time-share properties may require additional disclosures. At press time, 33 states have varying requirements for disclosure regarding residential real estate and all of these except Florida have specific forms. The official state disclosure forms are contained on the Forms-on-CD that accompanied this book. A basic real estate disclosure form is included in this chapter (and on the Forms-on-CD) for the following states that either do not have a specific statutory disclosure requirement or have not provided official forms: Alabama, Arkansas, District of Columbia (Washington D.C.), Florida, Georgia, Hawaii, Kansas, Massachusetts, Minnesota, Missouri, Montana, New Hampshire, New Mexico, North Dakota, Rhode Island, Utah, Vermont, West Virginia, and Wyoming. The states that have official state forms (on the Forms-on-CD) and the names of the forms are listed below (Note: California requires several different disclosure statements):

Alaska: Residential Real Property Transfer Disclosure Statement
Arizona: Affidavit of Disclosure
California: Smoke Detector Statement of Compliance, Military Ordnance Disclosure, Industrial Use Disclosure, Earthquake Hazards, Disclosure, Real Estate Transfer Disclosure Statement, Natural Hazard Disclosure Statement
Colorado: Seller's Property Disclosure
Connecticut: Residential Property Condition Disclosure Report
Delaware: Seller's Disclosure of Real Property Condition Report
Florida: Use the Basic Real Estate Disclosure Form (provided in this book) and the Florida Property Tax Disclosure Summary (not provided)
Idaho: Seller Property Disclosure Form
Illinois: Residential Real Property Disclosure Report
Indiana: Seller's Residential Real Estate Sales Disclosure
Iowa: Residential Property Seller Disclosure Statement
Kentucky: Seller's Disclosure of Property Conditions
Louisiana: Property Disclosure Document for Residential Real Estate, Addendum to Residential Property Disclosure
Maine: Property Disclosure Statement
Maryland: Residential Property Disclosure and Disclaimer Statement
Michigan: Seller's Disclosure Statement
Mississippi: Seller's Disclosure Statement
Nebraska: Seller Property Condition Disclosure Statement
Nevada: Seller's Real Property Disclosure Form
New Jersey: Seller's Property Condition Statement

New York: Property Condition Disclosure Statement
North Carolina: Residential Property Disclosure Statement
Ohio: Residential Property Disclosure Form
Oklahoma: Residential Property Condition Disclosure Statement
Oregon: Seller's Property Disclosure Statement or Statement of Exclusion
Pennsylvania: Seller's Property Disclosure Statement
South Carolina: Residential Property Condition Disclosure Statement
South Dakota: Seller's Property Condition Disclosure Statement
Tennessee: Residential Property Condition Disclosure
Texas: Seller's Disclosure of Property Condition
Virginia: Residential Property Disclosure Statement
Washington: Seller's Residential Property Disclosure Statement
Wisconsin: Real Estate Condition Report

Under the strictest laws, the seller is required to disclose all facts that materially affect the value or desirability of the property which are known or are accessible only to him or her. Please check the Real Estate Laws Appendix for information on any state requirements. Please note that there may also be local or municipal disclosure requirements. You are cautioned to consult a local real estate professional, lawyer, or your state's own statutes to determine if the following form fulfills your state's requirements. The following basic disclosure statement provides a detailed statement regarding most provisions required by most states. The provided statement covers questions relating to ownership of the property, water/sewer issues, possible site problems, possible defects in the home itself, and any prior inspections which may have been performed. The Agreement to Sell Real Estate and the Contract for Deed that are used in this book both contain a paragraph that provides that the seller will provide buyer with a Real Estate Disclosure Statement within five (5) days of the signing of the documents and that the disclosures will be made by the seller concerning the condition of the property and are provided on the basis of the seller's actual knowledge of the property on the date of this disclosure. The agreements also provide that the disclosures are not, in any way, be construed to be a warranty of any kind by the seller.

Basic Real Estate Disclosure Statement: Any seller that uses the included Agreement to Sell Real Estate or Contract for Deed must provide the buyer with a real estate disclosure statement, even if not required by statute in the seller's particular state. For those states that do not have an official disclosure statement, sellers may use the following form. A sample numbered version of this form is found on page 231. To complete the following form, you will need the following information:

① Provide a legal description of the property
② Do you have the legal right to sell this property?
③ Are there any leases or rental agreements?
④ Is there a survey for this property available?

(5) Are there any encroachments or boundary disputes?

(6) Any written easement or rights of way?

(7) Any assessments against the property?

(8) Any zoning or code violations or non-conforming uses?

(9) Any covenants, conditions, or restrictions?

(10) Any legal disputes?

(11) Any liens?

(12) Any planned zoning or use changes?

(13) Any planned changes in adjacent property?

(14) Any landslides or erosion present?

(15) Any landfill or dumps present?

(16) Any hazards or hazardous waste present?

(17) Any soil or drainage problems?

(18) Any fill material present?

(19) Any damage from fire, wind, floods, earthquakes, or landslides?

(20) Any environmental hazards present?

(21) Any storage tanks present?

(22) Any greenbelt or utility easement present?

(23) Is there a homeowner's association? Provide details.

(24) Has the property been flooded?

(25) Is it in a flood plain?

(26) What is the source of household water? Any problems?

(27) If serviced by well, provide details.

(28) Are there any irrigation rights?

(29) Is there an outdoor sprinkler system? Provide details.

(30) What is the sewage disposal system for property? Provide details.

(31) What is the age of roof? Provide details.

(32) Any additions, conversions, or remodeling? Provide details.

(33) What is the age of the home? Provide details.

(34) Are you aware of any defects in the structure or of any other improvements?

(35) Has there been a termite or pest inspection? Provide details.

(36) Has there been a dry rot or structural inspection? Provide details.

(37) Are you aware of any other conditions or defects to the property?

(38) Date of seller's signing of disclosure statement

(39) Signature of seller

(40) Printed name of seller

(41) Signature of seller (second seller if needed)

(42) Printed name of seller (second seller if needed)

(43) Date of buyer's receipt of disclosure statement

(44) Signature of buyer

(45) Printed name of buyer

(46) Signature of buyer (second buyer if needed)

(47) Printed name of buyer (second buyer if needed)

Agreement to Sell Real Estate

This agreement is made on ① _____ , 20 ___ , between

② _____ , seller,

address: ③

and ④ _____ , buyer,

address: ⑤

The seller now owns the following described real estate, located at

⑥ _____ ,City of ⑦ _____ ,

State of ⑧ _____ , and legally described as follows: ⑨

For valuable consideration, the seller agrees to sell and the buyer agrees to buy this property for the following price and on the following terms:

1.   The seller will sell this property to the buyer, free from all claims, liabilities, and indebtedness, unless noted in this agreement.

2.   The following personal property is also included in this sale: ⑩

3.   The buyer agrees to pay the seller the sum of $ ⑪ _____ , which the seller agrees to accept as full payment. This agreement, however, is conditional upon the buyer being able to arrange suitable financing on the following terms at least thirty (30) days prior to the closing date for this agreement: A mortgage in the amount of $ ⑫ _____ , payable in ⑬ _____ monthly payments, with an annual interest rate of ⑭ _____ % (⑮ _____ percent) .

4.   The purchase price will be paid as follows:
      Earnest deposit ....$ ⑯ _____
      Other deposit: ....$ ⑰ _____
      Cash or certified check on closing .....$ ⑱ _____
      (subject to any adjustments or prorations on closing)
      Total Purchase Price ....$ ⑲ _____

5.   The seller acknowledges receiving the earnest money deposit of $ ⑳ _____ _____ from the buyer. If buyer fails to perform this agreement, the seller shall retain this money. If seller fails to perform this agreement, this money shall

be returned to the buyer or the buyer may have the right of specific performance. If buyer is unable to obtain suitable financing at least thirty (30) days prior to closing, then this money will be returned to the buyer without penalty or interest.

6. This agreement will close on ㉑_____ , 20 ___ , at ㉒_____ o'clock ㉓___ . m., at ㉔_____ , City of ㉕_____ , State of ㉖_____ . At that time, and upon payment by the buyer of the portion of the purchase price then due, the seller will deliver to buyer the following documents:

   (a) A Bill of Sale for all personal property
   (b) A Warranty Deed for the real estate
   (c) A Seller's Affidavit of Title
   (d) A closing statement
   (e) Other documents: ㉗

7. At closing, pro-rated adjustments to the purchase price will be made for the following items:

   (a) Utilities
   (b) Property taxes
   (c) The following other items: ㉘

8. The following closing costs will be paid by the seller: ㉙

9. The following closing costs will be paid by the buyer: ㉚

10. Seller represents that it has good and marketable title to the property and will supply the buyer with either an abstract of title or a standard policy of title insurance. Seller further represents that the property is free and clear of any restrictions on transfer, claims, indebtedness, or liabilities except the following:

   (a) Zoning, restrictions, prohibitions, or requirements imposed by any governmental authority
   (b) Any restrictions appearing on the plat of record of the property
   (c) Public utility easements of record
   (d) Other: ㉛

   Seller warrants that there shall be no violations of zoning or building codes as of the date of closing. Seller also warrants that all personal property included in this sale will be delivered in working order on the date of closing.

11. At least thirty (30) days prior to closing, buyer shall have the right to obtain a written report from a licensed termite inspector stating that there is no termite infestation or termite damage to the property. If there is such evidence, seller shall remedy such infestation and/or repair such damage, up to a maximum cost of two (2) percent of the purchase price of the property. If the costs exceed two (2) percent of the purchase price and seller elects not to pay for the costs over two (2) percent, buyer may cancel this agreement and the escrow shall be returned to buyer without penalty or interest.

12. At least thirty (30) days prior to closing, buyer or their agent shall have the right to inspect all heating, air conditioning, electrical, and mechanical systems of the property, the roof and all structural components of the property, and any personal property included in this agreement. If any such systems or equipment are not in working order, seller shall pay for the cost of placing them in working order prior to closing. Buyer or their agent may again inspect the property within forty-eight (48) hours of closing to determine if all systems and equipment are in working order.

13. Between the date of this agreement and the date for closing, the property shall be maintained in the condition as existed on the date of this agreement. If there is any damage by fire, casualty, or otherwise, prior to closing, seller shall restore the property to the condition as existed on the date of this agreement. If seller fails to do so, buyer may:

    (a) accept the property, as is, along with any insurance proceeds due seller,

or

    (b) cancel this agreement and have the escrow deposit returned, without penalty or interest.

14. As required by law, the seller makes the following statement: "Radon gas is a naturally occurring radioactive gas that, when accumulated in sufficient quantities in a building, may present health risks to persons exposed to it. Levels of radon gas that exceed federal and state guidelines have been found in buildings in this state. Additional information regarding radon gas and radon gas testing may be obtained from your county health department."

15. As required by law, the seller makes the following Lead Warning Statement: "Every purchaser of any interest in residential real property on which a residential dwelling was built prior to 1978 is notified that such property may present exposure to lead from lead-based paint that may place young children at risk of developing lead poisoning. Lead poisoning in young children may produce permanent neurological damage, including learning disabilities, reduced intelligence

quotient, behavioral problems, and impaired memory. Lead poisoning also poses a particular threat to pregnant women. The seller of any interest in residential real estate is required to provide the buyer with any information on lead-based paint hazards from risk assessments or inspection in the seller's possession and notify the buyer of any known lead-based paint hazards. A risk assessment or inspection for possible lead-based paint hazards is recommended prior to purchase."

Seller's Disclosure

③② Presence of lead-based paint and/or lead-based paint hazards: (Seller to initial one).

_____ Known lead-based paint and/or lead-based paint hazards are present in building (explain):

_____ Seller has no knowledge of lead-based paint and/or lead-based paint hazards in building.

③③ Records and reports available to seller: (Seller to initial one).

_____ Seller has provided buyer with all available records and reports pertaining to lead-based paint and/or lead-based paint hazards are present in building (list documents):

_____ Seller has no records and reports pertaining to lead-based paint and/or lead-based paint hazards in building.

Buyer's Acknowledgment

③④(Buyer to initial all applicable).

_____ Buyer has received copies of all information listed above.

_____ Buyer has received the pamphlet "Protect Your Family From Lead in Your Home."

_____ Buyer has received a ten (10)-day opportunity (or mutually agreed-on period) to conduct a risk assessment or inspection for the presence of lead-based paint and/or lead-based paint hazards in building.

_____ Buyer has waived the opportunity to conduct a risk assessment or inspection for the presence of lead-based paint and/or lead-based paint hazards in building.

The seller and buyer have reviewed the information above and certify, by their signatures at the end of this agreement, that to the best of their knowledge, the information they have provided is true and accurate.

16. Seller agrees to provide Buyer with a Real Estate Disclosure Statement (or its equivalent that is acceptable in the State in which the property is located) within five (5) days of the signing of this Agreement. Upon receipt of the Real Estate Disclosure Statement from Seller, Buyer shall have five (5) business days within which to rescind this Agreement by providing Seller with a written and signed statement rescinding this Agreement. The disclosures in the Real Estate Disclosure Statement are made by the seller concerning the condition of the property and are provided on the basis of the seller's actual knowledge of the property on the date of this disclosure. These disclosures are not the representations of any real estate agent or other party. The disclosures themselves are not intended to be a part of any written agreement between the buyer and seller. In addition, the disclosure shall not, in any way, be construed to be a warranty of any kind by the seller.

17. The parties also agree to the following additional terms: ㉟

18. No modification of this agreement will be effective unless it is in writing and is signed by both the buyer and seller. This agreement binds and benefits both the buyer and seller and any successors. Time is of the essence of this agreement. This document, including any attachments, is the entire agreement between the buyer and seller. This agreement is governed by the laws of the State of ㊱_____ .

㊲_____
Signature of Seller

㊳_____
Printed Name of Seller

㊴_____
Signature of Witness for Seller

㊵_____
Printed Name of Witness for Seller

㊶_____
Signature of Witness for Seller

㊷_____
Printed Name of Witness for Seller

㊸_____
Signature of Buyer

㊹_____
Printed Name of Buyer

㊺_____
Signature of Witness for Buyer

㊻_____
Printed Name of Witness for Buyer

㊼_____
Signature of Witness for Buyer

㊽_____
Printed Name of Witness for Buyer

Contract For Deed

This contract is made on ①_____ , 20 ____ , between ②_____ , seller, address: ③
and ④_____ , buyer, address: ⑤

The seller now owns the following described real estate, located at ⑥_____
_____ , City of ⑦_____ , State of ⑧_____ :
and legally described as follows: ⑨

For valuable consideration, the seller agrees to sell and the buyer agrees to buy this property for the following price and on the following terms:

1.   The seller agrees to sell this property to the buyer, free from all claims, liabilities, and indebtedness, unless noted in this contract.

2.   The following personal property is also included in this sale: ⑩

3.   The buyer agrees to pay the seller the sum of $ ⑪_____ , which the seller agrees to accept as full payment, such total purchase price includes interest as noted below in Paragraph #4.

4.   The purchase price will be paid as follows:
      Total Purchase Price ....$ ⑫_____
      Less Down Payment ....$ ⑬_____
      Balance Due ....$ ⑭_____
      (subject to any adjustments or prorations on closing)

      Balance Due will be paid in ⑮_____ equal monthly payments of $ ⑯_____ each, until the Balance is paid in full. The monthly payments will be due and payable on the ⑰_____ day of each month, beginning on ⑱ _____
20____ . The total purchase price includes principal and interest of ⑲_____
% (percent) per year on the unpaid balance. The balance due under this contract is prepayable at any time, in whole or in part, without penalty

5.   The seller acknowledges receiving the down payment of $ ⑳ _____
from the buyer.

6. If buyer fails to perform any duties under this contract, including the failure to make any of the required payments within 30 days of when such payment is due, this contact shall be forfeited and terminated 30 days after the receipt by the buyer of a Declaration of Intent to Forfeit and Terminate Contract for Deed, which shall be sent to the buyer via Certified U.S. Mail. During the 30-day period after the receipt of this Declaration, Buyer shall have the right to cure the default. If the default is not satisfied within the 30-day period, then on the 31st day after receipt of the Declaration, Buyer shall forfeit all monies paid to the Seller under the Contract for Deed and Buyer shall immediately vacate the property. Seller shall, on that date, have the right to reenter and take full possession of the property, without being liable for any action or any costs incurred by the Buyer. Upon termination of this contract by the seller, the seller shall retain all money paid by the buyer to the seller as accumulated rent for the property.

7. If seller fails to perform this contract, all money paid to the seller by the buyer shall be returned to the buyer or, at buyer's option, the buyer may have the right of specific performance, including the performance by the seller of delivering a warranty deed to the buyer for full title to the property.

8. All closing costs will be paid by the buyer: Upon payment by the buyer of the entire purchase price when due and the fulfillment of all other contracts under this contract by the buyer, the seller will deliver to buyer the following documents:

   (a) A Bill of Sale for all personal property included in this sale
   (b) A Warranty Deed for the real estate
   (c) A Seller's Affidavit of Title
   (d) A closing statement
   (e) Other documents: ㉑

9. The buyer agrees to pay all property taxes and assessments against the property beginning with the tax year of ㉒_____.

10. Seller represents that it has good and marketable title to the property and, on request, will supply the buyer with an abstract of title. Seller further represents that the property is free and clear of any restrictions on transfer, claims, indebtedness, or liabilities except the following:
   (a) Zoning, restrictions, prohibitions, or requirements imposed by any governmental authority
   (b) Any restrictions appearing on the plat of record of the property
   (c) Public utility easements of record
   (d) Other: ㉓

Seller warrants that there shall be no violations of zoning or building codes as of the date of this contract. Seller also warrants that all personal property included in this sale has been delivered to the buyer in working order.

11. Between the date of this contract and the date for closing, the property shall be maintained by the buyer in the condition as existed on the date of this contract. In addition, if there is a structure on this property as of the date of this contract, the buyer agrees to maintain both general liability insurance and property insurance in the amount of the balance due under this contract, as specified in Paragraph #4 of this contract, naming the seller as owner of the property and recipient of all insurance settlements, If there is any damage by fire, casualty, or otherwise, prior to closing, buyer shall restore the property to the condition as existed on the date of this contract, and buyer shall be have the right to use any casualty or fire insurance proceeds for such restoration. If buyer fails to do so within a reasonable time, seller may declare this contract forfeit and terminated.

12. As required by law, the seller makes the following statement: "Radon gas is a naturally occurring radioactive gas that, when accumulated in sufficient quantities in a building, may present health risks to persons exposed to it. Levels of radon gas that exceed federal and state guidelines have been found in buildings in this state. Additional information regarding radon gas and radon gas testing may be obtained from your county health department."

13. As required by law, the seller makes the following Lead Warning Statement: "Every purchaser of any interest in residential real property on which a residential dwelling was built prior to 1978 is notified that such property may present exposure to lead from lead-based paint that may place young children at risk of developing lead poisoning. Lead poisoning in young children may produce permanent neurological damage, including learning disabilities, reduced intelligence quotient, behavioral problems, and impaired memory. Lead poisoning also poses a particular threat to pregnant women. The seller of any interest in residential real estate is required to provide the buyer with any information on lead-based paint hazards from risk assessments or inspection in the seller's possession and notify the buyer of any known lead-based paint hazards. A risk assessment or inspection for possible lead-based paint hazards is recommended prior to purchase."

Seller's Disclosure

㉔Presence of lead-based paint and/or lead-based paint hazards: (Seller to initial one).

_____ Known lead-based paint and/or lead-based paint hazards are present in building (explain):

_____ Seller has no knowledge of lead-based paint and/or lead-based paint hazards in building.

㉕ Records and reports available to seller: (Seller to initial one).

_____ Seller has provided buyer with all available records and reports pertaining to lead-based paint and/or lead-based paint hazards are present in building (list documents):

_____ Seller has no records and reports pertaining to lead-based paint and/or lead-based paint hazards in building.

Buyer's Acknowledgment

㉖ (Buyer to initial all applicable).

_____ Buyer has received copies of all information listed above.

_____ Buyer has received the pamphlet "Protect Your Family From Lead in Your Home."

_____ Buyer has received a ten (10)-day opportunity (or mutually agreed-on period) to conduct a risk assessment or inspection for the presence of lead-based paint and/or lead-based paint hazards in building.

_____ Buyer has waived the opportunity to conduct a risk assessment or inspection for the presence of lead-based paint and/or lead-based paint hazards in building.

The seller and buyer have reviewed the information above and certify, by their signatures at the end of this contract, that to the best of their knowledge, the information they have provided is true and accurate.

14. Seller agrees to provide Buyer with a Real Estate Disclosure Statement (or its equivalent that is acceptable in the State in which the property is located) within five (5) days of the signing of this Agreement. Upon receipt of the Real Estate Disclosure Statement from Seller, Buyer shall have five (5) business days within which to rescind this Agreement by providing Seller with a written and signed statement rescinding this Agreement. The disclosures in the Real Estate Disclosure Statement are made by the seller concerning the condition of the property and are provided on the basis of the seller's actual knowledge of the property on the date of this disclosure. These disclosures are not the representations of any real estate agent or other party. The disclosures themselves are not intended to be a part of

any written agreement between the buyer and seller. In addition, the disclosure shall not, in any way, be construed to be a warranty of any kind by the seller

15. The parties also agree to the following additional terms: ㉗

16. The buyer and seller agree that this contract or any assignment of this contract may not be recorded without the express written permission of the seller. If this contract is recorded contrary to the above provision, then any existing balance shall become immediately due and payable.

17. Buyer agrees that any construction on this property be limited to residences built of new materials and that all construction comply with all applicable building, health and zoning codes and laws.

18. No modification of this contract will be effective unless it is in writing and is signed by both the buyer and seller. No assignment of this contract by buyer will be effective without the written permission of the seller. This contract binds and benefits both the buyer and seller and any successors. Time is of the essence of this contract. This document, including any attachments, is the entire contract between the buyer and seller. This contract is governed by the laws of the State of ㉘_____ .

㉙_____
Signature of Seller

㉚_____
Printed Name of Seller

㉛_____
Signature of Witness for Seller

㉜_____
Printed Name of Witness for Seller

㉝_____
Signature of Witness for Seller

㉞_____
Printed Name of Witness for Seller

㉟_____
Signature of Buyer

㊱_____
Printed Name of Buyer

㊲_____
Signature of Witness for Buyer

㊳_____
Printed Name of Witness for Buyer

㊴_____
Signature of Witness for Buyer

㊵_____
Printed Name of Witness for Buyer

DECLARATION OF INTENT TO FORFEIT AND TERMINATE CONTRACT FOR DEED

Under the terms of the Contract for Deed, dated ①_____, 20_____
which exists between ② _____, seller
address: ③

and ④_____ , buyer,
address: ⑤

The seller now owns the following described real estate, located at
⑥_____ , City of _____ , State of _____:
and legally described as follows: ⑦

The seller declares that as of the date of ⑧_____, 20 _____,
Buyer is in default of this Contract for Deed for the following reasons: ⑨

Due to this default, Seller declares the existing Contract for Deed between Seller and Buyer to be forfeit and terminated 30 days after the receipt of this Declaration by the Buyer. Seller shall send a copy of this Declaration to Buyer at the above address, via Certified U.S. Mail, on the date of ⑩_____,
20 _____.

During the 30-day period after the receipt of this Declaration, Buyer shall have the right to cure the default noted above. If the default is not satisfied within the 30-day period, then on the 31st day after receipt of this Declaration, Buyer shall forfeit all monies paid to the Seller under the Contract for Deed and shall immediately vacate the property. Seller shall, on that date, have the right to reenter and take full possession of the property, without being liable for any action or any costs incurred by the Buyer.

Dated: ⑪_____

⑫_____
Signature of Seller
⑬_____
Printed Name of Seller

Option to Buy Real Estate

This option agreement is made on ①_____ , 20 ___ , between ②_____ , seller, address: ③
and ④_____ , buyer,
address: ⑤

The seller now owns the following described real estate, located at ⑥_____
_____ , City of ⑦_____ , State of ⑧_____ , and legally described as follows: ⑨

For valuable consideration, the seller agrees to give the buyer an exclusive option to buy this property for the following price and on the following terms:

1.   The buyer will pay the seller $ ⑩_____ for this option. This amount will be credited against the purchase price of the property if this option is exercised by the buyer. If the option is not exercised, the seller will retain this payment.
2.   The option period will be from the date of this agreement until ⑪_____ , 20 ___ , at which time it will expire unless exercised.
3.   During this period, the buyer has the option and exclusive right to buy the seller's property mentioned above for the purchase price of $ ⑫_____ . The buyer must notify the seller, in writing, of the decision to exercise this option.
4.   Attached to this Option Agreement is a completed Agreement to Sell Real Estate. If the buyer notifies the seller, in writing, of the decision to exercise the option within the option period, the seller and buyer agree to sign the Agreement to Sell Real Estate and complete the sale on the terms contained in the Agreement.
5.   No modification of this Option Agreement will be effective unless it is in writing and is signed by both the buyer and seller. This Option Agreement binds and benefits both the buyer and seller and any successors. Time is of the essence of this Option Agreement. This document, including any attachments, is the entire agreement between the buyer and seller. This Option Agreement is governed by the laws of the State of ⑬_____ .

Dated ⑭_____

⑮_____   ⑯_____
Signature of Seller   Signature of Buyer
⑰_____   ⑱_____
Printed Name of Seller   Printed Name of Buyer

Offer to Purchase Real Estate

This offer is made on ①_____ 20 _____ , by ②_____ , buyer,
address: ③
to ④_____ , owner,
address: ⑤

The owner now owns the following described real estate, located at ⑥ _____ ,
City of ⑦_____ , State of ⑧_____ , and legally
described as follows: ⑨

The buyer offers to purchase the above property under the following terms:

The following price is offered for the property: $ ⑩_____
Escrow deposit paid to the Owner with this Offer: $ ⑪_____
Further deposit to Owner upon signing of Sales Agreement: $ ⑫_____
Balance due at closing: $ ⑬_____
Total purchase price: $ ⑭_____

This Offer is conditioned on the following terms:

1. This Offer is conditional upon the Buyer being able to arrange a firm
commitment for suitable financing on the following terms within ninety (90)
days of acceptance of this Offer by the Owner:

Mortgage amount: $ ⑮_____
Term of Mortgage: ⑯_____ monthly payments
Interest rate of Mortgage: ⑰_____% (percent) per annum

2. This offer is conditional upon the Buyer obtaining a satisfactory termite report
and upon a satisfactory inspection of the property by Buyer within ninety (90)
days of acceptance of this Offer by the Owner.

3. Property will be sold free and clear of all encumbrances and with good and
marketable title.

4. The parties agree to execute a standard Agreement to Sell Real Estate within
ninety (90) days of acceptance of this Offer by the Owner.

5. The closing for this sale shall occur on or before ⑱_____ , at ⑲_____ m. , at ⑳_____ , City of ㉑_____ , State of ㉒_____.

6. Other terms: ㉓

7. This Offer shall remain open until ㉔_____m. , on ㉕_____.
If not accepted by the Owner by this time, this Offer is rescinded and the deposit money shall be returned.

㉖_____   ㉗_____
Signature of Buyer   Date signed

㉘_____
Printed Name of Buyer

㉙_____   ㉚_____
Signature of Owner   Date Signed

㉛_____
Printed Name of Owner

Lead Warning Statement

Every purchaser of any interest in residential real property on which a residential dwelling was built prior to 1978 is notified that such property may present exposure to lead from lead-based paint that may place young children at risk of developing lead poisoning. Lead poisoning in young children may produce permanent neurological damage, including learning disabilities, reduced intelligence quotient, behavioral problems, and impaired memory. Lead poisoning also poses a particular threat to pregnant women. The seller of any interest in residential real estate is required to provide the buyer with any information on lead-based paint hazards from risk assessments or inspection in the seller's possession and notify the buyer of any known lead-based paint hazards. A risk assessment or inspection for possible lead-based paint hazards is recommended prior to purchase. Initial your correct choices.

① SELLER'S DISCLOSURE
Presence of lead-based paint and/or lead-based paint hazards: (Seller to initial one).
_____ Known lead-based paint and/or lead-based paint hazards are present in building (explain). ②
_____ Seller has no knowledge of lead-based paint and/or lead-based paint hazards in building.

RECORDS AND REPORTS AVAILABLE TO SELLER: (Seller to initial one).
_____ Seller has provided Buyer with all available records and reports pertaining to lead-based paint and/or lead-based paint hazards that are present in building (list documents). ②
_____ Seller has no records and reports pertaining to lead-based paint and/or lead-based paint hazards in building.

③ BUYER'S ACKNOWLEDGMENT (Buyer to initial all applicable).
_____ Buyer has received copies of all information listed above.
_____ Buyer has received the pamphlet "Protect Your Family From Lead in Your Home."
④_____ Buyer has received a 10-day opportunity (or mutually-agreed on period) to conduct a risk assessment or inspection for the presence of lead-based paint and/or lead-based paint hazards in building.
④_____ Buyer has waived the opportunity to conduct a risk assessment or inspection for the presence of lead-based paint and/or lead-based paint hazards in building.

Dated: ⑤_____

⑥_____   ⑧_____
Signature of Seller   Signature of Buyer
⑦_____   ⑨_____
Printed Name of Seller   Printed Name of Buyer

Appraisal Report

This Appraisal Report is made on ① _____ , 20 _____ , by ② _____ , Appraiser, address: ③ _____ .

Appraiser states that at the request of ④ _____ , who employed him/her to appraise the property commonly known as ⑤ _____ _____ , and whose legal description is: ⑥

and after a careful and thorough inspection of the property and to the best of his or her knowledge, it is the professional opinion of the Appraiser that the market value of the property is as follows:

Land	$ ⑦	_____
Improvements	$ ⑧	_____
Total Market Value	$ ⑨	_____

The physical conditions of the improvements are based on a visual inspection only and no liability is assumed for the soundness of the structure as no engineering test were done or requested. Appraiser also states that he or she has no financial interest whatsoever in the property, and that his or her findings are in no way contingent upon the payment that he or she is to receive for making the appraisal, and that he or she is qualified to make the appraisal for the following reasons: ⑩

⑪ _____   ⑫ _____
Signature of Appraiser   Printed Name of Appraiser

225

Appraisal Affidavit

This Appraisal Affidavit is made on ①_____ , 20 _____ , by ②_____
_____ , Appraiser, address: ③_____.

Appraiser states that, at the request of ④_____,
who employed him/her to appraise the property commonly known as ⑤_____
_____, and whose legal description is: ⑥

and that after a careful and thorough inspection of the property and to the best
of his or her knowledge, it is the professional opinion of the Appraiser that the
market value of the property is as follows:

Land	$ ⑦	_____
Improvements	$ ⑧	_____
Total Market Value	$ ⑨	_____

Appraiser also states that he or she has no financial interest whatsoever in the
property, and that his or her findings are in no way contingent upon the payment
that he or she is to receive for making the appraisal, and that he or she is qualified to make the appraisal for the following reasons: ⑩

⑪_____   ⑫_____
Signature of Appraiser   Printed Name of Appraiser

⑬ State of _____
    County of _____

On _____ , 20 _____ , _____
personally came before me and, being duly sworn, did state that he or she is
the person described in the above document and that he or she signed the above
document in my presence.

_____
Signature of Notary Public
Notary Public, In and for the County of _____
State of _____

My commission expires: _____   Notary Seal

Recording requested by: ① _____   Space above reserved for Recorder
Document prepared by: When recorded, mail to:
Name ② _____   Name ③ _____
Address _____   Address _____

Quitclaim Deed

Property Tax Parcel/Account Number: ④ _____

This Quitclaim Deed is made on ⑤ _____ , 20 _____ , between
⑥ _____ , grantor, address: ⑦ _____
_____

and ⑧_____ , grantee, address: ⑨ _____
_____.

For valuable consideration, the grantor hereby quitclaims and transfers all right, title, and interest held by the Grantor in the following described real estate to the grantee, and his or her heirs or assigns, to have and hold forever, located at ⑩ _____ , City of _____ , State of _____ , and described as follows: ⑪

Subject to all easements, rights of way, protective covenants, and mineral reservations of record, if any. Taxes for the Tax year of ⑫ _____ shall be prorated between the Grantor and Grantee as of the date of recording this deed.

Dated:⑬ _____ , 20 _____

⑭_____   ⑮_____
Signature of Grantor   Printed Name of Grantor

⑯_____   ⑯_____
Signature of Witness 1   Printed Name of Witness 1

⑯_____   ⑯_____
Signature of Witness 2   Printed Name of Witness 2

⑰ **Notary Acknowledgement**

State of _____
County of _____

On _____ , 20 _____ , _____ personally came before me, is person-
ally known to me or has proved his or her identity to me on the basis of satisfactory evidence, and, being duly sworn, did
state that he or she is the person described in the above document and that he or she signed the above document in my
presence.

_____
Signature of Notary Public
Notary Public, In and for the County of _____
State of _____
My commission expires: _____   Notary Seal

Recording requested by: ① _____
Document prepared by:
Name ② _____
Address _____

Space above reserved for Recorder
When recorded, mail to:
Name ③ _____
Address _____

Warranty Deed

Property Tax Parcel/Account Number: ④ _____

This Warranty Deed is made on ⑤ _____ , 20 _____ , between
⑥ _____ , grantor, address: ⑦ _____
_____

and ⑧_____ , grantee, address: ⑨ _____
_____ .

For valuable consideration, the Grantor hereby sells, grants, and conveys the following described real estate, in fee simple, to the Grantee to have and hold forever, along with all easements, rights, and buildings belonging to the described property, located at ⑩ _____ , City of _____ , State of _____ , and described as follows: ⑪

The Grantor warrants that it is lawful owner and has full right to convey the property, and that the property is free from all claims, liabilities, or indebtedness, and that the Grantor and its successors will warrant and defend title to the Grantee against the lawful claims of all persons. Taxes for the tax year of ⑫_____ shall be prorated between the Grantor and Grantee as of the date of recording of this deed.

Dated:⑬ _____ , 20 _____

⑭_____
Signature of Grantor

⑮_____
Printed Name of Grantor

⑯_____
Signature of Witness 1

⑯_____
Printed Name of Witness 1

⑯_____
Signature of Witness 2

⑯_____
Printed Name of Witness 2

⑰ **Notary Acknowledgement**

State of _____
County of _____

On _____ , 20 _____ , _____ personally came before me, is personally known to me or has proved his or her identity to me on the basis of satisfactory evidence, and, being duly sworn, did state that he or she is the person described in the above document and that he or she signed the above document in my presence.

_____
Signature of Notary Public
Notary Public, In and for the County of _____
State of _____
My commission expires: _____   Notary Seal

Real Estate Disclosure Statement

Notice to the Buyer:

The following disclosures are made by the seller concerning the condition of the property and are provided on the basis of the seller's actual knowledge of the property on the date of this disclosure. These disclosures are not the representations of any real estate agent or other party. These disclosures are not intended to be a part of any written agreement between the buyer and seller. Unless you have waived the right of cancellation in your real estate sales agreement, you have five (5) business days from the date you receive this disclosure form to cancel your agreement by delivering to the seller a separate signed statement canceling your agreement. For a more comprehensive examination of this property, you are advised to obtain the services of a qualified specialists to inspect the property on your behalf. Examples of specialists are: architects, engineers, surveyors, plumbers, electricians, roofers, or real estate inspection services. The buyer and seller may wish to provide appropriate provisions in the sales agreement regarding any defects, repairs, or warranties. This disclosure shall not be construed to be a warranty of any kind by the seller.

This disclosure concerns the following property: (1)

This disclosure is intended to satisfy the real estate disclosure requirements of the state in which this property is located. If additional information is required, I have attached an explanation or information to this statement and intend that such attachments be considered as part of this disclosure statement.

YES or NO

1. Do you have legal authority to sell this property? (2)
2. Is the title to this property subject to any leases or rental agreements?
    a. If yes, explain: (3)
3. Is there a boundary survey available for this property?
    b. If yes, explain (4)
4. Are you aware of any of the following:
    If yes to any, please explain on an attachment.
    a. Encroachments or boundary disputes? (5)
    b. Any written agreements for easements or rights of way? (6)
    c. Pending or existing assessments against the property? (7)

d. Zoning or building code violations, or non-conforming uses? ⑧
e. Covenants, conditions, or restrictions that affect the property? ⑨
f. Any pending or anticipated legal disputes concerning the property? ⑩
g. Any liens against the property? ⑪
h. Any major changes planned in neighborhood zoning or uses? ⑫
i. Any planned or anticipated changes in adjacent properties? ⑬
j. Any landslides or erosion on this or adjacent property? ⑭
k. Any landfills or dumps within one mile of the property? ⑮
l. Any hazards or hazardous materials on or near the property? ⑯
m. Any soil settling, standing water, or drainage problems on the property? ⑰
n. Any fill material in or under the property? ⑱
o. Any damage to property from fire, wind, floods, earthquakes, or landslides? ⑲
p. Any environmental hazards on or near the property? ⑳
q. Any underground or aboveground storage tanks on the property? ㉑
r. Any greenbelt or utility easements affecting the property? ㉒

5. Is there a Home Owners' Association? ㉓
    a. If yes, the name of it is:
    b. Are there any regular assessments?
        Amount: $
    c. Are there any pending special assessments?
    d. Are there any association or other joint maintenance agreements?
        If yes, explain or attach:

6. Has the property ever been flooded? ㉔

7. Is the property within a designated flood plain or flood way? ㉕

8. The source of household water is: ㉖
    a. Are there any water pressure problems?

9. If the property is serviced by a water well: ㉗
    a. Is the well solely owned or shared?
    b. Are there any written agreements regarding well usage?
        If yes, explain or attach:
    c. Are there any known problems or repairs needed?
    d. Does the well provide adequate year-round water supply?
    e. Has water been tested recently?
    f. Is water treated before use?

10. Are there any irrigation water rights for the property? ㉘
11. Is there an outdoor sprinkler system for the property? ㉙
      a. Are there any defects in the system?

12. The sewage disposal system for this property is: ㉚
      a. Are there any known problems with this system?
      b. Do all plumbing fixtures, including floor or laundry drains, go to this system?
      c. If a septic tank system, when was it last pumped?
      d. If a septic tank system, when was it last inspected?
      e. If a septic tank system, is the drainfield located entirely on this property?
      f. If a septic tank system, was it approved and is the permit available?

13. What is the approximate age of the roof? ㉛
      a. Is there a roof warranty? If yes, explain or attach:
      b. If yes, is the warranty transferable?
      c. Does the roof leak?
      d. Has the roof ever been repaired?

14. Have there been any additions, conversions, or remodeling of the property? ㉜
      a. If yes, were all building permits and inspections obtained?

15. What is the age of the house? ㉝
      a. Has there been any settling or sliding of the house or any other structures?

16. Are you aware of any defects in any of the following: ㉞
      If yes to any, explain:
      a. Foundations?
      b. Decks or patios?
      c. Exterior walls?
      d. Chimneys and fireplaces?
      e. Interior walls?
      f. Fire alarms and smoke detectors?
      g. Windows or doors?
      h. Pools, hot tubs, or saunas?
      i. Sidewalks?
      j. Garage?
      k. Floors or walkways?

 l. Wood stoves? .
 m. Electrical system?
 n. Plumbing system?
 o. Hot water tanks?
 p. Garbage disposal?
 q. Appliances?
 r. Sump pump?
 s. Heating and cooling system?
 t. Security system?
 u. Other (explain)?

17. Has a termite and/or pest inspection been performed recently? ㉟
 a. If yes, when:

18. Has a dry rot or structural inspection been performed recently? ㊱
 a. If yes, when:

19. Are you aware of any other conditions or defects which affect this property?
㊲

The foregoing answers and attached explanations (if any) are complete and correct to the best of my knowledge on the date signed. I authorize all of my real estate licensees or agents to deliver a copy of this disclosure statement to other real estate licensees or agents and to all prospective buyers of the property.

㊳_____
Date of Seller's signing

㊴_____
Signature of Seller

㊵_____
Printed Name of Seller

㊶_____
Signature of Seller

㊷_____
Printed Name of Seller

Buyer's Acknowledgment

1. As buyer, I acknowledge my duty to pay diligent attention to any material defects which are known to me or can be known to me by using diligent attention and observation.

2. I understand that the disclosures set forth in this statement and any amendments and attachments are made only by the seller.

3. I hereby acknowledge receipt of a copy of this disclosure statement and any attachments bearing seller's signature.

Unless you have waived the right of cancellation in your real estate sales agreement, you have five (5) business days from the date you receive this disclosure form to cancel your agreement by delivering to the seller a separate signed statement canceling your agreement.

㊸_____
Date of receipt by Buyer

㊹_____
Signature of Buyer

㊺_____
Printed Name of Buyer

㊻_____
Signature of Buyer

㊼_____
Printed Name of Buyer

Chapter 11

Forms for Hiring Employees

In this chapter, there are various forms which are intended to be used to hire employees or independent contractors for work. An application for employment is the first step in the hiring process. After an applicant has completed an application, their references may need to be checked; an easy task using the Verification of Job References form. It may be wise to have an applicant sign the Consent to Release Employment Information. After the references have been verified, generally, an interview will take place. Finally, a hiring decision is made. When an applicant is offered a job, two additional forms are provided, depending on the type of job that the applicant is hired to perform. They may be hired as an 'employee' and an employee contract is provided for this situation.

The employment contract contained in this chapter may be used and adapted for virtually any employment situation. Of course, it is perfectly legal to hire an employee without a contract at all. In many businesses, this is common practice. However, as job skills and salaries rise and as employees are allowed access to sensitive and confidential business information, written employment contracts are often prudent business practice. They may also be hired as an 'independent contractor.' As opposed to an employee, this type of worker is defined as one who maintains his or her own independent business, uses his or her own tools, and does not work under the direct supervision of the person who has hired him or her. An agreement to this effect is provided.

A successful new hire must also complete an IRS Form W-4: Employee Withholding Allowance Certificate, noting their preference for federal income tax withholding. Two additional federal government forms are necessary to be completed by the employer for each new hire: an immigration eligibility form (USCIS Form I-9:

Employee Eligibility Verification) and a form that notifies multiple states of each new hire for possible child support purposes (Federal Multi-State Employer Notification Form for New Hires). These forms are provided in this book as samples only and can be obtained through the U.S. Citizenship and Immigration Services (USCIS) website (**www.uscis.org**) or the U.S. Internal Revenue Service (IRS) website (**www.irs.gov**).

In the event that an applicant is not hired, a model rejection letter is included. There is, additionally, a rejection letter that may be used for unsolicited applicants who may have sent a resume to your company.

Several other forms are provided for specific situations that may require that a new employee agree to certain conditions, such as confidentiality or agreeing not to compete after leaving employment. Finally, two forms are provided that deal with payroll situations: a form requesting direct paycheck deposit into an employee's bank and a form consenting to certain payroll deductions, such as retirement, union dues, etc.

Employer Hiring Checklist

- ❏ IRS Form SS-4: Application for Employer Identification Number
- ❏ Application for Employment
- ❏ Consent to Release Employment Information
- ❏ Verification of Job References
- ❏ Job Description Form
- ❏ Job Applicant Rejection Letter
- ❏ Unsolicited Applicant Rejection Letter
- ❏ Employment Contract
- ❏ Independent Contractor Agreement
- ❏ IRS Form W-4: Employee Withholding Certificate
- ❏ USCIS Form I-9: Employee Eligibility Verification
- ❏ Federal Multi-State Employer Notification Form for New Hires
- ❏ Employee Confidentiality Agreement
- ❏ Employee Patents and Inventions Agreement
- ❏ Employee Agreement Not to Compete
- ❏ Employee Request for Direct Deposit of Paycheck
- ❏ Employee Consent to Payroll Deductions

Instructions for Forms for Hiring Employees

Sample IRS Form SS-4: Application for Employer Identification Number: Employers can obtain the official IRS form by going to www.irs.gov or visiting your local government office for forms. A sample form is provided on the Forms-on-CD.

Application for Employment: This form may be used for any job applicant. This application provides notice that the employer is an equal opportunity employer and that the application will be considered without discrimination. A sample numbered version of this form is found on page 246. Although very basic, this application provides that an applicant complete the following information:

1. Applicant's name and address and phone number
2. Applicant's Social Security and driver's license numbers
3. Job applying for and date available
4. Applicant's special training or skills
5. Applicant's educational level with dates and places of attendance
6. Applicant's previous employer's addresses and phone numbers
7. Applicant's prior positions and reasons for leaving
8. Name, address, and phone of personal references
9. Applicant's emergency notification information
10. Any additional information by applicant
11. Certification of applicant of truth and authorization for references to release information
12. Signature of applicant

The employer then has room on the application to include the following information:

13. Name of person interviewing applicant
14. Name of person verifying applicant's references
15. Hiring decision and notification of hiring or rejection sent
16. Date applicant to start work and rate of pay, if hired

Consent to Release Employment Information: This form is used to obtain an applicant's consent to authorize a previous employer to release past job records regarding the applicant. Although the job application in this chapter includes an authorization, some previous employer's may require a separate form for this purpose. A sample numbered version of this form is found on page 248. To complete this form, have the applicant complete the following information:

① Name of applicant
② Address of applicant
③ Name of former employer
④ Address of former employer
⑤ Name of potential employer
⑥ Address of potential employer
⑦ Date of consent
⑧ Signature of applicant
⑨ Printed name of applicant

Verification of Job References: The following form may be used as a template for verifying the personal, educational, and employment references that an applicant has provided on his or her job application. A sample numbered version of this form is found on page 249. To complete this form, fill in the following information:

① Name of applicant
② Description of job applied for
③ Phone number of high school named by applicant and date called
④ Verification of high school graduation
⑤ Phone number of college named by applicant and date called
⑥ Verification of college attendance/graduation
⑦ Phone number of former employers
⑧ Verification of employment dates, position held, rate of pay, and reason for leaving and date called
⑨ Phone number of personal references and date called
⑩ Verification of personal references
⑪ Decision regarding clearance for hiring based on references
⑫ Date of form completion
⑬ Signature of person completing form

Job Description Form: This form is intended to be used by an employer to describe the actual details of a particular job that needs to be filled. Its purpose is to provide both the employer and the employee with a clear picture of the duties and relationships that apply to the particular job. The form details the major and minor duties that the employee will perform and the 'chain of command' of the job position. A sample numbered version of this form is found on page 250. To complete this form, fill in the following information:

① Date form was prepared
② Name of person preparing form
③ Title of person preparing form

④ Department of person preparing form
⑤ Name of person approving form
⑥ Title of job
⑦ Who person filling job will report to
⑧ Short description of job
⑨ List the major responsibilities of job holder
⑩ List minor duties of job holder
⑪ Name of department head for department which contains this job
⑫ Name of direct supervisor of this job position
⑬ Descriptions of personnel who are supervised by job holder

Job Applicant Rejection Letter: This letter is intended to be used by an employer to notify a job applicant that they have not been hired. Although this form is provided on the Forms-on-CD as a PDF document, you may wish to use the text version of this form and cut and paste this letter onto your company's own letterhead. A sample numbered version of this form is found on page 251. To complete this letter, fill in the following information:

① Date letter was prepared
② Name and address of job applicant
③ Name of applicant
④ Signature of person sending letter
⑤ Printed name of person sending letter

Unsolicited Resume Rejection Letter: This letter is intended to be used by an employer to notify a person that has sent an unsolicited resume to your company that they have not been hired. Although this form is provided on the Forms-on-CD as a PDF document, you may wish to use the text version of this form and cut and paste this letter onto your company's own letterhead. You should include the unsolicited resume in the envelope with this letter. A sample numbered version of this form is found on page 252. To complete this letter, fill in the following information:

① Date letter was prepared
② Name and address of unsolicited applicant
③ Name of unsolicited applicant
④ Signature of person sending letter
⑤ Printed name of person sending letter

Employment Contract: This form may be used for any situation in which an employee is hired for a specific job. The issues addressed by this contract are as follows:

- That the employee will perform a certain job and any incidental further duties
- That the employee will be hired for a certain period of time and for a certain salary
- That the employee will be given certain job benefits (for example, sick pay, vacations, etc.)
- That the employee agrees to abide by the employer's rules and regulations
- That the employee agrees to sign agreements regarding confidentiality and inventions
- That the employee agrees to submit any employment disputes to mediation

A sample numbered version of this form is found on page 253. The information necessary to complete this form is as follows:

1. Date of the contract
2. Name of employer
3. Address of employer
4. Name of employee
5. Address of employee
6. A complete description of the job
7. Part or full time
8. Date employee to start work
9. Length of time job to continue (can be 'indefinite')
10. Pay scale for employee
11. Description of any benefits for employee
12. Number of days employee incapacitated that terminates contract
13. Additional terms
14. The state whose laws will govern the contract
15. The date the contract is signed
16. Signature of employer
17. Printed name of employer
18. Signature of employee
19. Printed name of employee

Independent Contractor Agreement: This form should be used when hiring an independent contractor. It provides a standard form for the hiring out of specific work to be performed within a set time period for a particular payment. It also provides a method for authorizing extra work under the contract. Finally, this document provides that the contractor agrees to indemnify (reimburse or compensate) the owner against any claims or liabilities arising from the performance of the work. To complete this form, fill in a detailed description of the work; dates by which certain portions of the job are to be completed; the pay for the job; the terms and dates of payment; and the state whose laws will govern the contract. A sample numbered version of this form is found on page 255. The information necessary to complete this form is as follows:

1. Date of the agreement
2. Name of owner
3. Address of owner including city and state
4. Name of contractor
5. Address of contractor including city and state
6. A complete description of the job that the contractor is performing including all labor and materials
7. Describe portion of work being done
8. Date that above portion will be completed by
9. Amount of full payment
10. Specific work description to be completed before owner makes payment
11. Dates that work should be completed by before owner makes payment
12. The state whose laws will govern the agreement
13. Date of signatures
14. Signature of owner
15. Printed name of owner
16. Signature of contractor
17. Printed name of contractor

IRS Form W-4: Employee Withholding Certificate: This form must be completed by each person that you hire that will be subject to the withholding of federal income tax. The employer should keep a completed W-4 form in each employee's personnel file and forward a copy to the person in the company that handles the company payroll. This form does not need to be sent to the U.S. Internal Revenue Service. Employers can obtain the official IRS form by going to www.irs.gov or visiting your local government office for forms. A sample form is provided on the Forms-on-CD.

USCIS Form I-9: Employee Eligibility Verification: This form must be completed by each person that you hire. The employee completes Section 1 of the form. The employer is responsible for assuring that the employee completes that section. The employer then completes Section 2 of the form and must verify the identification material that is supplied by the employee. The second page of the instructions provides a list of the acceptable identification documents. The employer should keep a completed I-9 form in each employee's personnel file. This form does not need to be sent to the U.S. Citizenship and Immigration Service. Employers can obtain the official IRS form by going to www.irs.gov or visiting your local government office for forms. A sample form is provided on the Forms-on-CD.

Federal Multi-State Employer Notification Form for New Hires: New hire reporting is the process by which you, as an employer, report information on your newly hired employees to a designated state agency shortly after the date of hire. New hire reports are matched against child support records at the state and national levels to locate parents who owe child support. This is especially helpful for interstate cases (in which one parent lives in a different state from his or her child), which are often the most difficult cases for states to resolve.

This form must be completed by for each person that you hire if you are an employee that has locations in more than one state. If you are an employer that only has locations in one state, you will need to contact your own state's Directory of New Hires and notify them of any new hire. Individual state forms are not supplied with this book. A sample form is provided on the CD. To access information regarding new hire regulations in your own state, you may access the following website:

http://www.acf.hhs.gov/programs/cse/newhire/employer/contacts/nh_websites.htm

Employee Confidentiality Agreement: This form may be used in those situations in which it is prudent to have the employee agree not to divulge any business or trade secrets. An employer's business secrets include any information regarding the employer's customers, supplies, finances, research, development or manufacturing processes, or any technical or business information. This form also provides that the employee agrees not to make any unauthorized copies of information or take any business information from the employer's facilities. A sample numbered version of this form is found on page 257. To prepare this form, simply do the following:

1. Date of the agreement
2. Name of employer
3. Address of employer including city and state
4. Name of employee
5. Address of employee including city and state
6. Additional terms of the agreement
7. Date agreement is signed
8. Signature of Employer
9. Printed name of the employer
10. Signature of Employee
11. Printed Name of Employee

Employee Patents and Inventions Agreement: This form is for use in those situations in which a dispute may arise over who owns an invention which an employee created while on the job for an employer. By using this form, the employee agrees to provide the employer with any information about such an invention. In addition, this document serves as an assignment and transfer to the employer of any rights that the employee may have had in any invention created on the job. A sample numbered version of this form is found on page 258. To prepare this form, simply fill in the employer's and employee's names and addresses and any additional terms.

① Date of the agreement
② Name of employer
③ Address of employer including city and state
④ Name of employee
⑤ Address of employee including city and state
⑥ Additional terms of the agreement
⑦ Date agreement is signed
⑧ Signature of Employer
⑨ Printed name of the employer
⑩ Signature of Employee
⑪ Printed Name of Employee

Agreement Not to Compete: This form may be used prior to an employee leaving an employment situation if the employer desires to restrict the former employee's competition. It provides for the employee to agree not to operate a similar business which will compete with the employer. The terms include a geographical limitation (in terms of miles of radius from the employer's business) on how closely a competing business can be operated. Also included is a time limit (in terms of years) that such an agreement will be in effect. A sample numbered version of this form is found on page 259. To prepare this form, complete the following:

① The date of the agreement
② The name of the employer
③ Address of the employer
④ The name of the employee
⑤ Address of the employee
⑥ Type of business operated by employer
⑦ Name of business operated by employer
⑧ Address of business operated by employer
⑨ Number of years the restriction on competition will exist
⑩ Miles from existing business the restriction on competition will cover
⑪ Any additional terms
⑫ State in which employer's business is located
⑬ Date of agreement
⑭ Signature of employer

⑮ Printed name of employer
⑯ Signature of employee
⑰ Printed name of employee

Employee Request for Direct Deposit of Paycheck: This form may be used by an employee to authorize the direct deposit of all or a portion of their paycheck into their own bank account. It may also be used to cancel such direct deposit. You may need to supply a copy of this form to the bank in question in order to facilitate a direct deposit or electronic direct deposit. The employee should be given a copy of this form for their own records. The original of the form should be supplied to the person who handles your company's payroll. A sample numbered version of this form is found on page 260. To complete this letter, fill in the following information:

① Name of employee (as shown on bank account signature card)
② Social Security number of employee
③ Name of employee's bank
④ Address of employee's bank
⑤ Employee's bank account number
⑥ Employee should check the appropriate box and, if necessary fill in the requested information
⑦ Signature of employee
⑧ Date of completion of form
⑨ Note: Employee must attach a blank deposit slip to this form.

Employee Consent to Payroll Deductions: This form may be used by an employee to authorize deductions from their paycheck for various reasons, such as retirement, union dues, or other deductions. The employee should be given a copy of this form for their own records. The original of the form should be supplied to the person who handles your company's payroll. A sample numbered version of this form is found on page 261. To complete this letter, fill in the following information:

① Name of company
② Total amount of deduction from paycheck from total line later in form (Item ⑤)
③ Paycheck date to begin deductions
④ Employee to check type of deduction and fill in amount
⑤ Total of all deductions (fill in also on ②)
⑥ Signature of employee
⑦ Date of completion of form
⑧ Printed name of employee
⑨ Social Security number of employee

Application for Employment

Name ① _____

Address ① _____

Phone Number ① _____

Social Security number ② _____

Driver's License number ② _____

Position applying for:③ _____

Date available:③ _____

Full time _____ Part time _____ Flexible _____

Special job skills or qualifications: ④ _____ .

Education⑤	School	Course of study	Last year	Graduation date
High School				
College/ University				
Trade/ Vocational				
Other				

Employ-ment	Job description	Employer's Address	Employer's Phone	Employment dates	Reason for leaving
⑥					⑦

May we contact your present employer? Yes _____ No _____

References	Address	Phone	Relationship	Occupation
⑧				

Emergency Contacts	Address	Phone	Relationship
⑨			

Please list any additional information (such as licenses, professional certifications, etc.) that you consider important for the job to which you have applied: ⑩

I understand that should I be hired, either I or the employer may terminate my employment at any time or for any reason consistent with state or federal law. I certify that the information in this application is correct and complete to the best of my knowledge and I understand that intentionally falsifying information could result in refusal of employment or discharge from employment. I also understand that to be lawfully employed in the U.S., I must show the employer documents proving my legal authorization to work in the U.S. I also authorize the employers, schools, and individuals named above to provide information to my prospective employer regarding my employment, education, character, and qualifications and I release them from all liability for damages in providing this information. ⑪

Date:_____

⑫ _____
Signature of Applicant

This company is an equal opportunity employer. Your application will be considered without regard to race, age, color, gender, religion, national origin, marital status, ancestry, citizenship, veteran status, or physical or mental disability.

Applicants Please Do Not Write Below This Line

Interviewed by ⑬ _____
References checked by: ⑭ _____

Hiring Decision:⑮   ☐ Hired   ☐ Rejected

Applicant notified date: _____   ☐ Rejection letter sent

Starting Date: ⑯ _____   Rate of Pay: _____

Consent to Release Employment Information

I, ①_____ , of ②_____ , do
consent and authorize ③ _____ , of
④_____ , to release any and all
employment records of mine that they might have in their possession to
⑤_____ , of ⑥_____ .

I release the above party from any liability for the release of any information or
records based on this consent and authorization.

Dated: ⑦_____

⑧_____
Signature of Applicant

⑨_____
Printed Name of Applicant

Verification of Job References

Name of Applicant:①
Description of Potential Job:②
Education References:

High School Phone #: ③_____   Date Called: _____   Verified ☐ ④

College Phone #: ⑤_____   Date Called: _____   Verified ☐ ⑥

Employer References: ⑦

1st Employer Phone #: _____   Date Called: _____ Verified ☐ ⑧
Employment Dates_____   Position _____
Last Pay Rate _____   Reason for Leaving _____

2nd Employer Phone #: _____   Date Called: _____ Verified ☐
Employment Dates_____   Position _____
Last Pay Rate _____   Reason for Leaving _____

3rd Employer Phone #: _____   Date Called: _____ Verified ☐
Employment Dates_____   Position _____
Last Pay Rate _____   Reason for Leaving _____

Personal References

1st Personal Reference Phone #: ⑨____ Date Called: _____ Verified ☐ ⑩

2nd Personal Reference Phone #: _____ Date Called: _____Verified ☐

3rd Personal Reference Phone #: _____Date Called: _____ Verified ☐

Applicant cleared for hiring: ⑪   ☐ YES   ☐ NO

Date ⑫_____

Signature ⑬_____

Job Description Form

Date: ①_____
Prepared by: ②_____
Title: ③_____
Department: ④_____
Approved by: ⑤_____

Job Description:

Job title: ⑥_____
Reporting to: ⑦_____
Job statement: ⑧_____

Major Duties: ⑨

1. _____
2. _____
3. _____
4. _____
5. _____
6. _____

Minor Duties: ⑩

1. _____
2. _____
3. _____
4. _____
5. _____
6. _____

Relationships:

Department head: ⑪_____
Direct supervisor: ⑫_____
Personnel supervised: ⑬_____

Job Application Rejection Letter

Date: ①

To: ②

Dear ③_____:

Thank you for applying for a position with our company:

We interviewed many applicants for this position in our search process and have, unfortunately hired another applicant for the position for which you applied.

Thus, we will not be offering this position to you.

We thank you for your interest in working for our company and we will keep your application on file should another position become available.

Good luck in your job search.

Sincerely,

④_____
Signature

⑤_____
Printed Name

Unsolicited Resume Rejection Letter

Date: ①

To: ②

Dear ③_____:

We appreciate your interest in a position with our company.

Our company is not currently hiring anyone with your particular skills and qualifications.

We are returning your resume.

Good luck in your job search.

Sincerely,

④_____
Signature

⑤_____
Printed Name

Employment Contract

This Contract is made on ①_____, between ②_____ , Employer, of ③_____ , and ④_____ , Employee, of ⑤_____.

For valuable consideration, the Employer and Employee agree as follows:

1. The Employee agrees to perform the following duties and job description: ⑥

The Employee also agrees to perform further duties incidental to the general job description. This is considered a ⑦_____ time position.

2. The Employee will begin work on ⑧_____ . This position shall continue for a period of ⑨_____ .

3. The Employee will be paid the following: ⑩

The Employee will also be given the following benefits: ⑪

Sick pay :_____
Vacations:_____
Bonuses: _____
Retirement benefits:_____
Insurance benefits:_____

4. The Employee agrees to abide by all rules and regulations of the Employer at all times while employed.

5. This Contract may be terminated by:

(a) Breach of this Contract by the Employee
(b) The expiration of this Contract without renewal
(c) Death of the Employee
(d) Incapacitation of the Employee for over ⑫_____ days in any one year

6. Any dispute between the Employer and Employee related to this Contract will be settled by voluntary mediation. If mediation is unsuccessful, the dispute will

be settled by binding arbitration using an arbitrator of the American Arbitration Association.

7. Any additional terms of this Contract: ⑬

8. No modification of this Contract will be effective unless it is in writing and is signed by both the Employer and Employee. This Contract binds and benefits both parties and any successors. Time is of the essence of this Contract. This document is the entire agreement between the parties. This Contract is governed by the laws of the State of ⑭_____ .

Dated: ⑮_____

⑯_____
Signature of Employer

⑰_____
Printed Name of Employer

⑱_____
Signature of Employee

⑲_____
Printed Name of Employee

Independent Contractor Agreement

This agreement is made on ①_____ , 20 _____ , between
②_____ , owner, of
③_____ ,
City of _____ , State of _____ , and
④_____ , contractor, of
⑤_____ ,
City of _____ , State of _____ .

For valuable consideration, the owner and contractor agree as follows:

1. The contractor agrees to furnish all of the labor and materials to do the following work for the owner as an independent contractor: ⑥

2. The contractor agrees that the following portions of the total work will be completed by the dates specified:

Work: ⑦

Dates: ⑧

3. The contractor agrees to perform this work in a workmanlike manner according to standard practices. If any plans or specifications are part of this job, they are attached to and are part of this agreement.

4. The owner agrees to pay the contractor as full payment $ ⑨_____ , for doing the work outlined above. This price will be paid to the contractor on satisfactory completion of the work in the following manner and on the following dates:

Work: ⑩

Dates: ⑪

5. The contractor and the owner may agree to extra services and work, but any such extras must be set out and agreed to in writing by both the contractor and the owner.

6. The contractor agrees to indemnify and hold the owner harmless from any claims or liability arising from the contractor's work under this agreement.

7. No modification of this agreement will be effective unless it is in writing and is signed by both parties. This agreement binds and benefits both parties and any successors. Time is of the essence of this agreement. This document, including any attachments, is the entire agreement between the parties. This agreement is governed by the laws of the State of ⑫_____ .

Dated: ⑬_____ , 20 _____

⑭_____
Signature of Owner

⑮_____
Printed Name of Owner

⑯_____
Signature of Contractor

⑰_____
Printed Name of Contractor

Employee Confidentiality Agreement

This agreement is made on ①_____ , 20 _____ , between
②_____ , employer,
of ③_____ ,
City of _____ , State of _____ , and
④_____ , employee, of
⑤_____ ,
City of _____ , State of _____ .

For valuable consideration, the employer and employee agree as follows:

1. The employee agrees to keep all of the employer's business secrets confidential at all times during and after the term of employee's employment. Employer's business secrets include any information regarding the employer's customers, supplies, finances, research, development, manufacturing processes, or any other technical or business information.

2. The employee agrees not to make any unauthorized copies of any of employer's business secrets or information without employer's consent, nor to remove any of employer's business secrets or information from the employer's facilities.

3. The parties agree to the following additional terms: ⑥

Dated: ⑦_____ , 20 _____

⑧_____
Signature of Employer

⑨_____
Printed Name of Employer

⑩_____
Signature of Employee

⑪_____
Printed Name of Employee

Employee Patents and Inventions Agreement

This agreement is made on ①_____ , 20 _____ , between
②_____ , employer, of
③_____ ,
City of _____ , State of _____ , and
④_____ , employee, of
⑤_____ ,
City of _____ , State of _____ .

For valuable consideration, the employer and employee agree as follows:

1. The employee agrees to promptly furnish the employer with a complete record of any inventions or patents which the employee may create or devise during employment with the employer.

2. The employee grants and assigns to the employer her or his entire rights and interest in any inventions or patents that result in any way from any work performed while employed by the employer. The employee agrees that he or she does not have any past employment agreements, patents, or inventions that might conflict with this assignment. The employer also agrees to sign any further documents necessary to allow the employer the rights, title, or patent to any such inventions or creations.

3. The parties agree to the following additional terms: ⑥

Dated: ⑦_____ , 20 _____

⑧_____
Signature of Employer
⑨_____
Printed Name of Employer

⑩_____
Signature of Employee
⑪_____
Printed Name of Employee

Agreement Not to Compete

This Agreement is made on ①_____, between ②_____ ,
Employer, of ③_____ , and ④_____ , Employee, of ⑤___
_____ The Employer now owns and conducts a ⑥ business, under the
name of ⑦_____, located at ⑧_____.

For valuable consideration, the Employer and Employee agree as follows:

1. The Employee agrees not to compete, either directly or indirectly, with the
business of the Employer for a period of ⑨_____ years from the date
of this agreement.
2. This agreement will only extend for a radius of ⑩_____ miles from
the present location of the business of the Employer.
3. The Employee agrees that "not to compete" means that the Employee will not
engage in any manner in a business or activity similar to that of the Employer's.
4. If the Employee violates this agreement, the Employer will be entitled to an
injunction to prevent such competition, without the need for the Employer to post
any bond. In addition, the Employer will be entitled to any other legal relief.
5. Any additional terms: ⑪
6. No modification of this agreement will be effective unless it is in writing and is
signed by both the Employee and Employer. This agreement binds and benefits
both the Employee and Employer and any successors. Time is of the essence
of this agreement. This document, including any attachments, is the entire
agreement between the Employee and Employer regarding this issue. This
agreement is governed by the laws of the State of ⑫_____ .

Dated: ⑬_____

⑭_____
Signature of Employer

⑮_____
Printed Name of Employer

⑯_____
Signature of Employee

⑰_____
Printed Name of Employee

Employee Request for Direct Deposit of Paycheck

Full Legal Name of Employee: ①_____

Social Security Number: ②_____

Bank Name: ③_____

Bank Address: ④_____

Employee Bank Account Number: ⑤_____

Check the appropriate item: ⑥

❑   Direct deposit. The undersigned hereby requests and authorizes the entire amount of his or her paycheck each pay period to be deposited directly into the bank account named above.

❑   Direct payroll deduction deposit. The undersigned hereby requests and authorizes the sum of _____ dollars ($_____) be deducted from his or her paycheck each pay period and to be deposited directly into the bank account named above.

❑   Cancellation of direct deposit authorization. The undersigned hereby cancels the authorization for direct deposit or payroll deduction deposited previously submitted.

⑦_____   ⑧_____

Employee Signature   Date

⑨ (Please attach a blank copy of bank account deposit slip.)

Employee Consent to Payroll Deductions

The undersigned employee authorizes ① _____
to deduct $ ② _____ from his/her gross earnings each payroll period
beginning with the paycheck dated: ③ _____

Check all that apply and fill in amount of deduction: ④

In payment for:	Amount of deduction:
❑ Credit Union	$ _____.__
❑ Employee Savings Plan	$ _____.__
❑ 401 K Plan	$ _____.__
❑ Union Dues	$ _____.__
❑ _____	$ _____.__
❑ _____	$ _____.__
Total deductions ⑤	$ _____.__

Signature of Employee ⑥ _____ Date ⑦ _____

Printed Name of Employee ⑧ _____

Social Security Number of Employee ⑨ _____

Employee: Please keep a copy of this form for your records.

Chapter 12

Forms for Handling Employees

Once an employee has been hired, various forms may be used to keep track of the employee's performance and to handle situations that may arise during their tenure with your company. There is a main personnel record form that should be completed and placed in each new employee's file. A performance review form is provided to allow for periodic assessments of the employee's performance at their job. Three different employee consent forms are provided for situations that may arise during an employee's tenure with your company. Additionally, three forms are provided for use by an employee to request time off from work for various reasons. Finally, an absence report and an accident/injury report are also provided.

Instructions for Forms for Handling Employees

Personnel Form: The purpose of this form is to provide a central record of the hiring, job advancement, and end of employment of any employee. This form should be completed upon the hiring of any employee and should be periodically updated as required. A sample numbered version of this form is found on page 268. The following information is gathered on this form:

① Name of employee
② Social Security number of employee
③ Address of employee
④ Phone number of employee
⑤ Date employee was hired
⑥ Starting salary of employee
⑦ Date W-4 form completed

⑧ Date USCIS Form I-9 completed
⑨ Number of withholding allowances employee claimed on W-4 form
⑩ Whether employee has signed Employee Contract
⑪ Changes in salary with new salary rate and date new salary began
⑫ Changes in job position with new position title and date new position began
⑬ Any job review with date of review and status after review
⑭ Description of employee separation including date and reason for separation
⑮ Whether employee is eligible for being rehired
⑯ Signature of employer upon separation of employee
⑰ Date of employer signature
⑱ Signature of employee upon separation
⑲ Date of employee signature

Employee Performance Review: This form is to be used for the periodic monitoring of each employee's performance on the job. It may be used annually, semi-annually, or at some other periodic interval. It provides a clear and concise method to describe the employee's performance by providing a method to rate the following:
- Knowledge of the job, including equipment and systems
- Achievement on the job, including initiative and follow-up
- Employee relations with others, including coworkers and management
- Quality of employee's work, including ability and consistency
- Employee's attitude, including dependability and attendance

A sample numbered version of this form is found on page 270. Enter the following:

① Name of employee
② Social Security number of employee
③ Job title of employee
④ Department of employee
⑤ Current salary of employee
⑥ Date of last salary increase
⑦ Date of this review
⑧ Date of last review
⑨ Review of employee performance
⑩ Comments of reviewer
⑪ Signature of reviewer
⑫ Date of reviewer's signature
⑬ Whether performance review was discussed with employee
⑭ Employee's comments regarding review (if any)
⑮ Employee's signature
⑯ Date of employee's signature

Employee Consent to Drug and/or Alcohol Testing: This form may be used to obtain an employee's consent to submit to drug and/or alcohol testing. The employee should be given a copy of this form for their own records. The original of the form should be placed in an employee's personnel file. A sample numbered version of this form is found on page 273. To complete this letter, fill in the following information:

1. Name of company
2. Signature of employee
3. Date of completion of form
4. Printed name of employee
5. Social Security number of employee
6. Signature of witness to employee signing
7. Date of witnessing
8. Printed name of witness
9. A copy of this form should be provided to the employee

Employee Consent to Security Investigation: This form may be used to obtain an employee's consent to submit to a security investigation. The employee should be given a copy of this form for their own records. The original of the form should be placed in an employee's personnel file. A sample numbered version of this form is found on page 273. To complete this letter, fill in the following information:

1. Name of company
2. Signature of employee
3. Date of completion of form
4. Printed name of employee
5. Social Security number of employee
6. Signature of witness to employee signing
7. Date of witnessing
8. Printed name of witness
9. A copy of this form should be provided to the employee

Employee Consent to Medical Examination: This form may be used to obtain an employee's consent to submit to a medical examination. The employee should be given a copy of this form for their own records. The original of the form should be placed in an employee's personnel file. A sample numbered version of this form is found on page 274. To complete this letter, fill in the following information:

1. Name of company
2. Signature of employee
3. Date of completion of form

④ Printed name of employee
⑤ Social Security number of employee
⑥ Signature of witness to employee signing
⑦ Date of witnessing
⑧ Printed name of witness
⑨ A copy of this form should be provided to the employee

Employee Request for Vacation Time Form: This form may be used by an employee to request vacation time, if such time is a benefit of their employment The employee should be given a copy of this form for their own records. The original of the form should be placed in an employee's personnel file. A sample numbered version of this form is found on page 275. To complete this letter, fill in the following information:

① Vacation dates requested by employee
② Signature of employee
③ Date of completion of form
④ Printed name of employee
⑤ Approval or denial of request (and, if necessary, reason for denial of request)
⑥ Signature of employer
⑦ Date of employer signature
⑧ Printed name of employer
⑨ A copy of this form should be provided to the employee

Employee Request for Leave of Absence Form: This form may be used by an employee to request a leave of absence, if such leave is a benefit of their employment The employee should be given a copy of this form for their own records. The original of the form should be placed in an employee's personnel file. A sample numbered version of this form is found on page 276. To complete this letter, fill in the following information:

① Leave of absence dates requested by employee
② Signature of employee
③ Date of completion of form
④ Printed name of employee
⑤ Approval or denial of request (and, if necessary, reason for denial of request)
⑥ Signature of employer
⑦ Date of employer signature
⑧ Printed name of employer
⑨ A copy of this form should be provided to the employee

Family and Medical Leave Request Form: This form is to be used to comply with the Federal Family and Medical Leave Act which requires that eligible employees be entitled to up to 12 weeks of unpaid and job-protected leave for certain family and medical reasons. To be eligible, an employee must meet the following conditions:

- Have worked for the company for a total of 12 months (does not need to be consecutive)
- Have worked for the company at least 1,250 hours in the last 12 months
- Have a serious health condition that makes him or her unable to perform his or her job, OR
- Have a child, spouse, or parent with a serious health condition that requires the employee's full-time care, OR
- Have a child which after birth, adoption, or foster care requires full-time attention of the employee (whether employee is father or mother)

A sample numbered version of this form is found on page 277. To complete this form, please enter the following information:

① Date of request
② Name of employee
③ Social Security number of employee
④ Job title of employee
⑤ Department of employee
⑥ Date employee was hired
⑦ Eligibility for leave questionnaire
⑧ Reasons for requested leave questionnaire
⑨ Date of requested leave
⑩ Date employee agrees to return to work
⑪ Signature of employee
⑫ Date of signature employee
⑬ Approval or denial of requested leave
⑭ Signature of employer
⑮ Date of signature of employer

Employee Absence Report Form: This is a simple form to be completed for each instance of an employee's absence, whether for holiday, vacation, sickness, or otherwise. It provides a record of the reason for the absence, pay, and other comments regarding the incident. A sample numbered version of this form is found on page 279. To complete this form, the following information is necessary:

1. Name of employee
2. Social Security number of employee
3. Job title of employee
4. Department of employee
5. Date employee was hired
6. Dates and reasons for employee absence
7. Any comments regarding absence
8. Signature of employee
9. Date of employee signature
10. Name of person approving absence form
11. Signature of person approving absence form
12. Date of signature of person approving absence form

Employee Accident/Injury Report Form: This form provides a method to report a workplace accident and/or injury. The careful use of this form can provide an employer with important records in the event of the worker's compensation claims and/or other insurance-related matters. A sample numbered version of this form is found on page 280. This form requires the following information:

1. Date of accident/injury incident
2. Time of accident/injury incident
3. Name of employee
4. Social Security number of employee
5. Job title of employee
6. Department of employee
7. Date employee was hired
8. Type and nature of accident/injury incident and details of any medical assistance provided by employer
9. Signature of employer
10. Date of employer signature
11. Signature of employee
12. Date of signature of employee

Personnel Form

Employee Name	①
Social Security Number	②
Employee Address	③
Employee Phone Number	④

Date Hired: ⑤	Starting Salary: ⑥
W-4 Form completed: ⑦	USCIS I-9 Form completed: ⑧
Number of withholding allowances: ⑨	Employee Contract: ⑩ ____Yes ____ No

Changes in Salary	New Salary	Date Begun
⑪		
Changes in Position	New Position	Date Begun
⑫		
Job Reviews	Date	Status
⑬		
Separation	Date	Reason

⑭		Laid off: ____ Left voluntarily: ____ Discharged for cause: ____ Discharged - lack of work: ___ Other: ____

Eligible for rehire? ⑮ Yes ____ No ____

Signature of Employer Upon Separation ⑯_____

Date ⑰_____

Signature of Employee Upon Separation ⑱_____

Date ⑲_____

Employee Performance Review Form

Employee Name	①	
Social Security Number	②	
Job Title	③	
Department	④	

Current Salary: ⑤	Date of last salary increase: ⑥
Date of this review: ⑦	Date of last review: ⑧

Review Areas ⑨	Poor	Fair	Good	Excellent
Knowledge of Job				
Equipment				
Systems				
Achievement on job				
Initiative				
Follow-up				
Employee Relations				
With management				
With coworkers				
Quality of Work				
Ability				
Consistency				
Attitude				
Dependability				

Attendance				

Reviewer's Comments: ⑩

Signature of Reviewer ⑪ _____ Date ⑫ _____

Was this review discussed with employee? ⑬ Yes _____ No _____

Employee's Comments: ⑭

Signature of Employee ⑮ _____ Date ⑯ _____

Employee Consent to Drug and/or Alcohol Testing

In the interest of safety in the workplace, all employees of this company will be required to take a urine test for drug and/or alcohol use.

The undersigned employee has been fully informed of the reasons for a urine test for drug and/or alcohol use and of the procedure that is involved in the testing.

The undersigned employee fully and freely consents to the required urine test for the following company: ①_____.

In addition, the undersigned understands that the results of this test will become a permanent part of his or her personnel file and that positive results of this test may result in the termination of employment with this company. Finally, if the results of this test are positive, the employee understands that he or she will be given an opportunity to explain the results of this test.

Signature of Employee ②_____

Date ③ _____

Printed Name of Employee ④_____

Social Security Number of Employee ⑤_____

Signature of Witness ⑥_____Date ⑦_____

Printed Name of Witness ⑧_____

⑨ Employee: Please keep a copy of this form for your records.

Employee Consent to Security Investigation

In the interest of confidentiality and security in the workplace, certain employees of this company will be required to submit to a security investigation, which will be fully paid for by the company. This investigation is deemed necessary by this employer to protect its confidential and proprietary information and trade secrets and/or to investigate and uncover illegal conduct in the workplace.

The undersigned employee has been fully informed of the reasons for such security investigation and of the procedure that is involved in the investigation.

The undersigned employee fully and freely consents to the security investigation that the employer deems necessary for the following company: ①_____ _____.

In addition, the undersigned understands that the results of this investigation will become a permanent part of his or her personnel file and that the results of this investigation may result in disciplinary action and/or the termination of employment with this company. Finally, if the results of this investigation are negative, the employee understands that he or she will be given an opportunity to explain the results of this investigation.

The undersigned employee indemnifies, releases, forever discharges and agrees to hold the above-named employer, and any agents and/or employees or employer harmless from any and all claims, demands, judgements, and legal fees resulting or arising from any such investigation, its results, and any lawful use of such results.

Signature of Employee ②_____Date ③_____

Printed Name of Employee ④_____

Social Security Number of Employee ⑤_____

Signature of Witness ⑥_____Date ⑦_____

Printed Name of Witness ⑧_____

⑨ Employee: Please keep a copy of this form for your records.

Employee Consent to Medical Examination

In the interest of safety in the workplace, certain employees of this company will be required to take submit to a medical examination, which will be fully paid for by the company.

The undersigned employee has been fully informed of the reasons for such medical examination and of the procedure that is involved in the examination.

The undersigned employee fully and freely consents to the required medical examination for the following company: ①_____.

In addition, the undersigned understands that the results of this examination will become a permanent part of his or her personnel file and that negative results of this examination may result in the termination of employment with this company. Finally, if the results of this examination are negative, the employee understands that he or she will be given an opportunity to explain the results of this examination.

The undersigned employee indemnifies, releases, forever discharges and agrees to hold the above-named employer, and any agents and/or employees or employer harmless from any and all claims, demands, judgements, and legal fees resulting or arising from any such examination, its results, and any lawful use of such results.

Signature of Employee ②_____   Date ③_____

Printed Name of Employee ④_____

Social Security Number of Employee ⑤_____

Signature of Witness ⑥_____Date ⑦_____

Printed Name of Witness ⑧_____

⑨ Employee: Please keep a copy of this form for your records.

Employee Request for Vacation Time

The undersigned employee, under the terms of his or her employment, requests the following days of vacation time: ①
_____
_____
_____
_____

Signature of Employee ②_____
Date ③_____

Printed Name of Employee ④_____

This Employee Request for Vacation Time has been ⑤

❑ Approved

❑ Denied for the following reasons: _____
_____
_____
_____

Signature of Employer ⑥_____   Date ⑦_____

Printed Name of Employer ⑧_____

⑨ Employee: Please keep a copy of this form for your records.

Employee Request for Leave of Absence

The undersigned employee, under the terms of his or her employment, requests the following leave of absence dates: ①

_____
_____
_____
_____
_____

Signature of Employee ②_____Date ③_____

Printed Name of Employee ④_____

This Employee Request for Leave of Absence has been ⑤

❑ Approved

❑ Denied for the following reasons: _____
_____
_____
_____

Signature of Employer ⑥_____Date ⑦_____

Printed Name of Employer ⑧_____

⑨ Employee: Please keep a copy of this form for your records.

Family and Medical Leave Request Form

Date of Request:	①
Employee Name	②
Social Security Number	③
Job Title	④
Department	⑤
Date hired	⑥

Under the Federal Family and Medical Leave Act (FMLA), eligible employees are entitled to up to 12 (twelve) weeks of unpaid, job-protected leave for certain family and medical reasons. Please submit this request form to your supervisor at leave 30 (thirty) days before the leave is to begin, if possible. When submission of this form 30 (thirty) days in advance is not possible, submit the request as early as possible. The employer reserves the right to deny or postpone leave for failure to give appropriate notice whenever such denial or postponement would be permitted under federal or state law.

Eligibility ⑦	Yes	No
1. Have you worked for the company for a total of 12 months or more (whether or not consecutively)?		
2. During the past 12 months, have you worked at least 1,250 hours?		
3. Have you previously received medical or family leave?		
If yes: explain *Dates of previous leave:* *Purpose of previous leave:*		
4. Have you taken any intermittent leave?		
If yes: explain		
5. Have you taken other time off from your scheduled work?		
If yes: explain		

Check one	**Reasons for Requested Leave** ⑧	*Explanation*

	Serious health condition that makes you unable to perform your job	
	Serious health condition of child, spouse, or parent	
	Care for child after birth, adoption, or foster care	

Dates of Requested Leave ⑨	From:	To:

I Agree to return to work on:	⑩

If any circumstances change and I am unable to return to work on that date, I agree to inform my employer immediately in writing. I understand that my benefits will continue during my leave and that I will arrange to pay my share of any benefit premiums.

Signature of Employee ⑪ _____

Date ⑫ _____

Approved: ⑬	Denied:

Signature of Employer ⑭ _____

Date ⑮ _____

Employee Absence Report Form

Employee Name	①
Social Security Number	②
Job Title	③
Department	④
Date hired	⑤

Dates of Absence ⑥		
With Pay	Without Pay	Reason for Absence
		Holiday ____ Vacation ____ Sickness ____ Other ____
		Holiday ____ Vacation ____ Sickness ____ Other ____

Comments: ⑦

Signature of Employee ⑧_____

Date ⑨_____

Approved by ⑩_____

Signature of Approving Personnel ⑪_____

Date ⑫_____

Employee Accident/Injury Report

Date of Incident: ①	Time of Incident: ②
Employee Name ③	
Social Security Number ④	
Job Title ⑤	
Department ⑥	
Date hired ⑦	

Type of Accident or Injury ⑧	Medical Assistance Provided by Employer	Remarks

Signature of Employer ⑨ _____

Date ⑩ _____

Signature of Employee ⑪ _____

Date ⑫ _____

Chapter 13

Forms for Terminating Employees

There may come a time when an employee must, for many possible reasons, be terminated from employment. Two forms are provided in this chapter to track any disciplinary action that may be necessary regarding an employee's actions. Finally, two forms are provided to provide a written notice to an employee of their termination. The four forms provided are as follows:

Instructions for Forms for Terminating Employees

Employee Warning Notice: This form provides a method to warn an employee with a written notice regarding some violation of company policies, ranging from lateness and absence to misconduct and safety violations. The careful use of this form can provide an employer with important records in the event of the necessity to dismiss an employee for repeated warnings. The employee should be given a copy of this warning and the original should be placed in the employee's personnel file. A sample numbered version of this form is found on page 284. This form requires the following information:

1. Date of warning
2. Time of warning
3. Name of employee
4. Social Security number of employee
5. Job title of employee
6. Department of employee
7. Date employee was hired
8. Type and nature of violation and any remarks regarding violation

⑨ Signature of employer
⑩ Date of employer signature
⑪ Signature of employee
⑫ Date of signature of employee

Employee Final Warning Notice: This form provides a method to provide an employee with a final written notice regarding some violation of company policies, ranging from lateness and absence to misconduct and safety violations. This form should be used as a final warning to an employee that they may be terminated due to repeated warnings for some breach of the company's rules and/or standards. The employee should be given a copy of this warning and the original should be placed in the employee's personnel file.

A sample numbered version of this form is found on page 285. This form requires the following information:

① Date of warning
② Time of warning
③ Name of employee
④ Social Security number of employee
⑤ Job title of employee
⑥ Department of employee
⑦ Date employee was hired
⑧ Type and nature of violation and any remarks regarding violation
⑨ Signature of employer
⑩ Date of employer signature
⑪ Signature of employee
⑫ Date of signature of employee

Employee Notice of Dismissal Due to Job Elimination: This form provides a method to notify an employee that their job has been eliminated and that they are being dismissed from employment. As noted in this notice, the employee should be provided with an explanation of any accrued retirement, insurance, sick pay, and/or other benefits within 30 after the date of the employee's dismissal. The employee should be given a copy of this notice and the original should be placed in the employee's personnel file.

A sample numbered version of this form is found on page 286. This form requires the following information:

① Date of notice
② Name and address of employee

③ Name of employee
④ Last date of employment
⑤ Name of person in company who will explain any benefit issues to employee
⑥ Signature of employer
⑦ Printed name of employer

Employee Notice of Termination: This form provides a method to notify an employee that they have been terminated and that they are being dismissed from employment. The reason for termination should be explained in this form. Be certain that any reason for termination does not indicate any form of discrimination as explained in Chapter 2. As noted in this notice, the employee should be provided with an explanation of any accrued retirement, insurance, sick pay, and/or other benefits within 30 after the date of the employee's dismissal. The employee should be given a copy of this notice and the original should be placed in the employee's personnel file.

A sample numbered version of this form is found on page 287. This form requires the following information:

① Date of notice
② Name and address of employee
③ Name of employee
④ Reason for termination
⑤ Last date of employment
⑥ Name of person in company who will explain any benefit issues to employee
⑦ Signature of employer
⑧ Printed name of employer

Employee Warning Notice

Date of Warning: ①		Time of Warning: ②
Employee Name	③	
Social Security Number	④	
Job Title	⑤	
Department	⑥	
Date hired	⑦	

Type of Violation ⑧	Nature of Violation	Remarks
Lateness		
Conduct		
Absence		
Disobedience		
Carelessness		
Defective Work		
Cleanliness		
Attitude		
Safety		
Other		

Signature of Employer ⑨_____

Date ⑩_____

I have read and understand this warning.

Signature of Employee ⑪_____

Date ⑫_____

Employee Final Warning Notice

This is your final warning for serious violations of company policy. If any other violations of company policy occur, you will be <u>immediately</u> terminated from employment.

Date of Warning: ①		Time of Warning: ②
Employee Name	③	
Social Security Number	④	
Job Title	⑤	
Department	⑥	
Date hired	⑦	

Type of Violation ⑧	Nature of Violation	Remarks
Lateness		
Conduct		
Absence		
Disobedience		
Carelessness		
Defective Work		
Cleanliness		
Attitude		
Safety		
Other		

Signature of Employer ⑨_____ Date ⑩_____

I have read and understand this warning.
Signature of Employee ⑪_____ Date ⑫_____

Employee Notice of Dismissal Due to Job Elimination

Date: ①

To: ②

Dear ③_____:

We regret to inform you that, due to the elimination of your job position, you are being dismissed from employment. Your last day of work will be ④_____
_____.

Any severance pay will be in accordance with company policy. Any insurance benefits will continue in accordance with any state and federal law and/or provisions of company policy. You will be provided, within 30 days of your dismissal with a statement of any accrued benefits that may be due you. Please arrange to meet with ⑤_____ at your earliest convenience for an explanation of any benefit issues. If you have any company property, please be sure to return it prior to your last day of employment.

We regret that this action is necessary and we thank you for your work for our company. We will keep your name and personnel records on file and, should another position become available, we will contact you.

Thank you.

Sincerely,

⑥_____
Signature of Employer

⑦_____
Printed Name of Employer

Employee Notice of Termination

Date: ①

To: ②

Dear ③_____ :

We regret to inform you that you are being terminated from employment for the following reason: ④

 Your last day of work will be ⑤_____.

Any severance pay will be in accordance with company policy. Any insurance benefits will continue in accordance with any state and federal law and/or provisions of company policy. You will be provided, within 30 days of your dismissal with a statement of any accrued benefits that may be due you. Please arrange to meet with ⑥_____ at your earliest convenience for an explanation of any benefit issues. If you have any company property, please be sure to return it prior to your last day of employment.

We regret that this action is necessary and we thank you for your work for our company.

Thank you.

Sincerely,

⑦_____
Signature of Employer

⑧_____
Printed Name of Employer

Chapter 14

Business Credit Documents

The forms that are contained in this chapter relate to the extension of business credit to customers. In many business situations it is customary to offer credit to continuing customers on mutually agreeable terms. The prudent businessperson, however, should take certain steps to assure that the company that is being offered credit is a sound business risk. The various forms provided allow for the collection of credit information and for the evaluation of the credit potential of business customers.

Instructions for Business Credit Documents

Business Credit Application: This form is the basis of a check into the credit history of a customer. With this form a company desiring credit furnishes various information which may be checked further to ascertain the reliability and background of the credit applicant. A sample numbered version of this form is found on page 291. The credit applicant is requested to furnish the following information:

① Name of Company
② Mailing Address of Company
③ Phone number of Company
④ Fax number of Company
⑤ Email address of Company
⑥ Business entity type
⑦ Brief description of business
⑧ Year business was started
⑨ Yearly Gross Sales
⑩ Yearly Net Profits

⑪ Net Value
⑫ Names and Addresses of Owners, Partners, or Officers
⑬ Credit References - Names, addresses, phone and account numbers
⑭ Trade Credit References
⑮ Bank References
⑯ Credit Limit Requested
⑰ Credit Terms: Fill in the interest rate on overdue balances and number of days within which an invoice is to be paid
⑱ Date of Application
⑲ Credit Applicant Signature & Printed

Notice of Approval of Business Credit Application: This form is used to approve the above credit application. It should be sent only after the information in the credit application has been thoroughly checked and approved. This form reiterates the credit terms that your company is offering to the applicant. A sample numbered version of this form is found on page 293. Complete this form by inserting the following information:

① Date of notice
② Name and address of employee
③ Name of Company requesting credit
④ Date of Credit Application
⑤ Credit Limit
⑥ Fill in the interest rate on overdue balances
⑦ Fill in the number of days within which an invoice is to be paid
⑧ Signature of approving party
⑨ Printed name of approving party

Request for Bank Credit Reference: This form is intended to be used to contact the various banking references that a credit applicant has offered in his or her Business Credit Application. It requests the bank to provide confidential information regarding the applicant's banking and credit history with the bank. A copy of the applicant's Business Credit Application should be attached to this request when sending it to the bank. A sample numbered version of this form is found on page 294. Complete this form by inserting the following information:

① Date of Request
② Name of Bank
③ Name of Company that the Credit Reference is for
④ Account number of
⑤ Signature
⑥ Printed Name

Request for Trade Credit Reference: This form is intended to be used to contact the various trade references that a credit applicant has offered in his or her Business Credit Application. It requests that the trade vendor provide confidential information regarding the applicant's banking and credit history with the vendor. A copy of the applicant's Business Credit Application should be attached to this request when sending it to the vendor. A sample numbered version of this form is found on page 295. Complete this form by inserting the following information:

1. Date of Request
2. Name of Company that you are requesting information from
3. Name of Company that the Credit Reference is for
4. Account number
5. Signature
6. Printed Name

Request for Credit Information: This final form is designed to be used to obtain information regarding your personal credit history from any credit reporting agency. It is in accordance with the Federal Fair Credit Reporting Act. Fill in the appropriate information and forward it to the credit reporting agency from which you wish to obtain information. A sample numbered version of this form is found on page 296. Complete this form by inserting the following information:

1. Date of Request
2. Name of Company/Bank that you are requesting information from
3. Name of Company or Individual that the Credit Information is for
4. Previous Name and Address (optional)
5. Social Security Number
6. Phone Number
7. Signature
8. Printed Name

Business Credit Application

Company Name ① _____
Billing Address: ②
Phone ③ _____
Fax ④ _____
Email Address ⑤ _____

⑥　___ Corporation___ Partnership___ Proprietorship___ Other
If other, explain _____
Type of Business ⑦ _____　Year Established ⑧ _____

Yearly Gross Sales　　$ ⑨ _____
Yearly Net Profits　　$ ⑩ _____
Net Value　　　　　　$ ⑪ _____

⑫ **Names and Addresses of Owners, Partners, or Officers**

Name _____
SS# _____　Title _____
Address:

Name _____
SS# _____　Title _____
Address:

⑬ **Credit References**

Creditor Name _____
Account # _____　Phone _____
Address:

Creditor Name _____
Account # _____　Phone _____
Address:

⑭ Trade Credit References

Vendor Name _____

Account # _____   Phone _____

Address:

Vendor Name _____

Account # _____   Phone _____

Address:

⑮ Bank References

Bank Name _____

Account # _____   Phone _____

Address:

Bank Name _____

Account # _____   Phone _____

Address:

CREDIT LIMIT REQUESTED: $ ⑯_____

Credit Terms ⑰
- Payment on all invoices is due within _____ days of invoice date.
- All overdue invoices bear interest at _____ % (___ percent) per month on unpaid balance.
- Credit applicant agrees to pay all costs of collection, including court costs and attorneys fees.
- Credit terms and limit may be cancelled or changed by Creditor at any time without notice.
- All transactions are governed by the laws of the Creditor's state.
- All transactions are governed by the terms of the Creditor's documents.

The credit applicant accepts the above terms and states that all information contained in this credit application is true and correct. Credit applicant authorizes creditor to contact all references, inquire as to credit information, and receive any confidential information relevant to approving credit.

Dated: ⑱_____ , 20 _____

⑲_____   _____

Signature of Credit Applicant   Printed Name of Credit Applicant

Notice of Approval of Business Application

Date: ①_____ , 20 _____

To: ②_____
Address:

RE: Credit Application

Dear ③_____

Please be advised that, based upon your credit application which you filed with our firm dated ④_____ , 20 _____ , your credit has been approved.

Please be further advised that your initial credit limit is $ ⑤_____ .

The terms of this extension of credit to your company are as follows:

- Payment on all invoices is due within ⑥_____ days of invoice date.
- All overdue invoices bear interest at ⑦_____ % (_____ percent) per month on unpaid balance.
- Credit applicant agrees to pay all costs of collection, including court costs and attorneys fees.
- Credit terms and limit may be cancelled or changed by creditor at any time without notice.
- All transactions are governed by the laws of the creditor's state.
- All transactions are governed by the terms of the creditor's documents.

If you have any questions regarding this matter, please contact our accounting department. Thank you very much and we look forward to doing business with you.

Very truly,

⑧_____
Signature

_____
Printed Name

Request For Bank Credit Reference

Date: ①_____ , 20 _____

To: ②_____

RE: Credit Reference for ③_____ ,
        Account # ④_____ .

The above-named company has filed a credit application with our company naming your bank as a credit reference. By that application, the credit applicant has
authorized us to contact the stated references and receive confidential information
from them regarding their credit history. Attached please find a copy of the credit
application naming your bank as a reference and authorizing our company to
receive credit information.

We would, therefore, appreciate it if you could provide us with the following information:

    1. How long has the company had an account with your bank?
    2. What has been the average daily account balance?
    3. Is there a history of overdrafts on this account?
    4. Does this company currently have any loans with your bank?

        (a)   If so, what is the outstanding balance?
        (b)   Are they secured loans?
        (c)   What is the collateral?
        (d)   Has the repayment been satisfactory?

    5. Has this customer been a satisfactory banking client?

We would appreciate any further information that you might be able to provide
that may enable us to evaluate the credit history of this applicant. All information
will be held in strict confidence. Thank you very much for your assistance.

⑤_____
Signature

⑥_____
Printed Name

Request For Trade Credit Reference

Date: ① _____ , 20 _____

To: ② _____

RE: Credit Reference for ③ _____ ,
        Account # ④ _____ .

The above-named company has filed a credit application with our company naming your company as a credit reference. By that application, the credit applicant has authorized us to contact the stated references and receive confidential information from them regarding their credit history. Attached please find a copy of the credit application naming your company as a reference and authorizing our company to receive credit information.

We would, therefore, appreciate it if you could provide us with the following information:

1. How long has the company had an account with your company?
2. What has been the average credit line of this company?
3. Is there a history of past due payments by this company?
4. What is the current credit balance owed you by this company?
5. Has the repayment been satisfactory?
6. What are the credit terms that you have extended to this customer?
7. Has this customer been a satisfactory customer?

We would appreciate any further information that you might be able to provide that may enable us to evaluate the credit history of this applicant. All information will be held in strict confidence. Thank you very much for your assistance.

⑤ _____
Signature

⑥ _____
Printed Name

Request For Credit Information

Date: ①_____ , 20 _____

To: ②_____

RE: Disclosure of Credit Information

By this letter, I hereby request complete disclosure of my personal credit file as held within your agency records. This request is in accordance with the Federal Fair Credit Reporting Act. I request that this disclosure provide the names and addresses of any parties who have received a copy of my credit report, and the names and addresses of any parties who have provided information that is contained in my credit report.

Name ③_____
Address:

Previous Name ④_____
Previous Address:

Social Security # ⑤_____   Phone ⑥_____

⑦_____
Signature

⑧_____
Printed Name

Chapter 15

Business Financing Documents

The documents included in this chapter are designed for use in situations in which businesspersons will be using personal property as collateral for a loan. Loans for real estate, other than a simple promissory note and mortgage or deed of trust, are generally subject to more state regulations and, thus, should be handled by a real estate professional or attorney.

The legal documents for financing of business loans generally employ three key documents, each of which serves a different purpose. First, there is the actual Promissory Note by which the borrower promises to repay a debt. These documents are covered in Chapter 16. Next is the Security Agreement with which the borrower puts up specific property as collateral for repayment of a loan. Finally, there is the U.C.C. Financing Statement that is used to record a lien against personal property in the public records.

All states have adopted a version of the Uniform Commercial Code (U.C.C.). This code is a set of detailed regulations which govern the purchase and sale of goods and financing arrangements, along with many other commercial transactions. Every state has a method of filing (on the public record) various statements relating to financing arrangements. The value of making timely filings of financing statements and other U.C.C. related matter is that the date and time of filing the statement perfects (or legally locks in the time) the security interest that has been bargained for. The party with the earliest perfected security interest relating to a particular piece of property has priority claim to that property. You will need to check locally with your county clerk or recorder's office for any particular local and state rules regarding U.C.C. filings. The various forms included in this chapter are as follows:

Instructions for Business Financing Documents

Security Agreement: This document is the document that provides the secured party (the party providing a loan) with the right to the collateral that the borrower has put up as security for the repayment of the loan. The security agreement in this book provides for the following terms:

• That the borrower is granting the secured party a security interest in the property named
• That the security interest is to secure payment of a certain obligation
• That if the borrower defaults on the obligation, the secured party may accelerate the loan and make it immediately due and payable
• That if the borrower defaults, the secured party will have all the remedies under the U.C.C. (these may include selling the property or keeping the property)
• That the borrower will pay any costs of collection upon default
• That the borrower will be careful with the collateral and will not sell or dispose of it
• That the borrower will insure the collateral and keep it at a specified address for the term of the loan period
• That the borrower states that the property is owned free and clear, with no other liens against it, and that he or she has authority to use it as collateral
• That the borrower will sign any necessary financing statements
• That any changes to the agreement must be in writing

A sample numbered version of this form is found on page 304. Use the following information to fill out the Security Agreement:

① Date of Agreement
② Name of Borrower
③ Address of Borrower
④ Name of Secured Party
⑤ Address of Secured Party
⑥ Personal property which will be considered collateral
⑦ Description of Obligation
⑧ Collateral adequately insured and at this address
⑨ Name the State that this agreement is governed by
⑩ Signature & Printed Name of Borrower
⑪ Signature & Printed Name of Secured Party

Receipt for Collateral: If it is desired that the property offered as collateral be held by the secured party, it will be necessary to alter the above Security Agreement by deleting Paragraphs 5 and 6 and preparing this receipt for the collateral. This receipt provides:

- That the secured party has obtained the collateral and will hold it as security until the loan is repaid
- That if the borrower defaults on the obligation, the property may be disposed of to satisfy the obligation
- That the borrower will pay any costs and expenses relating to holding the property
- That the secured party does not acknowledge the value or condition of the property offered as collateral

A sample numbered version of this form is found on page 306. Use the following information to fill out the Receipt for Collateral:

① Date of Promissory Note
② Date of Security Agreement
③ Name of Borrower
④ Address of Borrower
⑤ Name of Noteholder/Secured Party
⑥ Address of Noteholder/Secured Party
⑦ Description of personal property used as collateral
⑧ Date of this Receipt
⑨ Signature & Printed Name of Borrower
⑩ Signature & Printed Name of Noteholder/Secured Party

General Guaranty: This form provides for a guarantor for the repayment of a debt. This *guarantor* is, in effect, a co-signer for the obligation. The guarantor agrees that he or she will make the payments if any of the payments are late or not paid. The guarantor also agrees to pay any costs of collection if the guaranty is not lived up to. The guarantor also agrees that the guaranty may be enforced without having to first sue the borrower for defaulting on the debt. A mere default by the borrower without any court action will suffice to require the guarantor to make good on the obligation. A sample numbered version of this form is found on page 307. Complete this form by inserting the following information:

① Date of Promissory Note
② Date of Security Agreement
③ Name of Guarantor
④ Address of Guarantor
⑤ Name of Noteholder/Secured Party
⑥ Address of Noteholder/Secured Party
⑦ Number of days that payments are due under this guaranty
⑧ Date of this Guaranty
⑨ Signature & Printed Name of Guarantor
⑩ Signature & Printed Name of Noteholder/Secured Party

Release of Security Interest: This form acts as a release of property from its nature as collateral for a loan. In addition, when the loan is repaid, the promissory note or obligation should also be released (See Chapter 16). A sample numbered version of this form is found on page 308. To fill in this form, simply provide the names and addresses of the parties and a description of the security interest being released.

1. Name of Secured party
2. Address of Secured party
3. Name of Borrower
4. Address of Borrower
5. Date of Security agreement
6. Date of Release
7. Signature & Printed Name of Secured Party
8. Signature & Printed Name of Borrower

U.C.C. Financing Statement: This form is a memorandum of the details of a security arrangement. It is designed to be filed with the appropriate state filing office in order to record the security interest. Once filed, this statement serves as a public record of the date and time that the security interest in the particular property was perfected. Please type or laser-print this form. Be sure it is completely legible. Read all Instructions, especially Instruction 1; correct Debtor name is crucial. Follow these Instructions completely. As this is an official form, the instructions for this form are somewhat more complex than others in this book. Fill in form very carefully; mistakes may have important legal consequences. If you have questions, consult an attorney. Filing offices cannot give legal advice. Do not insert anything in the open space in the upper portion of this form; it is reserved for filing office use.

When properly completed, send the Filing Office a copy, with required fee, to filing office. If you want an acknowledgment, complete item B and, if filing in a filing office that returns an acknowledgment copy furnished by filer, you may also send an Acknowledgment copy. If you want to make a search request, complete item 7 (after reading Instruction 7 below) and send Search Report copy, otherwise detach. Always print out two Debtor and Secured Party copies. If you need to use attachments, use 8-1/2 X 11 inch sheets and put at the top of each sheet the name of the first Debtor, formatted exactly as it appears in item 1 of this form; you are encouraged to use Addendum (Form UCC1Ad). Note: This Addendum form is not included on with this book or CD; versions of this form and other official U.C.C. forms are available from the International Organization of Commercial Administrators at **http://www.iaca.org/node/68**.

A sample numbered version of this form is found on page 309. Line by line instructions for the U.C.C. Financing Statement follow on the next few pages:

A. To assist filing offices that might wish to communicate with filer, filer may provide information in item A. This item is optional.

B. Complete item B if you want an acknowledgment sent to you. If filing in a filing office that returns an acknowledgment copy furnished by filer, present simultaneously with this form a copy of this form for use as an acknowledgment copy.

1. Debtor name: Enter only one Debtor name in item 1, an organization's name (1a) or an individual's name (1b). Enter Debtor's exact full legal name. Don't abbreviate.

1a. Organization Debtor. "Organization" means an entity having a legal identity separate from its owner. A partnership is an organization; a sole proprietorship is not an organization, even if it does business under a trade name. If Debtor is a partnership, enter exact full legal name of partnership; you need not enter names of partners as additional Debtors. If Debtor is a registered organization (e.g., corporation, limited partnership, limited liability company), it is advisable to examine Debtor's current filed charter documents to determine Debtor's correct name, organization type, and jurisdiction of organization.

1b. Individual Debtor. "Individual" means a natural person; this includes a sole proprietorship, whether or not operating under a trade name. Don't use prefixes (Mr., Mrs., Ms.). Use suffix box only for titles of lineage (Jr., Sr., III) and not for other suffixes or titles (e.g., M.D.). Use married woman's personal name (Mary Smith, not Mrs. John Smith). Enter individual Debtor's family name (surname) in Last Name box, first given name in First Name box, and all additional given names in Middle Name box.

For both organization and individual Debtors: Don't use Debtor's trade name, DBA, AKA, FKA, Division name, etc. in place of or combined with Debtor's legal name; you may add such other names as additional Debtors if you wish (but this is neither required nor recommended).

1c. An address is always required for the Debtor named in 1a or 1b.

1d. Debtor's taxpayer identification number (tax ID #) — social security number or employer identification number — may be required in some states.

1e,f,g. "Additional information re organization Debtor" is always required. Type of organization and jurisdiction of organization as well as Debtor's exact legal name can be determined from Debtor's current filed charter document. Organizational ID #, if any, is assigned by the agency where the charter document was filed; this is different from tax ID #; this should be entered preceded by the 2-character U.S. Postal identification of state of organization if one of the United States (e.g., CA12345, for a California corporation whose organizational ID # is 12345); if agency does not assign organizational ID #, check box in item 1g indicating "none." Note: If Debtor is a trust or a trustee acting with respect to property held in trust, enter Debtor's name in item 1 and attach Addendum (Form UCC1Ad) and check appropriate box in item 17. If Debtor is a decedent's estate, enter name of deceased individual in item 1b and attach Addendum (Form UCC1Ad) and check appropriate box in item 17. If Debtor is a transmitting utility or this Financing Statement is filed in connection with a Manufactured-Home Transaction or a Public-Finance Transaction as defined in applicable Commercial Code, attach Addendum (Form UCC1Ad) and check appropriate box in item 18.

2. If an additional Debtor is included, complete item 2, determined and formatted per Instruction 1. To include further additional Debtors, or one or more additional Secured Parties, attach either Addendum (Form UCC1Ad) or other additional page(s), using correct name format. Follow Instruction 1 for determining and formatting additional names.

3. Enter information for Secured Party or Total Assignee, determined and formatted per Instruction 1. If there is more than one Secured Party, see Instruction 2. If there has been a total assignment of the Secured Party's interest prior to filing this form, you may either (1) enter Assignor S/P's name and address in item 3 and file an Amendment (Form UCC3) [see item 5 of that form]; or (2) enter Total Assignee's name and address in item 3 and, if you wish, also attaching Addendum (Form UCC1Ad) giving Assignor S/P's name and address in item 12.

4. Use item 4 to indicate the collateral covered by this Financing Statement. If space in item 4 is insufficient, put the entire collateral description or continuation of the collateral description on either Addendum (Form UCC1Ad) or other attached additional page(s).

5. If filer desires (at filer's option) to use titles of lessee and lessor, or consignee and consignor, or seller and buyer (in the case of accounts or chattel paper), or bailee and bailor instead of Debtor and Secured Party, check the appropriate box in item 5. If this is an agricultural lien (as defined in applicable Commercial Code) filing or is otherwise not a UCC security interest filing (e.g., a tax lien, judgment lien, etc.), check the appropriate box in item 5, complete items 1-7 as applicable and attach any other items required under other law.

6. If this Financing Statement is filed as a fixture filing or if the collateral consists of timber to be cut or as-extracted collateral, complete items 1-5, check the box in item 6, and complete the required information (items 13, 14 and/or 15) on Addendum (Form UCC1Ad).

7. This item is optional. Check appropriate box in item 7 to request Search Report(s) on all or some of the Debtors named in this Financing Statement. The Report will list all Financing Statements on file against the designated Debtor on the date of the Report, including this Financing Statement. There is an additional fee for each Report. If you have checked a box in item 7, file Search Report Copy together with Filing Officer Copy (and Acknowledgment Copy). Note: Not all states do searches and not all states will honor a search request made via this form; some states require a separate request form.

8. This item is optional and is for filer's use only. For filer's convenience of reference, filer may enter in item 8 any identifying information (e.g., Secured Party's loan number, law firm file number, Debtor's name or other identification, state in which form is being filed, etc.) that filer may find useful.

Release of U.C.C. Financing Statement: This form is a memorandum detailing the release of a financing obligation and should be filed with the state filing office to clear the records once the obligation has been satisfied. To fill in this form, simply provide the names and addresses of the parties and a description of the financing statement being released. A sample numbered version of this form is found on page 310. The form will be completed by the filing office and stamped or sealed.

① Adopted in what state
② Name of Borrower
③ Address of Borrower
④ Name(s) of Secured Party
⑤ Address(es) of Secured Party
⑥ Describe personal property
⑦ File # of Original Financing Statement
⑧ Date of Release
⑨ Number and address where Original Financing Statement was filed
⑩ Date signed
⑪ Signature of Secured Party
⑫ Printed Name of Secured Party
⑬ Notary to fill out this section

Security Agreement

This agreement is made on ①_____ , 20 _____ , between
②_____ , borrower,
address: ③

and ④_____ , secured
party,
address: ⑤

For valuable consideration, the parties agree as follows:

1. The borrower grants the secured party a security interest under Article 9 of the Uniform Commercial Code (U.C.C.) in the following personal property which will be considered collateral: ⑥

2. This security interest is granted to secure payment by the borrower to the secured party on the following obligation: ⑦

3. In the event of default by the borrower in payment of any of the amounts due on the obligation listed under Paragraph 2, the secured party may declare the entire obligation immediately due and payable and will have all of the remedies of a secured party under the Uniform Commercial Code.

4. In the event of such default, borrower will also be responsible for any costs of collection, including court costs and attorney fees.

5. The borrower agrees to use reasonable care in using the collateral and agrees not to sell or dispose of the collateral.

6. The borrower agrees to keep the collateral adequately insured and at the following address for the entire term of this security agreement: ⑧

7. The borrower represents that the collateral is owned free and clear and that there are no other security agreements, indebtedness, or liens relating to the property offered as collateral. Borrower also states that it has full authority to grant this security interest.

8. Borrower agrees to sign any financing statements that are required by the secured party to perfect this security interest.

9. No modification of this agreement will be effective unless it is in writing and is signed by both parties. This agreement binds and benefits both parties and any successors.

10. Time is of the essence of this agreement. This document, including any attachments, is the entire agreement between the parties. This agreement is governed by the laws of the State of ⑨_____ .

The parties have signed this agreement on the date specified at the beginning of this agreement.

⑩_____
Signature of Borrower

_____
Printed Name of Borrower

⑪_____
Signature of Secured Party

_____
Printed Name of Secured Party

Receipt for Collateral

This receipt is made in connection with the promissory note dated ①_____ ,
20 _____ , and the security agreement dated ②_____ , 20 _____ , between
③_____ , borrower,
address: ④

and ⑤_____ , noteholder/
secured party,
address: ⑥

The noteholder/secured party acknowledges delivery of the following described
personal property as collateral under the security agreement: ⑦

This collateral is subject to the lien and all of the conditions of the security agreement. In the event of the borrower's default on any of the terms of the note or
security agreement, this property may be disposed of by the noteholder/secured
party to satisfy any of the borrower's obligations as allowed by law.

The borrower will continue to pay all costs and expenses relating to this property,
including any maintenance, storage fees, insurance, or taxes.

This receipt does not acknowledge the condition or the value of the property retained as collateral.

Dated: ⑧_____ , 20 _____

⑨_____
Signature of Borrower

_____
Printed Name of Borrower

⑩_____
Signature of Noteholder/Secured Party

_____
Printed Name of Noteholder/Secured Party

General Guaranty

This guaranty is made in connection with the promissory note dated ①_____ , 20 ___ , and the security agreement dated ②_____ , 20 ____ , between ③_____ _____ , guarantor

address: ④

and ⑤_____ , secured party/noteholder, address: ⑥

For value received, the guarantor unconditionally guarantees payment of all payments on the above promissory note when due and satisfaction of all terms of the security agreement.

The guarantor waives demand, presentment for payment, protest, and notice, and agrees that the secured party/noteholder does not have to exhaust all rights against the borrower before demanding payment under this guaranty.

In the event that all payments due under this guaranty are not paid on demand within ⑦_____ days of demand, guarantor will also be responsible for any costs of collection on this note, including court costs and attorney fees.

This guaranty both binds and benefits both parties and any successors.

Dated: ⑧_____ , 20 _____

⑨_____
Signature of Guarantor

_____
Printed Name of Guarantor

⑩_____
Signature of Secured Party/Noteholder

_____
Printed Name of Secured Party/Noteholder

Release of Security Interest

For valuable consideration,

① _____ , secured party,

address: ②

releases ③ _____ , borrower,

address: ④

from the following specific security agreement, dated: ⑤ _____ , 20 _____ :

Any claims or obligations that not specifically mentioned are not released by this release of security interest.

The secured party has not assigned any claims or obligations covered by this release to any other party.

The secured party will sign a release of U.C.C. financing statement if requested by borrower.

The party signing this release intends that it both bind and benefit any successors.

Dated: ⑥ _____ , 20 _____

⑦ _____

Signature of Secured Party

_____

Printed Name of Secured Party

⑧ _____

Signature of Borrower

_____

Printed Name of Borrower

UNIFORM COMMERCIAL CODE
FINANCING STATEMENT FORM

A. NAME & DAYTIME PHONE NUMBER OF CONTACT PERSON

B. SEND ACKNOWLEDGEMENT TO:
Name

Address

Address

City/State/Zip

THE ABOVE SPACE IS FOR FILING OFFICE USE ONLY

1. DEBTOR'S EXACT FULL LEGAL NAME – INSERT ONLY **ONE** DEBTOR NAME (**1a OR 1b**) – Do Not Abbreviate or Combine Names

1.a ORGANIZATION'S NAME			
1.b INDIVIDUAL'S LAST NAME	FIRST NAME	MIDDLE NAME	SUFFIX
1.c MAILING ADDRESS Line One	This space not available.		
MAILING ADDRESS Line Two	CITY	STATE POSTAL CODE	COUNTRY
1.d TAX ID#	REQUIRED ADD'L INFO RE: ORGANIZATION DEBTOR	1.e TYPE OF ORGANIZATION	1.f JURISDICTION OF ORGANIZATION	1.g ORGANIZATIONAL ID# ☐ NONE

2. ADDITIONAL DEBTOR'S EXACT FULL LEGAL NAME – INSERT ONLY **ONE** DEBTOR NAME (**2a OR 2b**) – Do Not Abbreviate or Combine Names

2.a ORGANIZATION'S NAME			
2.b INDIVIDUAL'S LAST NAME	FIRST NAME	MIDDLE NAME	SUFFIX
2.c MAILING ADDRESS Line One	This space not available.		
MAILING ADDRESS Line Two	CITY	STATE POSTAL CODE	COUNTRY
2.d TAX ID#	REQUIRED ADD'L INFO RE: ORGANIZATION DEBTOR	2.e TYPE OF ORGANIZATION	2.f JURISDICTION OF ORGANIZATION	2.g ORGANIZATIONAL ID# ☐ NONE

3. SECURED PARTY'S NAME (or NAME of TOTAL ASSIGNEE of ASSIGNOR S/P) – INSERT ONLY **ONE** SECURED PARTY (**3a OR3b**)

3.a ORGANIZATION'S NAME			
3.b INDIVIDUAL'S LAST NAME	FIRST NAME	MIDDLE NAME	SUFFIX
3.c MAILING ADDRESS Line One	This space not available.		
MAILING ADDRESS Line Two	CITY	STATE POSTAL CODE	COUNTRY

4. This FINANCING STATEMENT covers the following collateral:

5. ALTERNATE DESIGNATION (if applicable) ☐ LESSEE/LESSOR ☐ CONSIGNEE/CONSIGNOR ☐ BAILEE/BAILOR
☐ AG. LIEN ☐ NON-UCC FILING ☐ SELLER/BUYER

6. Florida DOCUMENTARY STAMP TAX – YOU ARE REQUIRED TO CHECK **EXACTLY ONE** BOX
☐ All documentary stamps due and payable or to become due and payable have been paid.

☐ No documentary stamps or taxes are required.

7. OPTIONAL FILER REFERENCE DATA

STANDARD FORM - FORM UCC-1 (REV.01/2009)   Filing Office Copy

Release of U.C.C. Financing Statement

This Release of Financing Statement is presented for filing under the U.C.C. (Uniform Commercial Code, as adopted in the following State of ①_____ .

(This Section for Use of the Filing Officer)

Date of filing _____ Time of filing _____
Number and address of filing office_____

Name(s) of Borrower ②_____
Address(es) of Borrower ③

Name(s) of Secured Party ④_____
Address(es) of Secured Party ⑤

The original financing statement covers the following personal property: ⑥

File # of Original Financing Statement ⑦_____

Dated: ⑧_____ , 20 _____

Number and address where Original Financing Statement was filed ⑨_____
_____

Dated: ⑩_____ , 20 _____   Seal

⑪_____   ⑫_____
Signature of Secured Party   Printed Name of Secured Party

⑬

State of _____

County of _____

On _____ , 20 _____ , _____
personally came before me and, being duly sworn, did state that he or she is
the person described in the above document and that he or she signed the above
document in my presence.

_____

Signature of Notary Public

Notary Public, In and for the County of _____

State of _____

My commission expires: _____   Notary Seal

Chapter 16

Promissory Notes

Contained in this chapter are various promissory notes. A *promissory note* is a document by which a borrower promises to pay the holder of the note a certain amount of money under specific terms. In the forms in this chapter, the person who borrows the money is referred to as the *borrower* and the person whom the borrower is to pay is referred to as the *noteholder*. The noteholder is generally also the lender, but this need not be so. The forms in this chapter are intended for use only by individuals who are not regularly in the business of lending money. Complex state and federal regulations apply to lending institutions and such rules are beyond the scope of this book. This chapter also contains various forms for demanding payments on a promissory note. *Note*: If you are at all unsure of the correct use of any forms in this chapter, please consult a competent attorney.

Instructions for Promissory Notes

Promissory Note (Installment Repayment): This type of promissory note is a standard unsecured note. Being *unsecured* means that the noteholder has no collateral or specific property to foreclose against should the borrower default on the note. If the borrower doesn't pay, the noteholder must sue and get a general judgment against the borrower. Collection of the judgment may then be made against the borrower's assets.

This particular note calls for the borrower to pay a certain annual interest rate on the note and to make periodic payments to the noteholder. It also has certain general terms:

- The borrower may prepay any amount on the note without penalty
- If the borrower is in default, the noteholder may demand full payment on the note
- The note is not assumable by anyone other than the borrower
- The borrower waives certain formalities relating to demands for payment
- The borrower agrees to pay any of the costs of collection after a default

A sample numbered version of this form is found on page 316. In order to complete this form, the following information is necessary:

① Amount of Note
② Date of Note
③ Name of borrower
④ Address of borrower
⑤ Name of noteholder
⑥ Address of noteholder
⑦ Principle amount
⑧ Interest rate
⑨ Number of installments
⑩ Amount of payments
⑪ What day of the "payment period" payment is due
⑫ The period for the installments (for example, monthly or weekly)
⑬ Payment in full by this date
⑭ The number of days a payment may be late before it is considered a default
⑮ Signature of borrower
⑯ Printed name of borrower

Promissory Note (Lump Sum Repayment): This note is also an unsecured promise to pay. However, this version of a promissory note calls for the payment, including accrued interest, to be paid in one lump sum at a certain date in the future. This note has the same general conditions relating to prepayment, defaults, and assumability as the Promissory Note with Installment Payments discussed on the previous page. A sample numbered version of this form is found on page 317. Complete this form by inserting the following information:

① Amount of Note
② Date of Note
③ Name of borrower
④ Address of borrower
⑤ Name of noteholder
⑥ Address of noteholder
⑦ Principle amount
⑧ Interest rate

⑨ Date that lump sum is due
⑩ The number of days a payment may be late before it is considered a default
⑪ Signature of borrower
⑫ Printed name of borrower

Promissory Note (on Demand): This also is an unsecured note. This type of promissory note, however, is immediately payable in full at any time upon the demand of the noteholder. This note has the same general conditions relating to prepayment, defaults, and assumability as the Promissory Note with Installment Payments discussed previously. A sample numbered version of this form is found on page 318. The following information is necessary to complete this form:

① Amount of Note
② Date of Note
③ Name of borrower
④ Address of borrower
⑤ Name of noteholder
⑥ Address of noteholder
⑦ Principle amount
⑧ Interest rate
⑨ The number of days past the demand date that payment may be made before the note is in default
⑩ Signature of borrower
⑪ Printed name of borrower

Release of Promissory Note: This release is intended to be used to release a party from obligations under a Promissory Note. There are several other methods by which to accomplish this same objective. The return of the original note to the maker, clearly marked "Paid in Full" will serve the same purpose. A Receipt in Full will also accomplish this goal (see Chapter 5: *Releases*). The Release of Promissory Note may, however, be used in those situations when the release is based on something other than payment in full of the underlying note. For example, the note may be satisfied by a gift from the bearer of the note of release from the obligation. Another situation may involve a release of the note based on a concurrent release of a claim that the maker of the note holds against the holder of the note. A sample numbered version of this form is found on page 319. Complete this form by inserting the following information:

① Date of original promissory note
② Amount of promissory note
③ Name of noteholder
④ Address of noteholder

⑤ Name of borrower
⑥ Address of borrower
⑦ Date of release signed
⑧ Signature of noteholder
⑨ Printed name of noteholder

Demand and Notice of Default on Installment Promissory Note: This form will be used to notify the maker of a promissory note of his or her default on an installment payment on a promissory note. Notice of default should be sent promptly to any account that falls behind in its payments on a note. This promissory note provides a legal basis for a suit for breach of the promissory note. A sample numbered version of this form is found on page 320. Complete this form by inserting the following information:

① Date of demand
② Name and address of borrower
③ Name of borrower
④ Date of original note
⑤ Amount of original note
⑥ Date of default payment
⑦ Amount of default payment
⑧ Signature of noteholder
⑨ Printed name of noteholder

Promissory Note (Installment Repayment)

$ ①_____

Dated: ②_____ , 20 _____

For value received,

③_____ , Borrower,
address: ④

promises to pay

⑤_____ , Noteholder,
address: ⑥

the principal amount of $ ⑦_____ , with interest at the annual rate of
⑧_____ percent, on any unpaid balance.

Payments are payable to the Noteholder in ⑨_____ consecutive
installments of $ ⑩ _____ , including interest, and continuing on the
⑪_____ day of each ⑫_____ until paid in full. If not paid off
sooner, this note is due and payable in full on ⑬_____ , 20 _____ .

This note may be prepaid in whole or in part at any time without penalty. If the
Borrower is in default more than ⑭_____ days with any payment, this
note is payable upon demand of any Noteholder. This note is not assumable
without the written consent of the Noteholder. The Borrower waives demand,
presentment for payment, protest, and notice. In the event of any default, the
Borrower will be responsible for any costs of collection on this note, including
court costs and attorney fees.

⑮_____
Signature of Borrower

⑯_____
Printed Name of Borrower

Promissory Note (Lump Sum Repayment)

$ ①_____

Dated: ②_____ , 20 _____

For value received,
③_____ , Borrower,
address: ④

promises to pay
⑤_____ , Noteholder,
address: ⑥

the principal amount of $ ⑦_____ , with interest at the annual rate of
⑧_____ percent, on any unpaid balance.

Payment on this note is due and payable to the Noteholder in full on or before
⑨_____ , 20 _____ .

This note may be prepaid in whole or in part at any time without penalty. If the Borrower is in default more than ⑩_____ days with any payment, this note is payable upon demand of any Noteholder. This note is not assumable without the written consent of the Noteholder. The Borrower waives demand, presentment for payment, protest, and notice. In the event of any default, the Borrower will be responsible for any costs of collection on this note, including court costs and attorney fees.

⑪_____
Signature of Borrower

⑫_____
Printed Name of Borrower

Promissory Note (on Demand)

$ ①_____

Dated: ②_____ , 20 _____

For value received,
③_____ , Borrower,
address: ④

promises to pay ON DEMAND to
⑤_____ , Noteholder,
address: ⑥

the principal amount of $ ⑦_____ , with interest at the annual rate of
⑧_____ percent, on any unpaid balance.

This note may be prepaid in whole or in part at any time without penalty. This note is not assumable without the written consent of the Noteholder. The Borrower waives demand, presentment for payment, protest, and notice. In the event of such default of over ⑨_____ days in making payment, the Borrower will be also be responsible for any costs of collection on this note, including court costs and attorney fees.

⑩_____
Signature of Borrower

⑪_____
Printed Name of Borrower

Release of Promissory Note

In consideration of full payment of the promissory note dated
①_____ , 20 _____ , in the face amount of $ ②_____ ,
③_____ , Noteholder,
address: ④

releases and discharges
⑤_____ , Borrower,
address: ⑥

from any claims or obligations on account of this note.

The party signing this release intends that it bind and benefit both itself and any successors.

Dated: ⑦_____ , 20 _____

⑧_____
Signature of Noteholder

⑨_____
Printed Name of Noteholder

Demand and Notice of Default on Installment Promissory Note

Date: ①_____ , 20 _____

To: ②_____

RE: Default on Installment Promissory Note

Dear ③_____ :

Regarding the promissory note dated ④_____ , 20 _____ , in the original amount of $ ⑤_____ , of which you are the maker, you have defaulted on the installment payment due on ⑥_____ , 20 _____ , in the amount of $ ⑦_____ .

Demand is made upon you for payment of this past-due installment payment. If payment is not received by us within ten (10) days from the date of this notice, we will proceed to enforce our rights under the promissory note for collection of the entire balance.

Very truly,

⑧_____
Signature of Noteholder

⑨_____
Printed Name of Noteholder

Chapter 17

Purchase of Goods Documents

The documents in this chapter are all related to the purchase and sale of goods from the perspective of the business doing the purchasing. The purchase and sale of goods in business situations is governed by the Uniform Commercial Code (U.C.C.) as it has been adopted by the various states. The forms in this chapter are intended to be used to comply with the provisions of the U.C.C. .

Instructions for Purchase of Goods Documents

Request for Price Quote: This form is used to obtain a firm price quote for particular goods. It allows the purchaser to lock in the price for a certain time period and bars the seller from raising the price during that period. A sample numbered version of this form is found on page 326. Complete this form with the following information:
1. Date of request
2. Name of person or business supplying quote
3. Name of person or business supplying quote
4. Goods/items to be quoted
5. Signature of person requesting quote
6. Printed name of person requesting quote

Notice of Acceptance of Order: This form provides for acceptance of an order and acknowledgment that the order has been inspected and approved by the purchaser. This form is found on page 327. Complete this form by inserting the following information:
1. Date of Notice
2. Name or company name that notice will be sent to
3. Name or company name that notice will be sent to
4. Purchase order #

⑤ Date of purchase order
⑥ List goods received
⑦ Provide invoice # and packing slip #
⑧ Signature & Printed Name of person accepting order

Notice of Conditional Acceptance of Non-Conforming Goods: When a purchaser receives a shipment of goods that does not conform to the order that was placed, the purchaser may offer to accept the goods on the condition that the purchase price be adjusted to accommodate for the non-conformity of the goods. The seller, of course, has the right to reject any discount and request that the goods be returned. This form allows for a conditional acceptance of the goods and requests that a price reduction be allowed within 10 days. A sample version of this form is found on page 328. Complete this form by inserting the following information:
① Date of Notice
② Name and address of person/company receiving notice
③ Name of person/company receiving notice
④ Date goods received
⑤ Purchase order #
⑥ Date of purchase order
⑦ Reasons items do not conform
⑧ Amount to credit account
⑨ Total price of goods after condition credit is applied
⑩ Signature
⑪ Printed Name

Notice of Rejection of Non-Conforming Goods: Use this form after the above form has been used and the 10-day period for acceptance of the price reduction terms has expired. This forms notifies the seller that the goods have been fully rejected for non-conformity with the original purchase order. It also gives the seller 10 days to return the money paid for the goods and 10 days to arrange for return of the goods. If the money is not returned, the advice of an attorney versed in business law should be sought. A sample numbered version of this form is found on page 329. Complete this form by inserting the following information:
① Date of Notice
② Name and address of person/company receiving notice
③ Name of person/company receiving notice
④ Date goods received
⑤ Purchase order #
⑥ Date of purchase order
⑦ Reasons items do not conform
⑧ Check # and date of check
⑨ Amount of check

⑩ Signature
⑪ Printed Name

Notice of Conditional Acceptance of Defective Goods: When a purchaser receives a shipment of goods that is defective or damaged in some manner, the purchaser may offer to accept the goods on the condition that the purchase price be adjusted to accommodate for the defect in the goods. The seller, of course, has the right to reject any discount and request that the goods be returned. This form allows for a conditional acceptance of the goods and requests that a price reduction be allowed within 10 days. A sample numbered version of this form is found on page 330. Complete this form by inserting the following information:

① Date of Notice
② Name and address of person/company receiving notice
③ Name of person/company receiving notice
④ Date goods received
⑤ Purchase order #
⑥ Date of purchase order
⑦ Reasons items are defective
⑧ Amount to credit account
⑨ New total after condition amount applied
⑪ Signature
⑫ Printed Name

Notice of Rejection of Defective Goods: This form should be used after using the above form and after the 10-day period for acceptance of the price reduction terms has expired. This form notifies the seller that the goods have been fully rejected because of defects. It also gives the seller 10 days to return the money paid for the goods and 10 days to arrange for return of the goods. If the money is not returned, the advice of an attorney versed in business law should be sought. A sample of this form is found on page 331. Complete this form by inserting the following information:

① Date of Notice
② Name and address of person/company receiving notice
③ Name of person/company receiving notice
④ Date goods received
⑤ Purchase order #
⑥ Date of purchase order
⑦ Reasons items are defective
⑧ Check # and date account paid
⑨ Amount paid
⑩ Signature
⑪ Printed Name

Notice of Rejection of Order: This form is a generic form for the rejection of an order by the purchaser. In addition to rejection of an order for non-conformity or for defective goods, orders may be rejected for unreasonable delay in shipment, damage, partial shipment only, that the price charged was not what was quoted, etc. It gives the seller 10 days to return the money paid for the goods. If the money is not returned, the advice of a business attorney should be sought. A sample of this form is found on page 332. Complete this form by inserting the following information:

① Date of Notice
② Name and address of person/company receiving notice
③ Name of person/company receiving notice
④ Date goods received
⑤ Purchase order #
⑥ Date of purchase order
⑦ Reasons items are rejected
⑧ Check # and date account paid
⑨ Amount paid
⑩ Signature
⑪ Printed Name

Notice of Refusal to Accept Delivery: This form should be used in those situations when the actual delivery of the goods is rejected (for example, when physical damage is evident on immediate inspection). A sample numbered version of this form is found on page 333. Complete this form by inserting the following information:

① Date of Notice
② Name and address of person/company receiving notice
③ Name of person/company receiving notice
④ Date goods received
⑤ Purchase order #
⑥ Date of purchase order
⑦ Reasons items are not accepted
⑧ Check # and date account paid
⑨ Amount paid
⑩ Signature
⑪ Printed Name

Notice of Demand for Delivery of Goods: The use of this form is required in situations in which goods have been ordered and paid for, but not delivered. This notifies the seller of a demand for immediate shipment of the goods or return of the money. A sample numbered version of this form is found on page 334. Complete this form by inserting the following information:

① Date of Notice
② Name and address of person/company receiving notice

③ Name of person/company receiving notice
④ Date goods were ordered
⑤ Purchase order #
⑥ Date of purchase order
⑦ Items/goods ordered
⑧ Check # and date account paid
⑨ Amount paid
⑩ Signature
⑪ Printed Name

Notice of Cancellation of Purchase Order: After the use of the previous form notifying the seller of a demand for delivery of goods and after the expiration of the 10-day period set for delivery by the above notice, this form should be sent to the seller. It effectively cancels the original purchase order for non-delivery and demands the return of any money paid. If the money is not returned, the advice of an attorney competent in business law should be sought. A sample of this form is found on page 335. Complete the form with the following information:
① Date of Notice
② Name and address of person/company receiving notice
③ Name of person/company receiving notice
④ Date goods were ordered
⑤ Purchase order #
⑥ Items/goods ordered
⑦ Check # and date account paid
⑧ Amount paid
⑨ Date of demand
⑩ Signature
⑪ Printed Name

Notice of Return of Goods Sold on Approval: When a purchaser receives goods *on approval*, he or she is allowed to examine the goods for a certain period and return them to the seller if desired within that time frame. This form is used to notify the seller of the decision to return the goods sold on approval. This form is found on page 336. Complete the form with the following information:
① Date of Notice
② Name and address of person/company receiving notice
③ Name of person/company receiving notice
④ Date goods were ordered
⑤ Purchase order #
⑥ Items/goods received on approval
⑦ Signature
⑧ Printed Name

Request For Price Quote

Date: ① _____ , 20 _____

To: ② _____

RE: Request for Price Quote

Dear ③ _____ :

We are interested in purchasing the following goods: ④

Please provide us with a firm quote for your standard price for these goods and the time period during which this quote will be good. Also, please provide us with your discount schedule for volume purchases. Please also provide us with the following information regarding any order that we might place with your company:

1. The standard terms for payment of invoices
  2. The availability of an open credit account with your firm. (If available, please provide us with the appropriate credit application)
3. Any delivery costs for orders. (If these costs are included in the price quote, please indicate on the quote)
4. Any sales or other taxes. (If these costs are included in the price quote, please indicate)
5. The usual delivery time for orders from the date of your receipt of a purchase order to our receipt of the goods

Very truly,

⑤ _____
Signature

⑥ _____
Printed Name

Notice of Acceptance of Order

Date: ① _____ , 20 _____

To: ② _____

RE: Acceptance of Order

Dear ③ _____ :

Please be advised that we have received the following goods, pursuant to our purchase order # ④ _____ , dated ⑤ _____ , 20 _____ : ⑥

The goods are further identified by invoice # ⑦ _____ and bill of lading/packing slip # _____ .

Please be advised that we have inspected the goods and they have been received in good condition, with no defects, and in conformity with our order.

Accordingly, we accept this shipment of goods.

Very truly,

⑧ _____
Signature

_____
Printed Name

Notice of Conditional Acceptance of Non-Conforming Goods

Date: ①_____ , 20 _____

To: ②_____

RE: Conditional Acceptance of Non-Conforming Goods

Dear ③_____ :

On ④_____ , 20 ___ , we received delivery from you on our purchase order #⑤_____ , dated ⑥_____ , 20 _____ . The goods which were delivered at that time do not conform to the specifications that were provided with our purchase order for the following reasons: ⑦

Although these goods are non-conforming and we are not obligated to accept them, we are prepared to accept these goods on the condition that you credit our account with you for $ ⑧_____ . This credit will make the total price of the goods under this purchase order $ ⑨_____ .

If you do not accept this proposal within ten (10) days from the date of this notice, we will reject these goods as non-conforming and they will be returned to you.

Please be advised that we reserve all of our rights under the Uniform Commercial Code and any other applicable laws.

Thank you for your immediate attention to this matter.

Very truly,

⑩_____
Signature

⑪_____
Printed Name

Notice of Rejection of Non-Conforming Goods

Date: ①_____ , 20 _____

To: ②_____

RE: Rejection of Non-Conforming Goods

Dear ③_____ :

On ④_____ , 20 _____ , we received delivery from you on our purchase order # ⑤_____ , dated ⑥_____ , 20 _____ .
The goods which were delivered at that time do not conform to the specifications that were provided with our purchase order for the following reasons: ⑦

We paid for these goods by our check # ⑧_____ , dated _____ , 20 _____ , in the amount of $ ⑨_____ .
This check has been cashed by you.

By this notice, we reject the delivery of these goods and demand the return of our money. Unless we receive a refund of our money within ten (10) days of the date of this letter, we will take immediate legal action for the return of our money. Please further advise us as to your wishes for the return of the rejected goods at your expense. Unless we receive return instructions within ten (10) days of this letter, we accept no responsibility for the safe storage of these goods.

Please be advised that we reserve all of our rights under the Uniform Commercial Code and any other applicable laws.

Thank you for your immediate attention to this matter.

Very truly,

⑩_____
Signature

⑪_____
Printed Name

329

Notice of Conditional Acceptance of Defective Goods

Date: ①_____ , 20 _____

To: ②_____

RE: Conditional Acceptance of Defective Goods

Dear ③_____ :

On ④_____ , 20 _____ , we received delivery from you on our purchase order # ⑤_____ , dated ⑥_____ , 20 _____ . The goods which were delivered at that time were defective for the following reasons: ⑦

Although these goods are defective and we are not obligated to accept them, we are prepared to accept these goods on the condition that you credit our account with you for $ ⑧_____ . This credit will make the total price of the goods under this purchase order $ ⑨_____ .

If you do not accept this proposal within ten (10) days from the date of this notice, we will reject these goods as defective and they will be returned to you.

Please be advised that we reserve all of our rights under the Uniform Commercial Code and any other applicable laws.

Thank you for your immediate attention to this matter.

Very truly,

⑩_____
Signature

⑪_____
Printed Name

Notice of Rejection of Defective Goods

Date: ①_____ , 20 _____

To: ②_____

RE: Rejection of Defective Goods

Dear ③_____ :

On ④_____ , 20 _____ , we received delivery from you on our pur-chase order # ⑤_____ , dated ⑥_____ , 20 _____ . The goods which were delivered at that time were defective for the following reasons: ⑦

We paid for these goods by our check # ⑧_____ , dated _____ _____ , 20 _____ , in the amount of $ ⑨_____ . This check has been cashed by you.

By this notice, we reject the delivery of these goods and demand the return of our money. Unless we receive a refund of our money within ten (10) days of the date of this letter, we will take immediate legal action for the return of our money. Please further advise us as to your wishes for the return of the rejected goods at your expense. Unless we receive instructions for their return within ten (10) days of this letter, we accept no responsibility for the safe storage of these goods.

Please be advised that we reserve all of our rights under the Uniform Commercial Code and any other applicable laws.

Thank you for your immediate attention to this matter.

Very truly,

⑩_____
Signature

⑪_____
Printed Name

Notice of Rejection of Order

Date: ①_____ , 20 _____

To: ②_____

RE: Rejection of Order

Dear ③_____ :

On ④ _____20 _____ , we received delivery from you on our purchase order # ⑤_____ dated ⑥_____ 20 _____ . We reject these goods for the following reasons: ⑦

We paid for these goods by our check # ⑧_____ , dated _____ _____ , 20 _____ , in the amount of $ ⑨_____ . This check has been cashed by you.

By this notice, we reject the delivery of these goods and demand the return of our money. Unless we receive a refund of our money within ten (10) days of the date of this letter, we will take immediate legal action for the return of our money. Please further advise us as to your wishes for the return of the rejected goods at your expense. Unless we receive instructions for their return within ten (10) days of this letter, we accept no responsibility for the safe storage of these goods.

Please be advised that we reserve all of our rights under the Uniform Commercial Code and any other applicable laws.

Thank you for your immediate attention to this matter.

Very truly,

⑩_____
Signature

⑪_____
Printed Name

Notice of Refusal to Accept Delivery

Date: ① _____ , 20 _____

To: ② _____

RE: Refusal to Accept Delivery

Dear ③ _____ :

On ④ _____ , 20 _____ , we received delivery from you on our purchase order # ⑤ _____ , dated ⑥ _____ , 20 _____ . We do not accept delivery of these goods for the following reasons: ⑦

We paid for these goods by our check # ⑧ _____ , dated _____ _____ , 20 _____ , in the amount of $ ⑨ _____ . This check has been cashed by you.

By this notice, we refuse to accept the delivery of these goods and demand the return of our money. Unless we receive a refund of our money within ten (10) days of the date of this letter, we will take immediate legal action for the return of our money.

Please be advised that we reserve all of our rights under the Uniform Commercial Code and any other applicable laws.

Thank you for your immediate attention to this matter.

Very truly,

⑩ _____
Signature

⑪ _____
Printed Name

Notice of Demand for Delivery of Goods

Date: ①_____ , 20 _____

To: ②_____

RE: Demand for Delivery of Goods

Dear ③_____ :

On ④_____ , 20 _____ , by our purchase order
⑤_____ , a copy of which is enclosed, we ordered the
following goods from you: ⑦

We paid for these goods by our check # ⑧_____ , dated _____
_____ , 20 _____ , in the amount of $ ⑨_____ . This
check has been cashed by you.

To date, the goods have not been delivered to us. We, therefore, demand the
immediate delivery of these goods. Unless the goods are delivered to us within
ten (10) days of the date of this letter, we will take action to cancel this purchase
order and have our money returned.

Please be advised that we reserve all of our rights under the Uniform Commercial
Code and any other applicable laws.

Thank you for your immediate attention to this matter.

Very truly,

⑩_____
Signature

⑪_____
Printed Name

Notice of Cancellation of Purchase Order

Date: ①_____ , 20 _____

To: ②_____

RE: Cancellation of Purchase Order

Dear ③_____ :

On ④ _____ 20 _____ , by our purchase order # ⑤_____ ,
a copy of which is enclosed, we ordered the following goods from you: ⑥

We paid for these goods by our check # ⑦_____ dated _____ 20 _____ ,
in the amount of $ ⑧_____ . This check has been cashed by you.

On ⑨_____ , 20 _____ , we demanded immediate delivery of
the goods. To date, the goods have not been delivered to us.

By this notice, we, therefore, cancel this order for late delivery and demand the
immediate return of our money. Unless we receive a refund of our money within
ten (10) days of the date of this letter, we will take immediate legal action for the
return of our money.

Please be advised that we reserve all of our rights under the Uniform Commercial
Code and any other applicable laws.

Thank you for your immediate attention to this matter.

Very truly,

⑩_____
Signature

⑪_____
Printed Name

Notice of Return of Goods Sold on Approval

Date: ① _____ , 20 _____

To: ② _____

RE: Return of Goods Sold on Approval

Dear ③ _____ :

On ④ _____ , 20 _____ , by our purchase order
⑤ _____ , a copy of which is enclosed, we received the
following goods from you on approval: ⑥

Please be advised that at this time we are electing to return these goods to you.

Thank you very much for the opportunity to examine the goods.

Very truly,

⑦ _____
Signature

⑧ _____
Printed Name

Chapter 18

Sale of Goods Documents

The various forms included in this chapter are also intended to be used for situations involving the sale of goods. However, these forms are prepared for use by the seller.

The first set are forms to be used in response to a buyer's action after goods have been shipped. Two legal contracts relating to the sale of goods are also included. Finally, two documents relating to the bulk sales of business inventory are also included.

In addition to the forms in this chapter, throughout this book there are other forms that may be used by a business which sells products. For example, Bills of Sale (Chapter 9), Promissory Notes (Chapter 16), Collection of Accounts (Chapter 19), etc. may all be valuable at some time during the normal course of business.

Instructions for Sale of Goods Documents

Demand for Explanation of Rejected Goods: Use of this form will follow a seller's notification that the buyer has rejected goods. It demands a satisfactory explanation for the rejection. To complete this form, specify the date, name of buyer, purchase order number, type of goods shipped, and date of rejection of the goods. A sample form is found on page 341. Complete this form by inserting the following:

① Date of Demand
② Name and address of person/company receiving demand
③ Name of person/company receiving demand

④ Date goods were shipped
⑤ Purchase order # and date of purchase order
⑥ Items/goods shipped
⑦ Date of notification of rejection
⑧ Signature
⑨ Printed Name

Notice of Replacement of Rejected Goods: This notice is to be used to replace goods that have been reasonably rejected by a buyer. It also instructs the buyer to return the rejected goods at the seller's expense. To complete this form, specify the date, name of buyer, purchase order number, type of goods shipped, and date of rejection of the goods. A sample numbered version of this form is found on page 342. Complete this form by inserting the following information:

① Date of Notice
② Name and address of person/company receiving notice
③ Name of person/company receiving notice
④ Date goods were shipped
⑤ Purchase order # and date of purchase order
⑥ Items/goods shipped
⑦ Date of notification of rejection
⑧ Signature
⑨ Printed Name

Notice of Goods Sold on Approval: When goods are sold to a buyer on approval, this form should be used to specify the time period that the buyer has to examine the goods and either accept or return them. A sample numbered version of this form is found on page 343. Complete this form by inserting the following information:

① Date of Notice
② Name and address of person/company receiving notice
③ Name of person/company receiving notice
④ Items/goods being delivered
⑤ # of days given to return items/goods
⑥ Signature
⑦ Printed Name

Contract for Sale of Goods: This basic contract is for the one-time sale of specific goods. A sample numbered version of this form is found on page 344. Complete this form by inserting the following information:

① Date of contract

② Name of seller
③ Address of seller with name of city and state
④ Name of buyer
⑤ Address of buyer with name of city and state
⑥ List the goods being sold
⑦ Specifications of goods sold
⑧ Price of goods sold
⑨ Date of delivery of goods sold
⑩ Amount shipping cost
⑪ Date of payment
⑫ Additional terms
⑬ Governed by the laws of what State (generally, the state of the seller)
⑭ Signature & printed name of seller
⑮ Signature & printed name of buyer

Contract for Sale of Goods on Consignment: For the sale of goods to a buyer on *consignment* (for resale), this form should be used. It provides that the seller will deliver goods to the buyer and that the buyer will display and attempt to resell the goods. It also provides that the goods remain the property of the seller until sold and that the buyer must return any unsold goods on demand. A sample form is found on page 346. The following information will be used to prepare this document:

① Date of contract
② Name of seller
③ Address of seller with name of city and state
④ Name of buyer
⑤ Address of buyer with name of city and state
⑥ List goods being sold on consignment
⑦ List price of goods that are to be sold on consignment
⑧ Price the buyer on consignment will pay for the goods
⑨ Date of delivery of goods
⑩ Amount shipping cost
⑪ Date of payment
⑫ Additional terms
⑬ Governed by the laws of what State (generally, the state of the seller)
⑭ Signature & printed name of seller
⑮ Signature & printed name of buyer

Bulk Transfer Affidavit: The Uniform Commercial Code (U.C.C.) contains provisions that are designed to protect both potential buyers and creditors of businesses that intend to make bulk transfers of their inventory. Failure to comply with the Bulk Sales or Transfers Act portion of the U.C.C. will generally mean that original creditors of a seller will have a lien against the *assets* (inventory) which are transferred to the buyer. This form is to be used by a seller to inform the buyer of all creditors of the business and the amount of their claims against the business. Attach a separate sheet detailing the names, addresses, and amount claimed by all known creditors. If there are no creditors or if the Bulk Sales and Transfers Act does not apply to a particular sale, this form may also be used as an affidavit to such facts by noting "None" on the attached sheet. A sample numbered version of this form is found on page 348. Complete this form by inserting the following information:

① State of affidavit
② County of affidavit
③ Name of person making affidavit
④ Address of person making affidavit with name of city and state
⑤ Name of person selling business assets
⑥ Address of person selling business assets with name of city and state
⑦ Name of person buying business assets
⑧ Address of person buying business assets with name of city and state
⑨ State of affidavit
⑩ Date signed
⑪ Signature of Seller
⑫ Printed name of Seller

Bulk Transfer Notice: This form is to be used to provide notice to the creditors of the intended bulk sale of goods. To complete, simply fill in the buyer's and seller's names and addresses, date of the sales agreement, proposed closing date of the sale, and the state in which the sale will take place. A copy of this completed form should be supplied to each creditor. A sample numbered version of this form is found on page 349. The following information will be used to prepare this document:

① Date of Notice
② Name of person/company receiving notice
③ Name of person/company receiving notice
④ Name of person/company that intends to make a bulk sale or transfer of business assets
⑤ Address of person/company that intends to make a bulk sale or transfer of business assets
⑥ Date of agreement
⑦ Name of person buying business assets
⑧ Address of person buying business assets with name of city and state
⑨ Date of intended sale
⑩ State of affidavit
⑪ Signature and printed name of Seller
⑫ Signature and printed name of Buyer

Demand for Explanation of Rejected Goods

Date: ① _____ , 20 _____

To: ② _____

RE: Explanation of Rejected Goods

Dear ③ _____ :

On ④ _____ , 20 _____ , we shipped the following goods to you pursuant to your purchase order # ⑤ _____ , dated _____ , 20 _____ : ⑥

On ⑦ _____ , 20 _____ , we received notice that you had rejected delivery of these goods without satisfactory explanation. We, therefore, request that you provide us with an adequate explanation for this rejection. Unless we are provided with such explanation within ten (10) days, we will take legal action to obtain payment for these goods.

Please be advised that we reserve all of our rights under the Uniform Commercial Code and any other applicable laws.

Thank you for your immediate attention to this matter.

Very truly,

⑧ _____
Signature

⑨ _____
Printed Name

Notice of Replacement of Rejected Goods

Date: ① _____ , 20 _____

To: ② _____

RE: Replacement of Rejected Goods

Dear ③ _____ :

On ④ _____ , 20 _____ , we shipped the following goods to you pursuant to your purchase order # ⑤ _____ , dated _____ , 20 _____ : ⑥

On ⑦ _____ , 20 _____ , we received notice that you had rejected delivery of these goods.

Please return the rejected goods to us at our expense using the same carrier that delivered the goods.

In addition, please be advised that we are shipping replacement goods to you at our expense.

If this correction of the rejected goods is not satisfactory, please contact us immediately. We apologize for any problems this may have caused.

Very truly,

⑧ _____
Signature

⑨ _____
Printed Name

Goods Sold on Approval

Date: ①_____ , 20 _____

To: ②_____

RE: Goods Sold on Approval

Dear ③_____ :

Please be advised that the following goods are being delivered to you on approval: ④

If these goods do not meet your requirements, you may return all or a part of them at our expense within ⑤_____ days of your receipt of the goods.

Any of these goods sold on approval that have not been returned to us by that time will be considered accepted by you and you will be charged accordingly.

We trust that you will find our goods satisfactory. Thank you very much for your business.

Very truly,

⑥_____
Signature

⑦_____
Printed Name

Contract for Sale of Goods

This contract for sale of goods is made on ① _____ , 20 ___ , between ② _____ , seller, address: ③

and ④ _____ , buyer, address: ⑤

For valuable consideration, the parties agree as follows:

1. The seller agrees to sell and the buyer agrees to buy the following goods: ⑥

2. The seller agrees to provide goods which meet the following specifications: ⑦

3. The buyer agrees to pay the following price(s) for the goods: ⑧

4. The seller agrees that the goods will be delivered to the buyer's place of business by ⑨ _____ , 20 _____ . The shipping costs are estimated at $ ⑩ _____ , and will be paid by the ⑪ _____ _____ .

5. The seller represents that it has legal title to the goods and full authority to sell the goods. Seller also represents that the property is sold free and clear of all liens, mortgages, indebtedness, or liabilities.

6. Any additional terms: ⑫

7. No modification of this contract will be effective unless it is in writing and is signed by both parties. Time is of the essence of this contract. This contract binds

and benefits both the buyer and seller and any successors. This document, including any attachments, is the entire agreement between the buyer and seller. This contract is governed by the laws of the State of ⑬_____ .

The parties have signed this contract on the date specified at the beginning of this contract.

⑭_____   ⑮_____
Signature of Seller   Signature of Buyer

⑭_____   ⑮_____
Printed Name of Seller   Printed Name of Buyer

Contract for Sale of Goods on Consignment

This contract for sale of goods on consignment is made on ①_____ , 20 __ , between ②_____ , seller address: ③

and ④_____ , buyer address: ⑤

For valuable consideration, the parties agree as follows:

1. The seller agrees to provide the following goods to the buyer on consignment: ⑥

2. The buyer agrees to display the goods at its place of business and use its best efforts to resell the goods at the following price(s): ⑦

3. The goods will remain the property of the seller until they are resold by the buyer. The buyer agrees to pay the following price(s) to the seller for any goods sold while held on consignment under this contract: ⑧

4. The seller agrees that the goods will be delivered to the buyer's place of business by ⑨_____ , 20 _____ . The shipping costs are estimated at $ ⑩_____ , and will be paid by the ⑪_____ _____ .

5. The buyer agrees to return any unsold goods, in good condition, to the seller on the seller's written demand.

6. The seller represents that it has legal title to the goods and full authority to sell the goods. Seller also represents that the property is sold free and clear of all liens, mortgages, indebtedness, or liabilities.

7. Any additional terms: ⑫

8. No modification of this contract will be effective unless it is in writing and is signed by both parties. Time is of the essence of this contract. This contract binds and benefits both the buyer and seller and any successors. This document, including any attachments, is the entire agreement between the buyer and seller. This contract is governed by the laws of the State of ⑬_____ .

The parties have signed this contract on the date specified at the beginning of this contract.

⑭_____
Signature of Seller

⑮_____
Signature of Buyer

⑭_____
Printed Name of Seller

⑮_____
Printed Name of Buyer

Bulk Transfer Affidavit

State of ①_____
County of ②_____

I, ③_____ , of
address: ④

being of legal age, make the following statements and declare that, on my own
personal knowledge, they are true:

1. I am the seller of business assets of
⑤_____ , located
at: ⑥_____ under an
agreement dated _____ , 20 _____ , with ⑦_____
_____ , buyer, located at ⑧_____
_____ .

2. This affidavit is provided to the buyer, under provisions of the Uniform Commercial Code, as enacted in the State of ⑨_____ , for the
purpose of providing creditors with notice of the intended sale under this agreement. Attached to and made part of this affidavit is a true and complete list of the
names, addresses, and amounts due all creditors of the seller's business as of
this date.

Signed under the penalty of perjury on ⑩_____ , 20 _____ .

⑪_____
Signature of Seller

⑫_____
Printed Name of Seller

Bulk Transfer Notice

Date: ① _____ , 20 _____

To: ② _____

RE: Notice to Creditors

Dear ③ _____ :

Please take notice that

④ _____ , located at

⑤ _____ ,

under an agreement dated ⑥ _____ , 20 _____ , with

⑦ _____ , buyer, locat-

ed at ⑧ _____ ,

intends to make a bulk sale or transfer of business assets. The seller has not done business under any other name for the past three (3) years. As part of this proposed sale, all debts of the seller are to be paid in full as due. This sale is intended to take place on ⑨ _____ , 20 _____ .

This notice is provided in compliance with the Bulk Sales or Transfers Act of the Uniform Commercial Code, as enacted in the State of ⑩ _____ .

As a creditor of the business being sold, you are notified to send verification of all bills, invoices, or records of accounts due to the buyer and seller at the above addresses.

⑪ _____
Signature of Seller

⑫ _____
Signature of Buyer

⑪ _____
Printed Name of Seller

⑫ _____
Printed Name of Buyer

Chapter 19

Collection Documents

The documents contained in this chapter are for use in the collection of past-due payments owed to you. Through the proper use of the documents in this chapter, your business should be able to collect on the majority of overdue and unpaid accounts without having to resort to the use of attorneys or collection agencies. Of course, if the initial attempts at collection using these documents fail, then it is advisable to turn the accounts over to parties who will be able to bring legal procedures to bear on the defaulting parties. The following forms are included in this chapter:

Instructions for Collection Documents

Request for Payment: This form should be used to make the initial request for payment from an overdue account payable. It should be sent when you have decided that an account is in delinquent status. It is intended to promote payment on the overdue account. To prepare this form, you will need to enter the name of the company or person with the delinquent account; the date, amount, and invoice numbers of the past-due invoices; any interest or late charges which have been assessed; and any credits or payments which have been made on the account. Be sure to keep a record of this request. Generally, making a copy of the actual request that is sent and placing in the file for the overdue account is the easiest method for this. A sample form is found on page 357. The following information will be used to prepare this document:

① Date of request
② Name and address of person request is made

③ Name of person request is made
④ Invoice number, Date and Amount
⑤ Interest percentage rate and amount
⑥ Late charge amount
⑦ Less credits & payments
⑧ Total amount
⑨ Signature
⑩ Printed Name

Second Request for Payment: You will generally use this form on the next billing date after you have sent the first request for payment. The information necessary for this form will be the same as the first request. You will need, however, to update any additions or subtractions to the account which have taken place during the period since the first request (for example, any payments on account, additional interest charges, additional late payments, additional invoices, etc.). A sample form is found on page 338. The following information will be used to prepare this document:

① Date of request
② Name and address of person request is made
③ Name of person request is made
④ Invoice number, Date and Amount
⑤ Interest percentage rate and amount
⑥ Late charge amount
⑦ Less credits & payments
⑧ Total amount
⑨ Date of first request for payment
⑩ Signature
⑪ Printed Name

Final Demand for Payment: This form should normally be used after one more billing cycle has elapsed since the second payment request was sent. It is a notice that collection proceedings will be begun if payment has not been received on the delinquent account within 10 days. (Please note that you may extend this period if you desire, for example, to allow for 30 days to pay). This notice should not be sent unless you actually plan on following up with the collection. However, it is often reasonable to wait a short while after the deadline before proceeding with assignment of the account for collection. This allows for delays in mail delivery and takes into account the tendency of companies and people with debt problems to push the time limits to the maximum. A sample form is found on page 359. The following information will be used to prepare this document:

① Date of Demand
② Name and address of person demand is made
③ Name of person request is made
④ Amount of delinquent account
⑤ Signature
⑥ Printed Name

Assignment of Account for Collection: This document is one of the methods to follow-up the final demand for payment. With this document, the past-due account is entirely turned over to either a collection agency or attorney for further collection procedures. This form is an actual assignment of the account to the firm who then actually owns the account and will continue any attempts at collection. It provides that the *assignee* (the firm who will be taking over the collection procedures) pays your company (the *assignor*, or the "one who assigns") an amount for the rights to collect the account. The fee paid is generally a percentage of the amount due. For example, if the fee is fifty percent and you are owed $4,000.00 on the account, the assignee firm will pay you $2,000.00 for taking over the account. Of course, if they are successful in collecting the entire amount they will have earned an additional $2,000.00. But at least you will have gotten half of the money owed to you. Under this method of collection, all future payments are to be paid to the assignee firm. Another method for handling collection is provided below in the Appointment of Collection Agent form. A sample form is found on page 360. The following information will be used to prepare this document:

① Date of assignment
② Name of assignor
③ Address of assignor with name of city and state
④ Name of assignee
⑤ Address of assignee with name of city and state
⑥ Name of customer
⑦ Address of customer with name of city and state
⑧ account receivable balance
⑨ Amount assignee agrees to pay to the assignor
⑩ Date signed
⑪ Signature of Assignor
⑫ Printed Name of Assignor
⑬ Signature of Assignee
⑭ Printed Name of Assignee

Notice of Assignment of Account for Collection: This form is used to notify the customer that the past-due account has been formally assigned to the collection firm. It tells the customer to make future payments on the account to the collection firm. A sample form is found on page 361. The following information will be used to prepare this document:

1. Date of notice
2. Name and address of person/company receiving notice
3. Name of person/company receiving notice
4. Date of assignment
5. Name of company being assigned account for collection
6. Address of company being assigned account for collection
7. Invoice #, date and amount
8. Interest and amount
9. Late charges and amount
10. Less credit & payment and amount
11. Total amount due
12. Signature
13. Printed Name

Appointment of Collection Agent: Through the use of this document, you appoint a collection agency to collect the delinquent account. This method of collection differs slightly from the actual assignment of the account for collection, in that the appointment of the agent for collection is only for a limited period of time and the fee which the collection agent earns is entirely dependent upon their ability to actually collect the money which is owed to you. This is known as a *contingent fee arrangement*. The collection agent may act on your behalf in attempting to collect the account, but does not have actual ownership of the account. You may limit the actions that the agent takes or spell out specific steps you wish taken with the special instructions. Generally, the payments will continue to be made to your company. A sample form is found on page 362. The following information will be used to prepare this document:

1. Date of appointment
2. Name of seller
3. Address of seller
4. Name of agent
5. Address of agent
6. Name of customer
7. Address of customer
8. Account receivable balance
9. Percentage rate
10. Special instructions
11. Total amount due
12. Signature & printed name of seller
13. Signature & printed name of buyer

Notice of Appointment of Collection Agent: This form should be used in conjunction with the above form. While the appointment form above is used between your business and the collection service, this form should be used to notify the delinquent account of the appointment of the collection agent for their account. It instructs the customer to make payments to your company or contact the collection agent. A sample form is found on page 363. The following information will be used to prepare this document:

1. Date of notice
2. Name and address of person/company sending notice to
3. Name of person/company sending notice to
4. Date of assignment
5. Name of collection agent
6. Address of collection agent
7. Invoice #, date & amount of accounts receivable being assigned
8. Interest & amount
9. Late charges & amount
10. Less credits & amount
11. Total amount due
12. Signature
13. Printed name

Notice of Disputed Account: This form should be used by you if you have received a statement with which you disagree. If you feel that the statement is in error, spell out your reasoning in the space provided and send this form to the creditor. A sample form is found on page 364. The following information will be used to prepare this document:

1. Date of notice
2. Name and address of person/company sending notice to
3. Name of person/company sending notice to
4. Date of statement
5. Balance due on disputed account
6. Reasons for the dispute of amount due
7. Signature
8. Printed name

Offer to Settle Disputed Account: This form is also intended to be used by your company if you dispute a statement sent to you by others. Through the use of this form, you can offer a compromise settlement on the account. A check in the amount of your compromised settlement can safely be sent with this offer, since, by the terms of the offer, cashing the check will be acceptance of the offer to compromise. Many companies will jump at the cash in hand and agree to concede the remaining balance. This document should only be used if there is an actual dispute regarding the amount owed. A sample form is found on page 365. The following information will be used to prepare this document:

① Date of offer
② Name and address of person/company sending offer to
③ Name of person/company sending offer to
④ Date of statement
⑤ Balance due on disputed account
⑥ Date of previous letter
⑦ Reasons for the dispute of amount due in previous letter
⑧ Amount of offer to settle account
⑨ Check number of enclosed check
⑩ Signature
⑪ Printed Name

Agreement to Settle Disputed Account: This is a formal version of the above letter agreement. This form may be used to spell out the terms of the compromise settlement more clearly. It should be used by your company if you have received an informal settlement offer from another party to settle an account. A sample form is found on page 366. The following information will be used to prepare this document:

① Date of agreement
② Name of seller
③ Address seller
④ Name of customer
⑤ Address customer
⑥ Date and amount of disputed account
⑦ Invoice #, date & amount of accounts being disputed
⑧ Amount seller will accept
⑨ Date agreement is signed
⑩ Signature of Seller
⑪ Printed Name of Seller
⑫ Signature of Customer
⑬ Printed Name of Customer

Notice of Dishonored Check: This document should be sent to anyone whose bad check has been returned to you from a bank. It is generally a good idea to attempt to have the check cleared twice before beginning the collection process with this letter. This provides time for last-minute deposits to clear and will often allow the check to clear. This document gives notice to the person of the dishonored check, notifies them of your policy and charges regarding service charges for bad checks, and provides a time limit for clearing up the bad check prior to legal action. Once the check has been paid, return the original check to the debtor. A sample form is found on page 367. The following information will be used to prepare this document:

① Date of notice
② Name and address of owner of dishonored check
③ Name of owner of dishonored check
④ Check number
⑤ Date on check
⑥ Amount of check
⑦ Bank name and address that refused check
⑧ Amount of service charge for dishonored check
⑨ Signature
⑩ Printed Name

Stop Payment on Check Order: This form is intended to be provided to a bank or similar financial institution to confirm a telephone stop-payment request. This form provides the institution with written confirmation of the oral request to stop payment on a check. A sample form is found on page 368. The following information will be used to prepare this document:

① Date of order
② Name and address of bank
③ Name of bank
④ Date of telephone conversation
⑤ Account name, account #, check #, date, amount and payable to who
⑥ Signature
⑦ Printed Name

Request for Payment

Date ①_____, 20 _____

To: ②_____

RE: Payment of Your Account

Dear ③_____ :

Regarding your loan, please be advised that we show the following outstanding balance on our books:

Invoice # ④_____ Date_____ Amount $ _____

Invoice # ④_____ Date_____ Amount $ _____

Interest on account at ⑤_____ percent   Amount $ _____

Late charges ⑥   Amount $ _____

Less credits and payments ⑦   Amount $ _____

TOTAL BALANCE DUE ⑧   AMOUNT $ _____

Please be advised that we have not yet received payment on this outstanding balance. We are certain that this is merely an oversight and would ask that you please send the payment now. Please disregard this notice if full payment has been forwarded to us.

Thank you for your immediate attention to this matter.

Very truly,

⑨_____
Signature

⑩_____
Printed Name

Second Request for Payment

Date: ① _____ , 20 _____

To: ② _____

RE: Payment of Your Account

Dear ③ _____ :

Regarding your account, please be advised that we continue to show the following outstanding balance on our books:

Invoice # ④ _____ Date_____ Amount $ _____

Invoice # ④ _____ Date_____ Amount $ _____

Interest on account at ⑤ _____ percent Amount $ _____

Late charges ⑥   Amount $ _____

Less credits and payments ⑦   Amount $ _____

TOTAL BALANCE DUE ⑧   AMOUNT $ _____

Please be advised that since our last request for payment dated ⑨ _____ ,
20 _____ , we have still not yet received payment on this outstanding balance.
We must request that you please send the payment immediately. Please disregard this notice if full payment has been forwarded to us.

Thank you for your immediate attention to this matter.

Very truly,

⑩ _____
Signature

⑪ _____
Printed Name

Final Demand for Payment

Date: ①_____ , 20 _____

To: ②_____

RE: Payment of Your Account

Dear ③_____ :

Regarding your delinquent account in the amount of $ ④_____ , we have requested payment on this account several times without success.

THIS IS YOUR FINAL NOTICE.

Please be advised that unless we receive payment in full on this account in this office within ten (10) days of the date of this letter, we will immediately turn this account over to our attorneys for collection proceedings against you without further notice.

These proceedings will include claims for pre-judgment interest on your account and all legal and court-related costs in connection with collection of this past-due account and will substantially increase the amount that you owe us. Collection proceedings may also have an adverse effect on your credit rating.

We regret the necessity for this action and urge you to clear up this account delinquency immediately. If full payment has been sent, please disregard this notice.

Thank you for your immediate attention to this serious matter.

Very truly,

⑤_____
Signature

⑥_____
Printed Name

Assignment of Account for Collection

This assignment of account for collection is made on ①_____ , 20 _____ , by and between ②_____ , assignor, address: ③

and ④_____ , assignee, address: ⑤

It is regarding the account receivable due to the assignor from a customer of the assignor, known as ⑥_____ , customer, address: ⑦

As of this date, the account receivable balance is $ ⑧_____ .

For valuable consideration, the parties agree as follows:

1. The assignee agrees to pay to the assignor on this day the sum of $ ⑨_____ _____ , in return for which the assignor assigns all rights, title, and interest in this account receivable to the assignee for collection.

2. Assignor shall indemnify and hold harmless the assignee from any and all claims arising from the account receivable or the underlying contract between the assignor and the customer. Assignor agrees to furnish the assignee all information required by the assignee in its collection efforts. Assignor agrees to notify the customer of this assignment and to pay to the assignee any payments on this account which are received from the customer after this date.

Dated ⑩_____ , 20 _____

⑪_____
Signature of Assignor

⑬_____
Signature of Assignee

⑫_____
Printed Name of Assignor

⑭_____
Printed Name of Assignee

Notice of Assignment of Account for Collection

Date: ① _____ , 20 _____

To: ② _____

RE: Assignment of Account for Collection

Dear ③ _____ :

Please be advised that as of ④ _____ , 20 _____ , the fol-
lowing account receivable balance has been assigned for collection to the firm of
⑤ _____ , of
address: ⑥

Invoice Number	Date	Amount
⑦ _____	_____	$ _____
⑦ _____	_____	$ _____

Interest on account at ⑧ _____ % $ _____

Late charges ⑨ $ _____

Less credits and payments ⑩ $ _____

TOTAL BALANCE DUE   ⑪ $ _____

Please contact the above firm regarding all future payments on this account.

Very truly,

⑫ _____   ⑬ _____
Signature   Printed Name

Appointment of Collection Agent

This agreement for the appointment of collection agent is made on ①_____ _____ , 20 _____ , by and between ②_____ , seller address: ③

and ④_____ , agent, address: ⑤

It is regarding the account receivable due to the seller from a customer of the seller, known as ⑥_____ , customer address: ⑦

As of this date, the account receivable balance is $ ⑧_____ .

For valuable consideration, the parties agree as follows:

1. Seller appoints agent to collect this account receivable from customer on behalf of seller. Agent will be entitled to a contingent fee of ⑨_____ % (_____ percent) of whatever amount of the account receivable is collected by agent, payable to the agent upon receipt of the collected amounts. Agent is also subject to the following special instructions: ⑩

2. Seller shall indemnify and hold harmless the agent from any and all claims arising from the account receivable or the underlying contract between the seller and the customer. Agent shall indemnify and hold harmless the seller from any and all claims arising from the agent's collection efforts. Seller agrees to furnish the agent all information required by the agent in its collection efforts. Seller agrees to notify the customer of this appointment.

Dated ⑪_____ , 20 _____

⑫_____
Signature of Seller

⑬_____
Signature of Agent

⑫_____
Printed Name of Seller

⑬_____
Printed Name of Agent

Notice of Appointment of Collection Agent

Date: ① _____ , 20 _____

To: ② _____

RE: Appointment of Collection Agent

Dear ③ _____ :

Please be advised that as of ④ _____ , 20 _____ , the firm
of ⑤ _____ ,
address: ⑥

has been appointed as agent for collection of the following account receivable
balance:

Invoice Number	Date	Amount
⑦ _____	_____	$ _____
⑦ _____	_____	$ _____
⑦ _____	_____	$ _____
⑦ _____	_____	$ _____

Interest on account at ⑧ _____ % $ _____
Late charges ⑨   Amount $ _____
Less credits ⑩   Amount $ _____

TOTAL BALANCE DUE ⑪ AMOUNT $ _____

You may continue to make your payments to our company or you may make
further payments to the collection agent. Thank you.

Very truly,

⑫ _____   ⑬ _____
Signature   Printed Name

Notice of Disputed Account

Date: ①_____ , 20 _____

To: ② _____

RE: Disputed Account

Dear ③_____ :

We are in receipt of your statement of our account dated ④_____ ,
20 _____ , indicating a balance due you of $ ⑤_____ .

We dispute this amount due for the following reasons: ⑥

Please contact us immediately to discuss the adjustment of our account.

Very truly,

⑦_____
Signature

⑧_____
Printed Name

Offer to Settle Disputed Account

Date: ① _____ , 20 _____

To: ② _____

RE: Disputed Account

Dear ③ _____ :

We are in receipt of your statement of our account dated ④ _____ , 20 _____ , indicating a balance due you of $ ⑤ _____ .

As noted in our previous letter dated ⑥ _____ , 20 _____ , we dispute this amount due for the following reasons: ⑦

Without admitting any liability on this account, but as an offer to compromise the amount due, we offer to settle this account in full by our payment to you of $ ⑧ _____ .

Our check # ⑨ _____ in that amount is enclosed. Your deposit of that check shall confirm your acceptance of our offer to settle this account and shall discharge the entire balance claimed.

Very truly,

⑩ _____
Signature

⑪ _____
Printed Name

Agreement to Settle Disputed Account

This agreement to settle disputed account is made on ① _____ , 20 _____ ,
by and between ② _____ , seller
address: ③

and ④ _____ , customer
address: ⑤

regarding a disputed account payable dated ⑥ _____ , 20 _____ ,
in the amount of $ _____ , based on the following invoices:

Invoice Number	Date	Amount
⑦ _____	_____	$ _____
⑦ _____	_____	$ _____
⑦ _____	_____	$ _____
⑦ _____	_____	$ _____

For valuable consideration, the parties agree as follows:

1. The seller will accept a lesser payment of $ ⑧ _____ , in full settle-
   ment of the claim on this account.

2. If the customer does not pay the seller this lesser payment within ten (10) days
   of receipt of a signed original copy of this agreement, the seller may sue the
   customer for the full amount of the disputed account payable.

3. If the customer pays the lesser payment within the time allowed for payment,
   both parties mutually release each other from any and all claims or rights to sue
   each other arising from their dispute over payment of this account payable.

4. This agreement binds and benefits both parties and any successors.

Dated ⑨ _____ , 20 _____

⑩ _____
Signature of Seller

⑫ _____
Signature of Customer

⑪ _____
Printed Name of Seller

⑬ _____
Printed Name of Customer

Notice of Dishonored Check

Date: ①_____ , 20 _____

To: ②_____

RE: Dishonored Check

Dear ③_____ :

Please be advised that payment on your check # ④_____ , dated
⑤_____ , 20 _____ , in the amount of $ ⑥_____ ,
has been refused by your bank, ⑦_____
address:

We have verified with your bank that there are insufficient funds to pay the
check.

Therefore, we request that you immediately replace this check with cash or a
certified check for the amount of the bad check and an additional $ ⑧_____ as
our service charge.

Unless we receive such payment within ten (10) days from the date of this letter,
or such further time as may be allowed by state law, we will immediately com-
mence appropriate legal action for recovery of our funds. Please be advised that
such legal proceedings may substantially increase the amount owed to us and
may include prejudgment interest and legal and court costs.

Upon receipt of payment, we will return your check to you. Thank you for your
prompt response to this serious matter.

Very truly,

⑨_____
Signature

⑩_____
Printed Name

Stop Payment on Check Order

Date: ① _____ , 20 _____

To: ② _____

RE: Stop Payment on Check

Dear ③ _____ :

Pursuant to our telephone conversation of ④ _____ , 20 _____ ,
please stop payment on the following check:

⑤
Account name
Account #
Check #
Check date
Check amount
Payable to

Thank you for your immediate attention to this matter.

Very truly,

⑥ _____
Signature

⑦ _____
Printed Name

Chapter 20

Miscellaneous Business Documents

Included in this chapter are various documents that may be used in a variety of circumstances. These documents range from a form for making sworn statements to an indemnity agreement that may be used by a party to accept responsibility for any claims or liability that may arise in a transaction. The forms that are included and the information necessary to prepare them are as follows:

Instructions for Miscellaneous Business Documents

Affidavit: This form is a basic form for an affidavit. An *affidavit* is a legal document with which a person can make a sworn statement regarding anything. It is essentially testimony under oath by the person making the affidavit. An affidavit may be used to document an aspect of a business transaction. It can be used for verification purposes. It may also be used as a supplement to a lawsuit, as the form provided is made under penalty of perjury.

The information necessary to prepare the basic affidavit is the name and address of the person making the affidavit and a written recital of the statement that the person is affirming. This form should be notarized as the statement is being made under oath and under penalty of perjury. If the person making the affirmed statement is acting in other than an individual capacity (as the director of a corporation, for example), substitute the appropriate signature and acknowledgment forms from Chapter 3. A sample form is found on page 372. The following information will be used to prepare this document:

① Name of person making affidavit
② Make statement
③ Date signed
④ Signature
⑤ Printed Name
⑥ Notary to fill out this section

Indemnity Agreement: This form may be used as a general supplement to certain business transactions. With this form, one party to a transaction agrees to indemnify and hold the other party harmless. What this means is that the party doing the indemnifying (the *indemnifier*) will pay for and defend against any legal claims or liabilities against the person being indemnified (the *indemnitee*) that may arise in the future based on the transaction. Unfortunately, there are no other English words that carry the precise meaning necessary to name the parties in this context.

The indemnifier, by this agreement, agrees to defend against any claims or liabilities arising from the transaction. The indemnitee agrees to promptly notify the indemnifier of any such claims. If the indemnifier does not pay for or defend against such claims, the indemnitee has the right to do so and demand reimbursement from the indemnifier. A sample form is found on page 373. The following information will be used to prepare this document:

① Date of agreement
② Idemnifier name & address
③ Idemnitee name & address
④ Describe activity
⑤ This agreement is governed by the laws of what state
⑥ Date agreement is signed
⑦ Signature of Idemnifier
⑧ Printed name of Idemnifier
⑨ Signature of Idemnitee
⑩ Printed name of Indemnitee

Waiver and Assumption of Risk: This form may be used in situations in which a customer is either using a business's facilities, receiving instruction, renting equipment, or participating in activities sponsored by a business. If there is any possibility of injury or harm, this form provides a method for the customer to assume the risk of the activity and waive any right to file a claim against the business.

By this form, a customer agrees that he or she has been informed of and understands the risks involved, and that he or she agrees to abide by any safety rules and to act in a non-negligent manner while using the facility or item or while participating in the instruction or activity. A sample form is found on page 374. The following information will be used to prepare this document:

① Name of customer
② Address of customer
③ Name of owner
④ Address of owner
⑤ Describe activities
⑥ Age of customer
⑦ Date of waiver signed
⑧ Signature of customer
⑨ Printed name of customer

Affidavit

I, ①_____ , being of legal age, make the following statements and declare that, on my own personal knowledge, they are true: ②

Signed under the penalty of perjury on ③_____ , 20 _____ .

④_____
Signature

⑤_____
Printed Name

⑥
State of _____
County of _____

On _____ , 20 _____ , _____ personally came before me and, being duly sworn, did state that he or she is the person described in the above document and that he or she signed the above document in my presence.

_____
Signature of Notary Public

Notary Public, In and for the County of _____
State of _____

My commission expires: _____   Notary Seal

Indemnity Agreement

This indemnity agreement is made on ①_____ , 20 _____ , between
②_____ , indemnifier,
address:

and ③_____ , indemnitee,
address:

For valuable consideration, the parties agree as follows:

1. The indemnifier agrees to indemnify and hold the indemnitee harmless from any claim or liability arising from the following activity: ④

2. In the event of any claim or asserted liability against the indemnitee arising from the above activity, the indemnitee agrees to provide the indemnifier with prompt written notice. Upon notice, the indemnifier agrees to defend and save the indemnitee harmless from any loss or liability. In the event the indemnifier fails to indemnify the indemnitee, the indemnitee has the right to defend or settle any claim on their own behalf and be fully reimbursed by the indemnifier for all costs and expenses of such defense or settlement.

3. No modification of this agreement will be effective unless it is in writing and is signed by both parties. This agreement binds and benefits both parties and any successors. This document, including any attachments, is the entire agreement between the parties. This agreement is governed by the laws of the State of
⑤_____ .

Dated ⑥_____ , 20 _____

⑦_____
Signature of Indemnifier

⑨_____
Signature of Indemnitee

⑧_____
Printed Name of Indemnifer

⑩_____
Printed Name of Indemnitee

Waiver and Assumption of Risk

I, ①_____ , customer,
address: ②

voluntarily sign this waiver and assumption of risk in favor of ③_____
_____ , owner,
address: ④

in consideration for the opportunity to use the owner's facilities and/or the opportunity to receive instruction from the owner or the owner's employees, and/or to engage in the activities sponsored by the owner, as follows: ⑤

I understand that there are certain risks and dangers associated with the activity and use of the facilities and that these risks have been fully explained to me. I fully understand the danger involved.

I fully assume the risks involved as acceptable to me and I agree to use my best judgment in undertaking these activities and follow all safety instructions.

I waive and release the owner from any claim for personal injury, property damage, or death that may arise from my use of the facilities or from my participation in the activities or instruction.

I am a competent adult, aged ⑥_____ , and I assume these risks of my own free will.

Dated ⑦_____ , 20 _____

⑧_____   ⑨_____
Signature of Customer   Printed Name of Customer

Glossary

Accounts payable: Money owed by a business to another for goods or services purchased on credit. Money that the business intends to pay to another.

Accounts receivable: Money owed to the business by another for goods or services sold on credit. Money that the business expects to receive.

Agent: A person who is authorized to act on behalf of another. A corporation acts only through its agents, whether they are directors, employees, or officers.

Aging: The method used to determine how long accounts receivable have been owed to a business.

Amend: To alter or change.

Articles of Incorporation: The charter of the corporation, the public filing with a state that requests that the corporation be allowed to exist. Along with the Corporate Bylaws, they provide details of the organization and structure of the business. They must be consistent with the laws of the state of incorporation.

Assets: Everything a business owns, including amounts of money that are owed to the business.

Assumed name: A name, other than a corporation's legal name as shown on the Articles of Incorporation, under which a company will conduct business. Most states require registration of the fictitious name if a company desires to conduct business under an assumed name. The corporation's legal name is not an assumed name.

Board of directors: The group with control of the general supervision of the corporation. They are elected by the shareholders and the directors, in turn, appoint the officers of the corporation.

Bookkeeping: The actual process of recording the figures in accounting records.

Business corporation laws: For each individual state, these provide the legal framework for the operation of corporations. The Articles of Incorporation and the Bylaws of a corporation must adhere to the specifics of state law.

Business liabilities: Business debts. Also the value of the owner's equity in his or her business.

Bylaws: The internal rules that govern the management of the corporation. They contain the procedures for holding meetings, appointments, elections and other management matters. If these conflict with the Articles of Incorporation, the provision in the Articles will be controlling.

C-corporation: A business entity owned by shareholders that is not an S-corporation. Subject to double taxation, unlike S-corporations.

Calendar year: Year consisting of 12 consecutive months ending on December 31st.

Capital: Initially, the actual money or property that shareholders transfer to the corporation to allow it to operate. Once in operation, capital also consists of accumulated profits. The net worth of the corporation, the owner's equity in a business, and/or the ownership value of the business.

Capital expense: An expense for the purchase of a fixed asset; an asset with a useful life of over one year. Generally, must be depreciated rather than deducted as a business expense.

Certificate of Incorporation: See Articles of Incorporation. Note, however, that some states will issue a Certificate of Incorporation after the filing of the Articles of Incorporation.

Chart of Accounts: A listing of the types and numbers of the various accounts that a business uses for its accounting records.

Check register: A running record of checks written, deposits made, and other transactions for a bank account.

Common stock: The standard stock of a corporation that includes the right to vote the shares and the right to proportionate dividends. See also *preferred stock.*

Consent Resolution: Any resolution signed by all of the directors or shareholders of a corporation authorizing an action, without the necessity of a meeting.

Corporation: A business entity owned by shareholders; can be a C-corporation or an S-corporation.

Cost basis: Total cost to a business of a fixed asset.

Cost of goods sold: The amount that a business has paid for the inventory that it has sold during a specific period. Calculated by adding beginning inventory and additions to inventory and then deducting the ending inventory value.

Credit: In double-entry accounting, an increase in liability or income accounts or a decrease in asset or expense accounts.

Debt: The amount that a business owes to another. Also known as "liability."

Depreciation: Cost of fixed asset deductible proportionately over time.

Dissolution: Methods by which a corporation concludes its business and liquidates. Dissolutions may be involuntary because of bankruptcy or credit problems or voluntary on the initiation of the directors or shareholders of a corporation.

Dividend: A distribution of money or property paid by the corporation to a shareholder based on the amount of shares held. A proportionate share of the net profits of a business that the board of directors has determined should be paid out to shareholders, rather than held as retained earnings. Dividends must be paid out of the corporation's net earnings and profits. The board of directors has the authority to declare or withhold dividends based on sound business discretion.

Domestic corporation: A corporation is a domestic corporation in the state in which it is incorporated. See also *foreign corporation.*

Equity: Any debt that a business owes. It is owner's equity if owed to the business owners and liabilities if owed to others.

Expenses: The costs to a business of producing its income. Any money that it has paid or will pay out during a certain period.

FEIN: Federal Identification Number, used for tax purposes.

FICA: Federal Insurance Contributions Act. Taxes withheld from employees and paid by employers for Social Security and Medicare.

Fictitious name: See *assumed name.*

Financial statements: Reports that summarize the finances of a business; generally a profit and loss statement and a balance sheet.

Fiscal year: A 12-month accounting period used by a business.

Fiscal-year reporting: For income tax purposes, reporting business taxes for any 12-month period that does not end on December 31 of each year.

Fixed assets: Assets of a business that will not be sold or consumed within one year. Generally, fixed assets (other than land) must be depreciated.

FUTA: Federal Unemployment Tax Act. Federal business unemployment taxes.

Gross pay: The total amount of an employee's compensation before the deduction of any taxes or benefits.

Gross profit: Gross sales minus the cost of goods sold.

Gross sales: The total amount received for goods and services during an accounting period.

Gross wages: The total amount of an employee's compensation before the deduction of any taxes or benefits.

Income: Any money that a business has received or will receive during a certain period.

Income statement: Financial statement that shows the income and expenses for a business. Also referred to as an "operating statement" or "profit and loss statement."

Incorporator: The person who signs the Articles of Incorporation. Usually a person, but some states allow a corporation or partnership to be an incorporator.

Indemnify: To reimburse or compensate. Directors and officers of corporations are often reimbursed or indemnified for all the expenses they may have incurred in incorporating.

Initial capital: The money or property that an owner or owners contribute to starting a business.

Intangible personal property: Generally, property not attached to land that you cannot hold or touch (for example: copyrights, business goodwill, etc.).

Inventory: Goods that are held by a business for sale to customers.

Invoice: A bill for the sale of goods or services that is sent to the buyer.

Ledgers: The accounting books for a business. Generally, refers to the entire set of accounts for a business.

Liabilities: The debts of a business.

Liquidity: The ability of a company to convert its assets to cash and meet its obligations with that cash.

Managers: In a limited liability company, those persons selected by the members of the company to handle the management functions of the company. Managers of limited liability companies may or may not be members/owners of the company. Managers are roughly analogous to the officers of a corporation.

Members: In a limited liability company, those persons who have ownership interests (equivalent to shareholders in a corporation). Most states allow single-member limited liability companies.

Minutes: A written record of the activities of a meeting.

Net income: The amount of money that a business has after deducting the cost of goods sold and the cost of all expenses. Also referred to as "net profit."

Net loss: The amount by which a business has expenses and costs of goods sold greater than income.

Net pay: The amount of compensation that an employee actually will be paid after the deductions for taxes and benefits.

Net profit: The amount by which a business has income greater than expenses and cost of goods sold. Also referred to as "net income."

Net sales: The value of sales after deducting the cost of goods sold from gross sales.

Net wages: The amount of compensation that an employee will actually be paid after the deductions for taxes and benefits.

Net worth: The value of the owner's share in a business. The value of a business determined by deducting the debts of a business from the assets of a business. Also referred to as "owner's equity."

Nontaxable income: Income that is not subject to any state or local sales tax.

Not-for-profit corporation: A corporation formed under state law that exists for a socially worthwhile purpose. Profits are not distributed but retained and used for corporate purposes. May be tax-exempt. Also referred to as "nonprofit."

Officers: Manage the daily operations of a corporation. Generally consists of a president, vice president, secretary, and treasurer. Appointed by the board of directors.

Operating margin: Net sales divided by gross sales. The actual profit on goods sold, before deductions for expenses.

Operating statement: Financial statement that shows the income and expenses for a business. Also referred to as "income statement" or "profit and loss statement."

Owner's equity: The value of an owner's share in a business. Also referred to as "capital."

Partnership: An unincorporated business entity that is owed by two or more persons.

Payee: Person or business to whom a payment is made.

Payor: Person or business that makes a payment.

Personal property: All business property other than land and the buildings that are attached to the land.

Physical inventory: The actual process of counting and valuing the inventory on hand at the end of an accounting period.

Piercing the corporate veil: A legal decision that allows a court to ignore the corporate entity and reach the assets of the shareholders, directors, or officers.

Plant assets: Long-term assets of a business. Those business assets that are subject to depreciation (other than land).

Posting: In double-entry accounting, the process of transferring data from journals to ledgers.

Pre-paid expenses: Expenses that are paid for before they are used (for example: insurance, rent, etc.).

Profit and loss statement: Financial statement that shows the income and expenses for a business. Also referred to as an "income statement" or "operating statement."

Quorum: The required number of persons necessary to officially conduct business at a meeting. Generally, a majority of the shareholders or directors constitutes a quorum.

Real property: Land and any buildings or improvements that are attached to the land.

Reconciliation: The process of bringing a bank statement into agreement with the business check register.

Registered agent: The person designated in the Articles of Incorporation who will be available to receive service of process (summons, subpoena, etc.) on behalf of the corporation. A corporation must always have a registered agent.

Registered office: The actual physical location of the registered agent. Need not be the actual principal place of business of the corporation.

Resolution: A formal decision that has been adopted by either the shareholders or the board of directors of a corporation.

Retail price: The price for which a product is sold to the public.

Revenue: Income that a business brings in from the sale of goods or services or from investments.

S-corporation: A type of business corporation in which all of the expenses and profits are passed through to its shareholders to be accounted for at tax time individually in the manner of partnerships. A specific IRS designation that allows a corporation to be taxed similarly to a partnership, yet retain limited liability for its shareholders.

Salary: Fixed weekly, monthly, or annual compensation for an employee.

Sales: Money brought into a business from the sale of goods or services.

Sales income: Revenue derived from selling a product of some type.

Salvage value: The value of an asset after it has been fully depreciated.

Service income: Income derived from performing a service for someone.

Service of process: To accept subpoenas or summonses for a corporation.

Shareholder's equity: In a corporation, the owner's equity of a business divided by the number of outstanding shares.

Shareholders: Owners of issued stock of a corporation and, therefore, owners of an interest in the corporation. They elect the board of directors and vote on major corporate issues.

Single-entry accounting: A business recordkeeping system that generally tracks only income and expense accounts. Used generally by small businesses, it is much easier to use and understand than double-entry accounting.

Sole proprietorship: An unincorporated business entity in which one person owns the entire company.

Stock transfer book: The ledger book (or sheets) in which the registered owners of shares in the corporation are recorded.

Straight-line depreciation: Spreads the deductible amount equally over the recovery period.

Supplies: Materials used in conducting the day-to-day affairs of a business (as opposed to raw materials used in manufacturing).

Tangible personal property: Property not attached to land that you can hold and touch (for example: machinery, furniture, equipment).

Taxes payable: Total of all taxes due but not yet paid.

Wages: Hourly compensation paid to employees, as opposed to salary.

Wages payable: Total of all wages and salaries due to employees but not yet paid out.

Wholesale price: The cost to a business of goods purchased for later sale to the public.

Working capital: The money available for immediate business operations. Current assets minus current liabilities.

Index

Nova Publishing Company
Small Business and Consumer Legal Books and Software

Legal Toolkit Series

Business Start-Up Toolkit	ISBN 978-1-892949-43-1	Book w/CD	$39.95
Estate Planning Toolkit	ISBN 978-1-892949-44-8	Book w/CD	$39.95
Legal Forms Toolkit	ISBN 978-1-892949-48-6	Book w/CD	$39.95
No-Fault Divorce Toolkit	ISBN 978-1-892949-35-6	Book w/CD	$39.95
Personal Bankruptcy Toolkit	ISBN 978-1-892949-42-4	Book w/CD	$29.95
Will and Living Will Toolkit	ISBN 978-1-892949-47-9	Book w/CD	$29.95

Law Made Simple Series

Personal Legal Forms Simplified (3rd Edition)	ISBN 978-0-935755-97-8	Book w/CD	$28.95
Powers of Attorney Simplified (2nd Edition)	ISBN 978-1-892949-56-1	Book w/CD	$29.95

Small Business Made Simple Series

Limited Liability Company: Start-up Kit (4th Edition)	ISBN 978-1-892949-54-7	Book w/CD	$29.95
Real Estate Forms Simplified (2nd Edition)	ISBN 978-1-892949-49-3	Book w/CD	$29.95
S-Corporation Small Business Start-up Kit (4th Edition)	ISBN 978-1-892949-53-0	Book w/CD	$29.95
Small Business Accounting Simplified (5th Edition)	ISBN 978-1-892949-50-9	Book w/CD	$29.95
Small Business Bookkeeping System Simplified	ISBN 978-0-935755-74-9	Book only	$14.95
Small Business Legal Forms Simplified (5th Edition)	ISBN 978-1-892949-62-2	Book w/CD	$29.95
Small Business Payroll System Simplified	ISBN 978-0-935755-55-8	Book only	$14.95
Sole Proprietorship: Start-up Kit (3rd Edition)	ISBN 978-1-892949-59-2	Book w/CD	$29.95

Legal Self-Help Series

Divorce Yourself: The National Divorce Kit (6th Edition)	ISBN 978-1-892949-12-7	Book w/CD	$39.95
Prepare Your Own Will: The National Will Kit (6th Edition)	ISBN 978-1-892949-15-8	Book w/CD	$29.95

National Legal Kits

Simplified Divorce Kit (3rd Edition)	ISBN 978-1-892949-39-4	Book w/CD	$19.95
Simplified Family Legal Forms Kit (2nd Edition)	ISBN 978-1-892949-41-7	Book w/CD	$19.95
Simplified Incorporation Kit	ISBN 978-1-892949-33-2	Book w/CD	$19.95
...mplified Limited Liability Company Kit	ISBN 978-1-892949-32-5	Book w/CD	$19.95
...lified Living Will Kit (2nd Edition)	ISBN 978-1-892949-45-5	Book w/CD	$19.95
...fied S-Corporation Kit	ISBN 978-1-892949-31-8	Book w/CD	$19.95
...d Will Kit (3rd Edition)	ISBN 978-1-892949-38-7	Book w/CD	$19.95

Ordering Information

Phone orders with Visa/MC: (800) 462-6420
Fax orders with Visa/MC: (800) 338-4550
Internet: www.novapublishing.com
Free shipping on all internet orders (within in the U.S.)